Prepared
to
Answer

Second Edition

GORDON FERGUSON

PREPARED
TO
ANSWER

SECOND EDITION

ipi

PREPARED TO ANSWER (SECOND EDITION)

Book cover and interior design: Toney C. Mulhollan

Printed in the United States of America

Former ISBN: 1-57782-070-3
NEW ISBN: 978-0-9824085-0-6

The paper used in this publication meets the minimum requirements of the American National Standard for Information Sciences—Permanence of Paper for Prnted Library Materials, ANSI Z39.48-1992.

Illumination Publishers International
www.ipibooks.com
6010 Pinecreek Ridge Court
Spring, Texas 77379-2513, USA

DEDICATION

To my family:

Theresa, the wife of my youth and dearly loved partner of 44 years, the one who has influenced me more for God than any other human—by far.

Bryan and Joy Ferguson—my firstborn and his wife, who is now my daughter, thanks for your love for me and your grace towards me—I treasure those things from you so much.

Jeff and Renee Klinkhammer—my daughter and her husband, who is now my son, thanks for your love for me and your encouragement almost daily—as we live only three miles apart.

Bryce, Blayze and Ronan Ferguson—my Hawaiian grandsons, who have been so blessed through the wonderful blending of American and Asian cultures—and who are such a blessing to me as your Pop Pop.

Aleea and Cody Klinkhammer—my Arizona grandchildren who live nearby, thus providing much love and comic relief—you help keep your Pop Pop young(er).

TABLE OF CONTENTS

TABLE OF CONTENTS

ACKNOWLEDGEMENTS

The first edition of this book, written in 1995, was my first attempt at writing a full length book. I was 52 at the time. I recall some writer saying years ago that no one should write a book before he is at least 40 years old, since he is too likely to change viewpoints prior to that age. Maybe there is wisdom in that statement generally, but any writer that doesn't continue to change at least some things about his viewpoints is not growing. I know that I have changed a lot in the past 14 years, and I hope that those changes signal spiritual growth and maturity. The basic doctrinal views expressed in this edition remain essentially the same as those in the first edition. *How* I state them has changed, in a genuine desire to be more gracious toward those with whom I differ doctrinally.

In addition, other changes have also been made, of which you need to be made aware. I added an Introduction to Section One on Catholicism, not because the general doctrinal areas I address have changed, but enough changes have occurred in more peripheral areas since Vatican II that some would overestimate what actually has changed—hence the need to explain the nature of the changes. I changed the title of the chapter on what I have called the Mainline Church of Christ to reflect a broader perspective on what I have now termed *Restoration Churches*, which includes two key issues with both Christian Churches and the Mainline Church of Christ, and leaves intact a (better) treatment of three other issues more unique to the Mainline Church. Perhaps most significant is the addition of a new chapter on Evangelicalism in the 21st Century, which has made, and is making, quite an impact on much of Protestant religion generally. Among the minor changes are additional comments on my earlier interpretation of two passages: Matthew 16:18 (within the treatment of Catholicism) and 1 Corinthians 13:10 (within the treatment of Pentecostalism).

I have added an Appendix treating the teachings of Watchman Nee and Witness Lee, whose teachings have not produced any large independent religious group, yet have influenced the thinking of many people who have read their writings. I believe the overall influence of their teaching to be subtle in its errors, but because of this subtlety, more dangerous. That Appendix is entitled "Watchman Nee's Teaching On Soul And Spirit: A Form Of Neo-Gnosticism." A final Appendix entitled "Matters of Conscience: A Deeper Look" was also added, to help those among us who are prone to demand changes in others while resisting changes in their own thinking through an erroneous appeal to what the Bible says about the conscience.

Many things have influenced my desire to be less judgmental in attitude and tone. Nothing has affected me more than changes within my own church affiliation. This group of churches, often called the ICOC (International Churches of Christ), has gone through a significant upheaval in the past several years. It has taken some time to sort out what was good about our past and what was bad—what was correct before God and what was incorrect, and therefore, unbiblical. I have often described this movement as being like a barbell, with equally large weights at either end—one end representing the amazingly good things accomplished by God's grace and the other end representing the regrettably bad things done in our human wisdom and pride. With hindsight, I would say now that many (not all) of the bad things were actually good things done in wrong ways. We are doing our best before God to distinguish what was good and bad, in order to "hate what is evil and cling to what is good" (Romans 12:9).

With that background in mind, we must ask if accuracy in Biblical doctrines is still worth striving for? On this point, I am absolutely unchanged: I believe it matters significantly to God what we believe and practice. The real test is in defending right doctrines against those I believe to be wrong without trying to claim God's judgment throne. I can argue strongly for biblical doctrines without making final judgments regarding the eternal destiny of those with whom I disagree. God is the Judge, and I am more than happy to leave that job up to him. My aim in life as a teacher of his Word is to teach and persuade everyone I can to believe and practice what I believe the Bible to teach, no matter where they are on their spiritual journey, whether a Christian or a not-yet-Christian. We all need teaching and persuading to help us become more like Christ and get more in line with his Word. I personally need it, and as I receive it, I want to pass it on. That is the stuff of which discipleship is made.

At this juncture, some of what I said in my original Foreword is worth repeating, at least in condensed form. I am grateful for the biblical training I received at two institutions, the Preston Road School of Preaching in Dallas, Texas, and the Harding Graduate School of Religion in Memphis, Tennessee. The former provided a very practical, in-depth foundation of basic Bible knowledge, and the latter gave me more of the academic foundation, which led to a master's degree in New Testament Studies.

As I look back over my life, it is clear that certain people exerted a major influence on my spiritual directions and accomplishments. My mother always believed that the Bible was God's Word, and she held its truths to be priceless. Although I did not fully appreciate her views when I was a young man, I grew to value the impact she made on my belief system. Later, when I was in rebellion against God, it was my wife who pointed me back to my religious roots. From that day until now, no one has influenced me more for God. She has lived a *Jesus life* before me for well over forty years.

When I was in my early twenties, God sent an unusual man into my life by the name of Richard Hostetler. His refreshing lack of a "preacher demeanor" opened me up to the concept that one could love God without being a stuffy, stained-glass type clergyman. He was an open and loving man who made a major contribution to my spiritual development. His focus on evangelism, total commitment and the grace of God set my course for a life of seeking to implement these things and to encourage others to do the same.

As a young preacher, an older preacher named J.T. Bristow became my mentor and spiritual father figure. Characterized by strong preaching and the ability to move people to repentance, he became a model for my own development as a speaker. Few in that fellowship of churches had the courage to speak as fearlessly as he did.

In 1981, Tom Brown introduced me to the fellowship of churches that I became a part of several years later. For several years following that introduction, many others were very helpful influences. Joe Woods was a key personal friend who answered many questions with both his doctrine and life. Ron Brumley and George Havins, elders of the San Diego church at the time, invited us to move there and work with them, which we did in 1985. They and their wives became wonderful friends for time and eternity. Of these key people mentioned above, four of them have graduated to glory: J.T. Bristow, George Havins, Richard Hostetler and Joe Woods. May a part of their reward come from the blessing they were in my life, and continue to be through the principle expressed in Hebrews 11:4 regarding Abel—for by faith, they still speak even though they are dead.

We moved to Boston at the beginning of 1988 and were trained and discipled by many during our 16 years there. Names like Al and Gloria Baird, Bob and Pat Gempel, Wyndham and Jeanie Shaw, Randy and Kay McKean and Tom and Sheila Jones are among those who come immediately to mind. Working with the staff of DPI (*Discipleship Publications International*) through the years has been one of my greatest joys in my ministry. Tom Jones was the editor when I wrote all of the books

I have written to this point, and once he retired as editor, I all but retired as a writer of books for some years. I intend to write more at the semi-retirement stage of life which I have recently entered, but I never hoped to have had such a delightful experience as the one we had in the process of laboring together as writer and editor, long-term friends and brothers in Christ.

The members of the Boston Church of Christ were for many years my brothers and sisters, my sons and daughters. Their love called me higher and filled my heart with gladness. They played a unique role in God's plan, and for that reason, developed into a unique people and a true family. For the last five years, I have labored as an evangelist, teacher and elder with the Phoenix Valley Church of Christ, and have been blessed with many new relationships that are deepening day by day.

When I wrote the first edition of this book, I had a wonderful and beautiful wife, Theresa, and two very special children, Bryan and Renee. Now I have two additional children (by virtue of them being married to Bryan and Renee)—Joy and Jeff, who are as much children to us as are their mates. And to top it off, we now have four grandsons and a granddaughter: Bryce, Blayze and Ronan Ferguson, and Aleea and Cody Klinkhammer. To all ten of you, thank you for loving me the way that you have. You are precious beyond words!

As I now begin to work with Toney Mulhollan of Illumination Publishers International in producing books and other materials, I am grateful for his long-term friendship, his desire to help me in my present efforts and his total commitment to the production of spiritual materials in all forms and formats—written, audio and video. His longevity and perseverance as a disciple of Jesus are truly exemplary and inspiring. His commitment to God and his kingdom knows no bounds.

Finally, as always, to God be the glory for anything good that comes from my life and my pen. He has given me the gifts of teaching and writing and has provided some unique training to develop them. He is my Father, my friend and my life. In the hope of living and conveying his truths, I offer this book in the name of his Son, Jesus the Christ.

Phoenix, Arizona
February 2009

FOREWORD

The Lord said, "Always be prepared to give an answer to everyone who asks you to give the reason for the hope that you have…"

—1 Peter 3:15 NIV

Answers. Do they exist? Is it really possible to have them? In an age when the very idea of absolute truth is quickly labeled as audacious and intolerant, do we dare look for "the" answers? Or is it better just to shrink back and decide not to "go there." But if answers do exist, where do we go? Isn't that what Oprah's show is for? And in an age when every question can be "googled" and answers are flashed by the thousands in a nanosecond, do we really need a book like this? I believe, yes, even now more than ever.

We live in a time when all forms of religion are lumped together and considered by many influential people to be basically the same. Then there are many wearing the name Christian who regard the different Christian denominations and movements in the same way, saying, "Don't we all believe and practice basically the same things"? Are there really any differences? Are they significant? Preparing yourself to answer these questions can seem like a daunting task. This book provides all of us with the information to be, and to feel, adequately equipped.

In a time when pseudo-Christian philosophies are appearing overnight, we desperately need the biblical lighthouse to help us navigate through the fog. In our readings, we must not allow ourselves to become so infatuated with the latest and most popular "spiritual" philosophies and teachings that the Bible becomes ancillary rather than primary. We must always critically analyze and interpret what we read and hear in light of God's Word, and not the other way around. I am thankful that my dear friend and brother, Gordon Ferguson, has been willing to tackle this challenge and give us biblical perspective. In his own inimitable style, Gordon gives us the facts and the scriptural view to cut through the haze and come to clarity.

Every disciple needs to have this edition of "Prepared to Answer" in their home for two reasons:

1) As disciples, Christ has commissioned us to go and make disciples of all nations. That includes millions of people who are in some form of "Christian" group and yet lack the full truth about how to become a true disciple of Jesus Christ. For us to effectively help them learn the truth, we need a basic knowledge of these groups and their beliefs. "Prepared to Answer" provides just that.

2) There are also times in each of our lives when we need to be "prepared to answer" the questions that arise in our own minds about other "Christian" groups. I am thankful that Gordon's book gives us the tools to do both.

I hope everyone will take the time to sit at the feet of this great teacher as he helps us all become better "Prepared to Answer."

Bruce Williams
Los Angeles

INTRODUCTION
Life and Doctrine

"Don't even think about skipping this introduction." That is a statement I thought about putting at the top of this page in large bold letters. Every book has an introduction or foreword, and its value varies depending on the nature of the book and its author's intent. This introduction is *highly* important, and, in my judgment, it is absolutely necessary to read it before proceeding with the rest of the book. As an elder and teacher in the kingdom of God and part of a worldwide movement to restore biblical Christianity, I am writing this book to equip disciples of Jesus Christ to respond effectively to confusion in the religious world. However, if the contents are viewed and used wrongly, harm will be done to the ones using them and to the ones with whom they are used.

Doctrine is important to anyone intent on pleasing God and helping others to please God. Religion without doctrine is like a human body without a skeletal system. A coherent body of belief that reflects the thinking of God must be the starting point if our lives are to be lived differently and have impact. See how Paul put it in 1 Timothy 4:16:

Watch your life and doctrine closely. Persevere in them, because if you do, you will save both yourself and your hearers.

It is clear that life and doctrine go hand in hand. Both must receive careful attention. Whoever first said they are like the two wings of an airplane was on the right track. Try to have the right life without doctrine and you will end up with some sort of "mushy moralism" that will neither help people nor please God. On the other hand, become a doctrinal expert and give no attention to your own inner person—your heart and your attitudes—and you will do more harm than good. Listen again to Paul's words to Timothy:

As I urged you when I went into Macedonia, stay there in Ephesus so that you may command certain men not to teach false doctrines any longer nor to devote themselves to myths and endless genealogies.

These promote controversies rather than God's work—which is by faith. The goal of this command is love, which comes from a pure heart and a good conscience and a sincere faith. Some have wandered away from these and turned to meaningless talk. They want to be teachers of the law, but they do not know what they are talking about or what they so confidently affirm (**1 Timothy 1:3-7**).

The man who wants to be a teacher and straighten out others, but wanders away from a pure heart, a good conscience and a sincere faith, will make a lot of meaningless noise.

As Paul demanded that correct doctrine be used, he sometimes referred to it as *sound* doctrine. The word translated *sound* is a word whose primary meaning is "healthy." Thus, Paul is saying that correct doctrine is necessary in order to be spiritually healthy. Sound doctrine promotes good spiritual health—but there is a danger. We cannot be healthy without holding to Christ's teaching, true enough: but we must hold to it with healthy attitudes. *A distorted emphasis on doctrinal issues will absolutely choke out our spirituality.* We will turn into legalists unless we find the right balance.

Actually, this proper balance is well-defined in the text from which the book title comes, 1 Peter 3:15-16:

But in your hearts set apart Christ as Lord. Always be prepared to give an answer to everyone who asks you to give the reason for the hope that you have. But do this with gentleness and respect, keeping a clear conscience, so that those who speak maliciously against your good behavior in Christ may be ashamed of their slander.

Peter gives us some extraordinary insights into being "ready to answer":

- We must have a heart committed to Jesus. He must be our Lord if we are to help anyone else become a disciple. Before we fill our heads with the answers to man-made doctrines, we had better first fill our hearts with Jesus. Then we will not become like the Pharisees.
- It's essential we have trained minds. Being prepared to answer others demands that we know what we believe and why we believe it!
- We must have controlled speech. "A gentle answer turns away wrath, but a harsh word stirs up anger" (Proverbs 15:1). Arguments are not productive when studying with others, but unshakable convictions expressed with calmness and

gentleness will move hearts to truth. "Through patience a ruler can be persuaded, and a gentle tongue can break a bone" (Prov. 25:15).
- We must have an exemplary life. People *will* slander us, and nothing will ever change that overall reaction to truth. But we can win some people to the truth with our godly example of a perseverance that keeps teaching the truths of God's Word.

This book is not designed to make anyone an expert on denominational doctrines. I do not personally claim to be an expert. Nor is this book aimed at making you a skillful debater of those with whom you disagree doctrinally. Debating ends up in quarrels about words and produces poor attitudes toward those we are debating. This book has two key purposes:

- To strengthen the biblical convictions of disciples: we need to know what we believe and why we believe it. We who are striving to build biblical churches are often accused of being narrow-minded and having exclusive attitudes. However, the challenge is to be confident and knowledgeable without being arrogant.

- To help us understand what is wrong about the doctrinal *backgrounds* of the people we are teaching: it is not enough to use the "proof-text" approach (our verses against theirs) to help those caught in the web of denominational teaching. We need to know the basic philosophies behind their erroneous teaching if we are to explain and dismantle it in their minds. Therefore, we must be aware of at least some of the basic issues in denominationalism.

Over twenty years ago, I first became associated with the discipling churches as a minister with the San Diego Church of Christ. After one sermon, a young woman came up to me with some real doctrinal concerns. She explained that she had been studying with some of our members and wanted to be a true disciple. However, one of her past denominational doctrines was causing her confusion. She did not want to hold on to that teaching if it were wrong biblically; but on the other hand, she was too intellectually honest to dismiss it with some of the shallow answers she had been given thus far. It took no more than twenty minutes to dismantle that doctrine in her mind and heart. She left feeling relieved and joyful and was baptized into Christ a short time later. This example demonstrates how the teachings in this book can help. If a person is prideful and argumentative, no amount of arguing will likely convince him of the truth. However, if a person is genuinely seeking the truth but is caught in the web of false teaching, you knowing how to answer that teaching will make a tremendous difference.

Yes, let's get ready to answer and stay ready to answer. And let's do it with the spirit and demeanor expressed by our brother, Peter. When we do that, we will spend our lives making a real impact on hearts and, therefore, on eternity. **Prepared to give an answer**—it is the path of a disciple! May God grant us this preparation of mind and heart, and may he glorify himself through our proclamation of his Word!

SECTION ONE

CATHOLIC
RELIGION

INTRODUCTION:
Section One

In the first edition of this book, I used references from the most current Catechism of the Catholic Church, which reflected the changes from Vatican II, and I also quoted directly from Documents of Vatican II. However, I did not mention these changes, since they were primarily liturgical changes and did not affect the doctrines discussed in my book. The majority of my quotes were from an older Catholic writer, James Cardinal Gibbons, former Archbishop of Baltimore. His highly popular book, *The Faith of Our Fathers*, was written in the late 1800s and has gone through well over 100 editions and sold millions of copies in dozens of languages. Although more recent Catholic writings have stated their major doctrines in less direct language, in an attempt to be less offensive to non-Catholics, the same doctrines I address remain essentially unchanged.

What has changed in the Catholic Church? That is an interesting question, and the answers are not easy to ascertain. One reason that the answers are unclear is that Catholicism has different faces in different nations. Catholic churches in many nations outside the United States have changed their practice of Catholicism far less than churches in the United States. Traditions have been clung to with fervor, as an inherent part of their cultures. Catholicism in these cases is not simply a religion—it is a way of life, of family, of nationality. Thus, even peripheral areas have not been nearly as affected in those cultures.

Then you have issues of age to consider. In any culture, younger Catholics are more accepting of changes than older members are. That should come as no surprise, since it is basic human nature reflected in almost any generation in almost any culture. Applying that principle to the United States as a whole, we are a young country in comparison to most others, which likely explains why changes in Catholicism have been more readily accepted here than almost anywhere else. But the question remains: what are those changes?

The most notable change has been that masses are now conducted in the current language of the people instead of in Latin, as had been the case for centuries. More freedoms are allowed in priestly vestments and the configuring of church services. In spite of the continuation of the teaching that the only infallible interpretation of Scriptures comes from the official clergy, Vatican II led to more openness and even encouragement of reading the Bible for oneself. Attitudes toward science became more relaxed, especially in areas where an aspect of science was generally accepted as proven fact. Interest in evangelism was reawakened, with Pope John Paul II leading the way in this emphasis. Women began having more important roles, as demonstrated by the fact that, whereas in the past there were only altar boys, now there are both altar boys and altar girls.

A slight doctrinal shift has occurred regarding one of the seven sacraments—Extreme Unction. It is now more often called "Anointing of the Sick." More recognition is given to the original context of James 5:14-15 in which healing is promised, rather than viewing this sacrament to be only for those facing immediate death. However, in practice, little change can be recognized in spite of the changes in terminology.

One of the changes most likely to be misunderstood by Catholics and non-Catholics alike is the Catholic admission that all religions bring benefits to their adherents. That does not mean that the official Catholic Church teaches that those in other religions in Christendom are saved eternally, but rather that some benefits of grace are conferred to them, and could lead the way for their ultimate acceptance of Catholicism (and salvation). Jews and Muslims are specifically mentioned as having some common links with Christianity, and while the wording used is obviously an attempt to build bridges rather than burning them, it falls far short of admitting the possibility of them being saved. The same is true in the case of those in non-Catholic Christendom, except the wording is even more ecumenical and thus more susceptible to misunderstanding by non-Catholics and even Catholics themselves—many of whom would like to blur these distinctions and are themselves convinced of the salvation of those outside their faith. But regardless of what broadminded Catholics think and say, that does not change the official position of the Catholic Church. While we can commend their desire to be less condemning of non-Catholics, we can in no way commend their basic doctrines—the very doctrines that are examined in detail in this book and refuted biblically. With that brief explanation, let's begin that journey into a deeper examination of Catholicism.

CHAPTER ONE

THE FALLING AWAY WAS FORETOLD BY GOD

A Comfort for the Pain

One of the most puzzling, frustrating and heart-rending issues in the religious world is the issue of division. If a person had read the Bible carefully *before* becoming aware of the multiplicity of churches in the so-called Christian world, he would be baffled once he discovered that the religion of Christendom is made up of literally hundreds of groups with differing doctrines and practices. Just imagine: a first-century disciple is suddenly transported through time, landing in a large city in America today. No doubt he or she would be shocked at the technological nature of our generation; but perhaps a greater shock would occur when that person began looking for the church of Jesus Christ! Can you just picture the confusion and emotional pain suffered by such a misplaced disciple?

In reality, anyone who has made any effort to find God has been perplexed by the existence of such a divided religious world. When we become aware of the tremendous plea that Jesus made for unity, we are even more dismayed. It has often been said that the cost of a divided Christendom is an unbelieving world. Jesus' prayer in John 17:20-23 shows how clearly he understood this:

> My prayer is not for them alone. I pray also for those who will believe in me through their message, that all of them may be one, Father, just as you are in me and I am in you. May they also be in us so that the world may believe that you have sent me. I have given them the glory that you gave me, that they may be one as we are one: I in them and you in me. May they be brought to complete unity to let the world know that you sent me and have loved them even as you have loved me.

The only situation worse than confronting this division would be to confront it without a warning from God that it was coming. Praise God he did not leave us without such warning! Being warned may not correct the departures and the division, but it does show that: (1) none of this took God by surprise; (2) he is not the author of such confusion; and (3) we do not have to be a part of it! If God stands against division (and he clearly does), then our insistence on interpreting and following his inspired Word as the early church did cannot be wrong. Such an approach on our part is neither naive nor arrogant—it is biblical to the core!

Predicted and Predictable

Not only did God predict a departure from his Spirit-inspired message, but such a departure was humanly predictable, given the nature of both man and the universe. One of the well-recognized laws in science is the second law of thermodynamics. That law describes the way available energy is used up. Generally stated, this law demonstrates that *order* always gives way to *disorder*, unless something or someone intervenes to prevent it. Examples in our lives abound, from the condition of our yards, to our desks, to our bodies! Without intervention and careful attention, everyone and everything simply deteriorates on a gradual but predictable basis.

Since this firmly established principle operates in the physical world, we should not be surprised that it operates just as predictably in the spiritual realm. Look back to the example of the Israelite nation in their early days. We read on one page of the Bible that they were strong in their faith; and then we turn a few pages and read that they were weakening and abandoning the very principles which had blessed their lives. The Book of Judges shows this tendency over and over—as people repented, did well for a while, but then gradually lost their convictions and went backwards.

This same backward progression is clearly seen in the first-century church. As John wrote to the seven churches of Asia (Revelation 1-3), he described their departure from Jesus in doctrine, practice, convictions and heart. This departure came, even though the church had been led by inspired apostles and prophets, and had been warned by them about such departures. "First love" mellows into lukewarm behavior, desire is replaced by duty and zeal gives way to tradition and ritual. Since we are not different in our human nature and tendencies today, we must find out what occurred in the early church that led to the falling away, and then avoid it like the plague it is. If we do not learn from history, we are doomed to repeat it!

The Specific Passages Predicting Apostasy

Numerous New Testament (NT) passages predicted the falling away (apostasy). Make sure that you read both the passages and their explanations carefully, even if you think you are familiar with them. One of the basic principles of discipleship is *assume nothing*! We must develop both knowledge and deep convictions if we are going to successfully wade into the morass of religious error and help others escape it.

> At that time many will turn away from the faith and will betray and hate each other, and many false prophets will appear and deceive many people. Because of the increase of wickedness, the love of most will grow cold (**Matthew 24:10-12**).

In Matthew 24, Jesus describes Jerusalem's destruction, which would come some 40 years later in 70 A.D. Throughout those decades, false prophets would come to deceive people who might otherwise have been true followers of Jesus. As Jesus said in the previous chapter, "You shut the kingdom of heaven in men's faces. You yourselves do not enter, nor will you let those enter who are trying to" (Matthew 23:13). Notice the progression in Matthew 24—the false prophets water down the commands of God, which results in an increase of sin, which in turn leads to their love for God and their love for each other turning cold. It is true that lukewarmness produces sin, and here Jesus tells us that sin produces lukewarmness!

We have been raised in a religious atmosphere in which truth has been diluted beyond recognition. Our society is on the verge of chaos because people are ignoring the moral demands of God, largely because of smooth-speaking, conflict-avoiding preachers who long ago quit proclaiming God's demands with authority and without apology! Were Jesus to preach in our society as he did on this earth nearly 2,000 years ago, the result would be the same, but most likely in much *less time*! People would not accept the truth, and would react especially to the forceful way he delivered it. The false prophets of his time and ours will face God for their smooth but incredibly weak and damnable teaching.

> I know that after I leave, savage wolves will come in among you and will not spare the flock. Even from your own number men will arise and distort the truth in order to draw away disciples after them (**Acts 20:29-30**).

Paul, like Jesus, traces the departure from truth back to leaders in error, some from within the true church. People from the ranks will not simply wander off doctrinally and start their own movement based on false teachings; it takes *leaders* to do that kind of damage. This explains the Bible's numerous warnings about false teachers and leaders, and why they must be exposed and avoided (Romans 16:17-18; Titus 3:9-11).

Concerning the coming of our Lord Jesus Christ and our being gathered to him, we ask you, brothers, not to become easily unsettled or alarmed by some prophecy, report or letter supposed to have come from us, saying that the day of the Lord has already come. Don't let anyone deceive you in any way, for that day will not come until the rebellion occurs and the man of lawlessness is revealed, the man doomed to destruction. He will oppose and will exalt himself over everything that is called God or is worshipped, so that he sets himself up in God's temple, proclaiming himself to be God...And then the lawless one will be revealed, whom the Lord Jesus will overthrow with the breath of his mouth and destroy by the splendor of his coming (**2 Thessalonians 2:1-4, 8**).

This passage leaves no doubt about an evil power arising to oppose God, claiming God's authority and God's glory. Because he identifies himself with God, he is clearly a heretical and apostate *religious* leader. While questions may be raised about the original application of this text, its warning applies to any group or individual who assumes a glory and power which belongs only to God. And it shows just how prone men are to wanting that exaltation by other men.

The Spirit clearly says that in later times some will abandon the faith and follow deceiving spirits and things taught by demons. Such teachings come through hypocritical liars, whose consciences have been seared as with a hot iron. They forbid people to marry and order them to abstain from certain foods, which God created to be received with thanksgiving by those who believe and who know the truth (**1 Timothy 4:1-3**).

In this passage, Paul is very specific in both the prediction of an apostasy and in his depiction of the teachings which lead to it: "The Spirit *clearly* says..." These teachings were *Gnostic* in nature. Gnosticism (from the Greek word *gnosis*, for knowledge) was based on the belief that material things are evil; those of this persuasion were either *libertines* or *ascetics*.

Libertines claimed that, since the flesh was inherently evil, then one could do with the body whatever one wanted; as long as one held the right knowledge, the moral behavior mattered little. See 2 Peter 2 for a description of these libertines.

The latter type of Gnostic is described in 1 Timothy 4 (see also Colossians 2:20-23). Some people might view the prohibitions against marriage and foods as less than ideal, but not overly dangerous. God, on the other hand, traces these prohibitions back to deceiving spirits and demons! God says the people who teach these false doctrines, thus becoming pawns of the demons, are hypocritical liars with seared consciences.

To downplay false doctrines is to be unlike God in heart, and quite dangerous to ourselves and to others. It does take both life and doctrine to be righteous and to guide others into righteousness (1 Timothy 4:16).

> In the presence of God and of Christ Jesus, who will judge the living and the dead, and in view of his appearing and his kingdom, I give you this charge: Preach the Word; be prepared in season and out of season; correct, rebuke and encourage—with great patience and careful instruction. For the time will come when men will not put up with sound doctrine. Instead, to suit their own desires, they will gather around them a great number of teachers to say what their itching ears want to hear. They will turn their ears away from the truth and turn aside to myths (**2 Timothy 4:1-4**).

Once again, we see a very clear prediction of an apostasy, showing the human tendency to water down the demands of true discipleship. Without strong convictions based on biblical authority, we will look for the easy ways in life. As always, there will be false teachers who are more concerned with men's approval than with God's approval. Those of Isaiah's day were charged with similar motives, as they supposedly made this request of the prophets: "Give us no more visions of what is right! Tell us pleasant things, prophesy illusions" (Isaiah 30:10). Modern men may say the same things in a more reasonable and pious way, but God is not fooled. He clearly recognizes our desire to "have it our way," and he condemns it.

> But there were also false prophets among the people, just as there will be false teachers among you. They will secretly introduce destructive heresies, even denying the sovereign Lord who bought them—bringing swift destruction on themselves. Many will follow their shameful ways and will bring the way of truth into disrepute. In their greed these teachers will exploit you with stories they have made up. Their condemnation has long been hanging over them, and their destruction has not been sleeping (**2 Peter 2:1-3**).

Here again, the coming of false teachers is described. They will be secretive and deceptive about how they introduce their destructive heresies. Their influence will be widespread, and the reputation of spiritual truth will suffer. These teachers will be motivated by greed as their imaginations run wild. Initially, these false teachers were libertine Gnostics whose morality was extremely worldly. A careful reading of this chapter will demonstrate that these false teachers were already at work in Peter's time.

Dear children, this is the last hour; and as you have heard that the anti-christ is coming, even now many antichrists have come. This is how we know it is the last hour...Dear friends, do not believe every spirit, but test the spirits to see whether they are from God, because many false prophets have gone out into the world (**1 John 2:18; 4:1**).

The antichrist described in John's writing was not some future world leader, as modern speculators so confidently assert. Rather, *many* antichrists were already doing their work at the end of the first century. The letters of John show that some false teachers were denying that Jesus had been a true man, possessing a flesh-and-blood body. They are called *Docetists* (from *dokeo*, "to seem"). Gnostic beliefs had prompted them to originate the idea that Jesus was not really material (which they viewed as inherently evil), but pure spirit who "seemed" to be flesh and blood. Hence, John writes this in 2 John 1:7: "Many deceivers, who do not acknowledge Jesus Christ as coming in the flesh, have gone out into the world. Any such person is the deceiver and the antichrist."

Summary on the Apostasy

These passages, and others like them, make it abundantly plain that a falling away from the revealed truths of God would occur. This apostasy was beginning in the latter part of the first century and was led by false teachers espousing a variety of different errors. The Gnostic-related doctrines were very noticeable, and they eventually led to certain practices in the Roman Catholic Church. Since these false doctrines were resisted strongly by the Spirit-inspired apostles and prophets of the first century, they must be resisted with the same fervor by true disciples today. The division produced by abandoning biblical principles is an ugly thing in God's sight, to be sure, but it helps us to know that he anticipated division and gave inspired warnings about the nature of apostasy. To be forewarned is to be forearmed.

An Escape from the Confusion

Despite centuries of biblical departures and false teaching, complete with the hundreds of denominations produced by it, there is a way out of the confusion. It is biblically and practically possible to have one church just like the one described in the Book of Acts. In teaching about the kingdom of God, Jesus said: "This is the meaning of the parable: The seed is the word of God" (Luke 8:11). One of the laws of nature is that the seed reproduces its own kind. We would not plant corn and expect watermelons to grow, because we know that the seed always reproduces its kind. Similarly, when the word of God, in its purity, is planted in the hearts of men and women, it will produce exactly what it did when the church first began. However, the existence of hundreds of denominations offers a challenge to the thinking of modern man. How could we have just one church again?

Keep in mind that the NT is quite clear on the "one church" concept. In the short book of Ephesians, we find "one body" mentioned four times (2:16; 3:6; 4:4; 4:25); in chapter 1:22-23, we find that the body is the church. "And God placed all things under his feet and appointed him to be head over everything for the church, which is his body, the fullness of him who fills everything in every way."

But the question lingers—how could we have only one church in our setting today? How could any group be the church of the Bible rather than a denomination? Perhaps some illustrations would be of help in showing how a true non-denominational church is possible. Keep in mind that we do not mean *inter-denominational*, although that is what *non-denominational* means in our society. We mean a unified church which is unified *like* the Bible teaches *by what* the Bible teaches. Now, let's look at some illustrations.

A Church on an Island

Imagine that 300 people are marooned on an uninhabited island (like Gilligan's Island!). Suppose that they were not religious beforehand, but they find a Bible in the shipwreck and start studying it for the first time. They then come to faith in Jesus, repent of their sins and are baptized into Christ. What do they become, and of what church are they a part? Let's look at the following diagram and explanation:

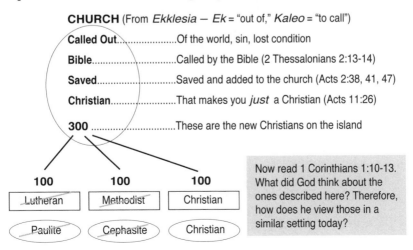

CHURCH (From *Ekklesia* — *Ek* = "out of," *Kaleo* = "to call")

Called Out......................Of the world, sin, lost condition

Bible...............................Called by the Bible (2 Thessalonians 2:13-14)

Saved..............................Saved and added to the church (Acts 2:38, 41, 47)

Christian..........................That makes you *just* a Christian (Acts 11:26)

300 ....These are the new Christians on the island

100   100   100

Lutheran   Methodist   Christian

Paulite   Cephasite   Christian

Now read 1 Corinthians 1:10-13. What did God think about the ones described here? Therefore, how does he view those in a similar setting today?

As we look at the diagram, it shows that the church means the "called out." Those in the church have been called out of the world, out of sin and out of a lost condition. The means of calling is the word of God, according to 2 Thessalonians 2:13-14:

> But we ought always to thank God for you, brothers loved by the Lord, because from the beginning God chose you to be saved through the sanctifying work of the Spirit and through belief in the truth. He called you to this through our gospel, that you might share in the glory of our Lord Jesus Christ.

Once we have been called by the word of God, we respond to it and are baptized, at which point we are saved and added to the church (Acts 2:38, 41, 47). When the people on the island do that, to which church are they added? Since they are simply following the Bible and do not even know of any denominations, they had to be added simply to the church of Jesus Christ, the family of God. What kind of Christians are they? They could not have become Baptists or Lutherans, because they had only the Bible. Therefore, they were simply Christians like the ones in the Book of Acts (Acts 11:26).

But now, let's suppose that the 300 on the island are rescued and return to the mainland. Being now in a spiritual mindset, they notice all of the different kinds of churches, and some of them start looking into joining other groups. One-hundred of them join the Lutheran Church, and 100 join the Methodist Church. Since they are already Christians from their experience on the island, it is obvious that, to become Lutherans and Methodists, they have to do something different, or in addition to, what they have already done. What they did on the island did not make them Lutherans or Methodists. The remaining 100 say, "We are already Christians. Why should we join another group? We'll just find a place to meet and just carry on like we did on the island."

From the example, we can see that being the church of the NT is still possible. But how does God feel about the 200 who joined the Lutherans and Methodists? 1 Corinthians 1:10-13 answers this question.

> I appeal to you, brothers, in the name of our Lord Jesus Christ, that all of you agree with one another so that there may be no divisions among you and that you may be perfectly united in mind and thought. My brothers, some from Chloe's household have informed me that there are quarrels among you. What I mean is this: One of you says, "I follow Paul"; another, "I follow Apollos"; another, "I follow Cephas"; still another, "I follow Christ." Is Christ divided? Was Paul crucified for you? Were you baptized into the name of Paul?

God demands unity and forbids division. Paul also condemns men's tendencies to want to exalt and follow men—even good men! The only way we should follow someone is for that person to have been crucified for us and then for us to be baptized into their name. Therefore, since God did not want Paulites or Cephasites in the first century, he certainly does not want Lutherans or Wesleyans in our day!

Religion in Early Rural America

Even if we see the possibility of having a present-day, non-denominational church, another question often arises: "Why do we have all of the different churches—don't all churches follow the Bible"? An illustration from the early days of rural America will help us answer this question.

In most frontier towns, there was often only one public building available for assemblies. Combined with the scarcity of available ministers, a rotation of denominational services developed in these towns. For example, in a certain town on the first Sunday of the month, a Methodist circuit-riding preacher would come to town and conduct Methodist services. On the second Sunday of the month, a Baptist preacher would arrive and conduct Baptist services. On the third Sunday, the Presbyterian minister would hold his services, and on the fourth, a Catholic priest would hold Mass. The problem is that only members of the minister's denominational group attended that particular service, with the result being that most religious people attended church services only once per month. People began asking why this situation had developed. They also asked, "Aren't all of the groups preaching the Bible"? The diagram below helps us to see the problem.

1. Methodists	Bible + the Methodist Discipline = **Methodists**
2. Baptists	Bible + the Baptist Manual = **Baptists**
3. Presbyterians	Bible + their Confession of Faith = **Presbyterians**
4. Catholics	Bible + their Catechism = **Catholics**

It was true that the ministers preached the Bible when they came to town, but along with it, they taught their particular denominational creed. Thus, it was the Bible *plus* the creed which made the difference. These groups needed unity badly, but the solution called for some serious decisions. You could never expect a Baptist to accept a Methodist Discipline, nor a Methodist to accept a Catholic Catechism, nor a Presbyterian to accept a Baptist Manual. But all of them could accept the Bible. Therefore, if all of them left their denominational creeds and simply followed the Bible, then unity would be possible and everyone could worship and work together. The Bible alone does not make

Methodists or Baptists or Catholics. It takes creeds to do that. Thus, doing away with creeds also does away with denominations, making unity and non-denominationalism possible.

Ferguson's Church

Another illustration shows that, while a church may preach the Bible in some way, this does not make it a true, Bible-based church. Actually, anyone can start a church. Just for the sake of illustration, let's suppose that I decided to start my own church. I might come up with the elements of the creed for my church in the following way, as seen in the diagram below:

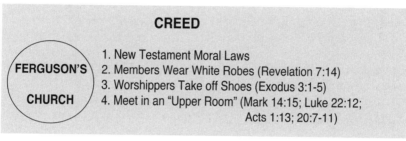

CREED

FERGUSON'S CHURCH

1. New Testament Moral Laws
2. Members Wear White Robes (Revelation 7:14)
3. Worshippers Take off Shoes (Exodus 3:1-5)
4. Meet in an "Upper Room" (Mark 14:15; Luke 22:12; Acts 1:13; 20:7-11)

If you came to my church on a given Sunday, my sermon might be on some NT moral law, in which case I would be preaching right from the Bible. You would leave saying, "Ferguson just preaches the Bible at his church," and on that day, this statement would be absolutely true. But on the next Sunday, I might read Revelation 7:14, a verse which describes (in a symbolic way) the purity of those in heaven who have washed their robes spiritually in the blood of Christ. It might sound reasonable to a person who knew little about the Bible (which covers most people in our society). You might still leave my services saying, "Well, it sounded a little different, but Ferguson did use the Bible."

I could also make a case out of going barefoot and meeting in an upper room. In the first instance, I would go to Exodus 3:1-5 and show how God told Moses to take off his shoes because the ground on which he stood was holy ground. Therefore, since we want to be holy, we will take off our shoes in worship. Of course, God did not tell us to follow that example, but to the biblically illiterate, it would sound at least reasonable. As for the part about meeting in upper rooms, a number of Scriptures show that the early disciples often met in upper rooms. Every specific reference to the Lord's Supper has an "upper room" as the setting. Since we want to imitate Jesus and the early disciples, and since it "gets us nearer to heaven," then we should want to observe the same practice.[1]

The point of this illustration is that many churches may seem to preach the Bible, but in reality, they are not consistently doing that. On any given Sunday, the Bible might be preached exactly. On any other Sunday, the Bible might be appealed to, but misapplied. The biblically uninformed might not know the difference, and they might believe they are really a part of a Bible church. The need for each person to study the Bible is an obvious application, but the main point is that a church may seem to be biblically based when it actually is not. Our goal must be *unity* and not simply *union*, to be *non-denominational* and not simply *inter-denominational*.

QUICK REFERENCE GUIDE: _____

1. The unity of everyone who desires to follow Christ is the will of God (John 17:20-23).

2. Jesus said that many would lose their love for him and for others within about 40 years from the time he spoke (Matthew 24:10-12).

3. From among the true church, false leaders would arise soon after Paul left Ephesus (Acts 20:29-30).

4. False leaders would reach the point where they assumed position and power reserved only for God himself (2 Thessalonians 2:1-8).

5. The Holy Spirit was quite clear about the impending apostasy, which would include teachings forbidding marriage and the eating of certain foods (1 Timothy 1-4).

6. The time would come when men would seek false teachers who would water down the truth, thereby making them comfortable in their sins (2 Timothy 4:1-4).

7. False teachers were motivated by greed (2 Peter 2:1-3).

8. The antichrists were already teaching false doctrines about the nature of Christ (1 John 2:18; 4:1).

Notes _____

[1]These illustrations came originally from an old friend, J.T. Bristow, of Gospel Outreach Publishers in Vancouver, Washington. With his permission, I included and adapted them for this book.

CHAPTER TWO

AUTHORITY IN RELIGION: FROM GOD OR FROM MEN?

Scripture vs. Tradition

One of the basic tenets of Catholic theology is that tradition is on equal footing with Scripture. The current *Catechism of the Catholic Church* states it in this way: "Both Scripture and Tradition must be accepted and honored with equal sentiments of devotion and reverence."[1] Herein lies the real issue: are the Scriptures totally sufficient as a guide of belief and practice, or is Catholic teaching correct when it says we must have "the living voice of the living church"?

The religious atmosphere of our present time exalts broad-mindedness and tolerance. Most religious groups avoid stating their true beliefs in a straightforward manner; most likely because they are afraid of being out of step with current trends and opinions. The Catholic Church is no exception to this approach. However, this approach is a very recent one, for former Catholic writers were much bolder in stating their doctrines in a dogmatic way.

One such writer of the past was James Cardinal Gibbons, former Archbishop of Baltimore. He wrote a highly popular book entitled *The Faith of Our Fathers*[2] in the late 1800s, which has gone through well over 100 editions and sold millions of copies in dozens of languages.[3] Gibbons expressly attempts to influence non-Catholics by arguing the validity of Catholicism. In his book, we see the real convictions behind the religion, enabling us to focus on the real issues.

The Catholic position, as stated by Gibbons, begins with the assumption that the Catholic Church is infallible. "The Church is One, Holy, Catholic, and Apostolic. Preaching the same creed everywhere and at all times; teaching holiness and truth, she is, of course, essentially enerring in her doctrine; for what is one, holy or unchangeable must be infallibly true."[4] He goes on to make an amazing assertion with these words: "If only one instance could be given in which the Church ceased to teach a doctrine of faith which had been previously held, that single instance would be the death blow of her claim to infallibility."[5]

From this assumed premise, Gibbons goes on to argue that God never intended his Word to be interpreted by the ordinary person, but only by the official clergy of the church. "Thus we see that in the Old and the New Dispensation, the people were to be guided by a living authority, and not by their private interpretation of the Scriptures."[6] The current *Catechism of the Catholic Church* states it less blatantly, but no less definitively with this comment: "The task of giving an authentic interpretation of the Word of God, whether in its written form or in the form of Tradition, has been entrusted to the living, teaching office of the Church alone...This means that the task of interpretation has been entrusted to the bishops in communion with the successor of Peter, the Bishop of Rome."[7]

As if to ensure that individuals cannot be trusted to study the Bible on their own, Gibbons seeks to undermine not only the ability of the ordinary person to read and understand the Bible, but whether the Bible can be understood at all! "Is the Bible a book intelligible to all? Far from it; it is full of obscurities and difficulties not only for the illiterate, but even for the learned."[8] He goes on to state, unequivocally, that the Bible is *not* sufficient to guide faith and practice. "Now the Scriptures alone do not contain all the truths which a Christian is bound to believe, nor do they explicitly enjoin all the duties which he is obliged to practice."[9]

Further, Gibbons asserts that the Bible cannot be trusted to even be the Word of God in its present condition. "What assurance have you that the book he hands you is the inspired Word of God; for every part of the Bible is far from possessing intrinsic evidences of inspiration: It may, for ought you know, contain more than the Word of God, or it may not contain all the Word of God."[10] Now let's consider the final step in this attempt to undermine trust in the Bible: "But even when you are assured that the Bible contains the Word of God, and nothing but the Word of God, how do you know that the translation is faithful?"[11]

While Catholic writers will say that the Scriptures are the Word of God, the above statements show that they trust far more in the infallibility of the Church and the Pope than in the infallibility of the Bible. Mark it down—churches based on traditions will hold to those traditions regardless of how they contradict the Bible. Jesus felt tremendous frustration as he tried to help religious people of his day choose God over tradition. The dogma is Scripture *plus* Tradition, until a choice must be made between the two: then it is Tradition *minus* Scripture!

The Scriptures Are Inspired

Gibbons may seem convincing when he uses human logic to discount the Bible as complete and trustworthy. But, no matter how persuasive human reasoning may be, the real issue is what the Bible actually declares about itself, and its declarations are unmistakable!

First, let's look at the *claim* of inspiration. The classic passage in this connection is 2 Timothy 3:16-17: "All Scripture is God-breathed and is useful for teaching, rebuking, correcting and training in righteousness, so that the man of God may be thoroughly equipped for every good work." The word translated God-breathed (*theopneustos*) in the New International Version is translated "inspired" in most of the older versions. It means that God was behind the message in a way which guaranteed that it was written exactly as he intended.

The word "Scripture" normally refers to the Old Testament (OT), but in this context, it most likely refers to both Old and New Testaments. Paul's second letter to Timothy was the last one he wrote before dying. With this letter, he completed his work as an inspired writer, and he expressed confidence that Timothy had all that he needed to be thoroughly equipped for every good work. Therefore, it seems both obvious and necessary that *Scripture* here refers to both the preparation for the coming of Christ (the OT) and the declaration that he had come (the NT). Both testaments are a part of the *one* written revelation of God to man— the Bible. The New is in the Old *concealed*, and the Old is in the New *revealed*. It is clear that the term "Scripture" can refer to the NT, because in 1 Timothy 5:17-18, Paul quoted Luke 10:7 and called it "Scripture." In 2 Peter 3:16, Peter referred to Paul's writing as part of the *Scriptures*.

Second, let's look at the *process* of inspiration. It is helpful to distinguish between *revelation* and *inspiration*. Revelation has more to do with the *content* of the message given by God, and inspiration has more to do with the delivery of that message, although the distinction is not absolute. Concerning revelation, Paul wrote this in Ephesians 3:2-5:

Surely you have heard about the administration of God's grace that was given to me for you, that is, the mystery made known to me by revelation, as I have already written briefly. In reading this, then, you will be able to understand my insight into the mystery of Christ, which was not made known to men in other generations as it has now been revealed by the Spirit to God's holy apostles and prophets.

Several important points about revelation are made in this text.

• God's mystery was made known to Paul by revelation.
• This revealed message could be read and understood by the disciples at Ephesus (and they were neither PhD's nor clergymen!).
• The inspired writers were "carried along" by the Spirit. This makes it clear that the writers were subordinate to the

Spirit, belying the claim by liberal theologians that the Bible is only a record of man's search for God. On the contrary, the Bible is the record of God's search for men, expressing his deep desire to have a relationship with them.

• This revelation was given to the apostles and prophets. In this context, *prophets* were those in the early church: a prophet was simply one who spoke for God, an inspired man. All apostles were also prophets, but most prophets were not apostles.

According to Hebrews 1:1-2, God had spoken through the prophets at various times and in various ways—but he now speaks through Jesus! Of course, Jesus revealed himself through his Spirit-inspired apostles and prophets. The progression was Father, Son, Spirit, prophet. (See John 16:12-16 for this progression.) Therefore, when Paul admonishes us to let the word of Christ dwell in us richly (Colossians 3:16), he was not talking simply about the *red letter* words of the Gospels and Revelation. All of the words in the NT are the words of Christ, delivered through the Spirit to the inspired prophets.

Was everything in the Bible inspired? Yes! Did everything in the Bible have to be revealed? Actually—no! Some information was already known by the writers, such as historical and geographical facts. But the spiritual truths were revealed, and then the process of inspiration protected the inspired men from error in all realms as they spoke and wrote. The revealed, inspired message of Jesus progressed through three distinct stages: the inspired message was only in the inspired men to begin with; then, this message was in both the men and the book as the NT started being recorded in writing (2 Thessalonians 2:1-2); and, finally, the inspired message was only to be found in the inspired book. However, the message was *available*, regardless of which stage and form the message was in.

The Holy Spirit used the inspired writers' own personalities. For example, the writers had different vocabularies. Luke, the physician, used a much more complex vocabulary than did John the fisherman. Paul dictated at least some of his writing to a recording secretary (sometimes called an *amanuensis*—see Romans 16:22). However, the Holy Spirit was still in control of the final product, and it was still God's word. The writers of the Gospel accounts wrote from different perspectives and emphasized different things. Matthew wrote from a Jewish perspective; Mark to a Roman mindset (lots of action); Luke to a Gentile audience; and John to a later universal audience. God chose the specific writers to say *what* he wanted *in the way* he wanted it said.

The process of inspiration did not reduce the NT writers to secretaries taking dictation, nor did it open them up to become mistake-prone individualists. God chose them, revealed his spiritual message to them, allowed them to work within their own personalities and vocabularies and protected their writing so that the final product was his message, without error. Therefore, Paul could confidently write: "This is what we speak, not in words taught us by human wisdom but in words taught by the Spirit, expressing spiritual truths in spiritual words" (1 Corinthians 2:13). From this passage, the phrase *plenary* (full) verbal (words) *inspiration* is used to describe this divine process.

The Scriptures Are Complete

The Scriptures are complete in both *content* and *effect*. The Bible contains error-free inspired writings, and it contains exactly the books God wanted. There were many books of a religious nature written during the same years that the NT was written. In fact, at least two of these books were written by Paul (1 Corinthians 5:9 mentions an earlier letter written to the church at Corinth, and Colossians 4:16 describes a letter to the Laodiceans). But God selected just the ones he wanted to provide the church in all ages with a complete message. Jesus promised the apostles that they would be guided by the Spirit into *all truth* (John 16:12-15). And Paul claimed that the Scriptures would provide the man of God with all that was needed for every good work (2 Timothy 3:16-17).

A preacher friend of mine from many years ago (now deceased) once participated in a public debate with a well-trained Catholic priest. At the beginning of the debate, my friend introduced a large banner with the words of 2 Timothy 3:16-17 clearly displayed. In his first speech, he referred to the banner and the passage, and noted how it destroyed the Catholic doctrine that questions the all-sufficiency of the Scriptures. He challenged the Catholic priest to directly deal with the passage in his next speech, but predicted that the priest would not do it. He was entirely correct. During the entire debate of several nights, my friend repeatedly referred to the banner, and he continued to challenge the priest to deal with the passage—but he never would. He could not accept the plain wording of the passage without rejecting his own Catholic doctrine.

Peter wrote that God has given us *everything* that we need in the spiritual realm: "His divine power has given us everything we need for life and godliness through our knowledge of him who called us by his own glory and goodness" (2 Peter 1:3). Jude said much the same thing in his brief letter: "Dear friends, although I was very eager to write to you about the salvation we share, I felt I had to write and urge you to contend for the faith that was once for all entrusted to the saints" (Jude 3). Both passages make it clear that the complete truth was already available. It had been *given* and *delivered*. Nothing else was yet to come, and nothing else was needed. The Scriptures of the OT and the NT were inspired and complete.

In Catholic versions of the Bible, one finds seven books in addition to the normal 66 with which we are familiar. These books come from the Apocrypha, the Jewish writings from the intertestamental period. Although widely used by the Jews, they were never accepted as Scripture by them, and were not officially proclaimed to be a part of the Catholic Bible until the 16th century. For a further discussion on why these books should not be seen as Scripture, see Appendix I on page 215.

Bible Authority: A Serious Matter!

The Bible, as an inspired book, is *precise* in its accuracy. In John 10:35, Jesus said the Scripture cannot be broken. In Matthew 22:23-33, he based his argument with the Jews on the tense of a verb. Verse 32 quotes Exodus 3:6, which records God saying, "I am the God of Abraham, the God of Isaac, and the God of Jacob." It does not say that God *was* their God. It says I *am* their God. Thus, these men were alive in the spirit world, and not dead (except physically). Jesus trusted the accuracy of Scripture down to the verb tenses! Similarly, Paul made an argument based on the difference between a singular and plural noun in Galatians 3:16. The Scriptures are precise, and we cannot afford to take them lightly nor treat them carelessly.

Since the Bible is authoritative, it must be carefully followed. Jesus spoke of the narrow road which few find and the broad road which many are on, and he made it clear that claiming to be his follower does not make it true (Matthew 7:13-14, 20). John 15:10 shows that we must obey Jesus' commands in order to remain in his love. Obviously, a failure to obey his commands separates us from his love! Consider these inspired words of Paul in Galatians 1:6-8:

> I am astonished that you are so quickly deserting the one who called you by the grace of Christ and are turning to a different gospel—which is really no gospel at all. Evidently some people are throwing you into confusion and are trying to pervert the gospel of Christ. But even if we or an angel from heaven should preach a gospel other than the one we preached to you, let him be eternally condemned!

There are two Greek words for "another." One means another of the same kind, and the other means another of a completely different kind. In this passage, Paul uses both to say that those who were turning to a different gospel were not turning to a gospel of a slightly different kind. They were turning to a gospel of a totally different kind. When the gospel (good news) is perverted, it ceases to be good news for those who pervert it. Consider also 2 John 9, which reads: "Anyone who runs ahead and does not continue in the teaching of Christ does not have God; whoever continues in the teaching has both the Father and the Son." God is serious about man holding carefully to his message!

Thankfully, the Bible can be understood. Paul said that we could read what he wrote and understand what he understood (Ephesians 3:3-5). Therefore, he went on to admonish us not to be foolish, but to understand the Lord's will (Ephesians 5:17). If we are not able to understand the Bible (as the Catholics claim), then it must be for one of two reasons. One, God did not want us to understand it (but he clearly does—1 Timothy 2:4). Or, two, he simply was not able to make it understandable! (Do you want to charge God with either of those?) All can agree that *some parts* of the Bible are difficult to understand (2 Peter 3:16 says exactly that), but most of it is easy enough to grasp if we *want* to understand and obey! In the case of the more difficult passages (which are actually few), we should be motivated even more to *study* rather than to entrust our study (and soul) to some professional clergyman.

Finally, the Bible must be understood *and* obeyed by anyone who expects to please God. We must hold to the teaching of Jesus in order to know the truth and to be set free from sin (John 8:32). Although Jesus died for all mankind (Hebrews 2:9), only those who *obey* him will be saved (Hebrews 5:9). It is through our obedience to the truth that our souls are purified (1 Peter 1:22). With a hurting heart and an uncompromising spirit, Jesus said, "Why do you call me, 'Lord, Lord,' and do not do what I say" (Luke 6:46)? The Scriptures are inspired; they are complete; they are authoritative; and they are most certainly the standard by which we shall be judged (John 12:48; James 2:12).

Let us be determined to have a noble heart before God, and to urge everyone to have the same. This heart is described beautifully in Acts 17:11 with these words:

> Now the Bereans were of more noble character than the Thessalonians, for they received the message with great eagerness and examined the Scriptures every day to see if what Paul said was true.

QUICK REFERENCE GUIDE: _____

1. **Catholic Claim**: the Bible cannot be totally understood by the average person. **Bible Truth**: John 8:32; Acts 17:11; Ephesians 3:3-5; 5:17; 1 Timothy 2:4.

2. **Catholic Claim**: the Bible plus traditions are needed to find salvation. **Bible Truth**: Matthew 15:7-9; John 16:13; 2 Timothy 3:16-17; 2 Peter 1:3; Jude 3.

3. The truths of the Bible were revealed by the Holy Spirit to inspired prophets (John 16:12-16; Ephesians 3:3-5; 2 Peter 1:21; 1 Corinthians 2:13).

4. The Bible is precise in its accuracy (John 10:35; Matthew 22:23-33; Galatians 3:16).

5. It must be followed very carefully (Matthew 7:13-14, 21; John 15:10; Galatians 1:6-8; 2 John 9).

6. If the Bible cannot be understood, then either God did not want us to understand (see 1 Timothy 2:4), or he was not powerful enough to make it understandable!

7. Without understanding and responding to the Bible's message, we cannot go to heaven (Luke 6:46; John 8:32; Hebrews 2:9 and 5:9; 1 Peter 1:22).

Notes _____

[1]*Catechism of the Catholic Church*, English Translation United States Catholic Conference, Inc. (Liguori, Missouri: Liguori Publications 1994) 26.

[2]James Cardinal Gibbons, *The Faith of Our Fathers* (New York: P. J. Kenedy & Sons, 1917).

[3]*Catechism of the Catholic Church*, 26.

[4]Gibbons, p. 54.

[5]Gibbons, p. 61.

[6]Gibbons, p. 66.

[7]*Catechism of the Catholic Church*, p. 54.

[8]Gibbons, p. 70.

[9]Gibbons, p. 72.

[10]Gibbons, p. 67.

[11]Gibbons, p. 68.

CHAPTER THREE

THE EXALTATION OF MEN

Did Jesus Really Ordain a Pope?

As we saw in Chapter One, the Bible predicted that leaders would be most responsible for the falling away. A number of times in the NT, leaders are warned about man's tendency to desire exaltation. Peter admonished elders to be on their guard against greed and not to lord it over their flock (1 Peter 5:1-3). His description of false teachers in 2 Peter 2 showed that some had not heeded his admonition. Our sinful nature enjoys the limelight and praise. Any leader in any group who says he is not tempted in this way is either out of touch with his own heart or dishonest. For men and women to lead in a powerful and godly way, their motivations must be brought into the light and purified by the Holy Spirit

Sadly, the Catholic Church illustrates what occurs when these sinful tendencies are not adequately addressed. The exaltation of men (and Mary!) is one of the religion's key characteristics. Gibbons takes four chapters of his book to justify a pope, his basic assertion being that Peter was the first Pope and has had successors up to the present day. Human logic and reason are the basis of the arguments, with the Bible used (actually *misused*) in an attempt to shore up the logic. Gibbons, as usual, assumes the very point to be proved.

> In like manner, the Church, besides an invisible Head in heaven, must have a visible head on earth. The body and members of the Church are visible; why not also the Head? The Church without a supreme Ruler would be like an army without a general, a navy without an admiral, a sheepfold without a shepherd, or like a human body without a head.[1]

He continues by correctly showing that God often called kings and other leaders to the forefront of his people. But the office of the Pope claims authority far beyond that of any such biblical leader. The Catholic

Church claims nothing short of infallibility for the Pope. Consider Gibbons' explanation:

> What, then, is the real doctrine of Infallibility? It simply means that the Pope, as successor of St. Peter, Prince of the Apostles, by virtue of the promises of Jesus Christ, is preserved from error of judgment when he promulgates to the Church a decision on faith or morals.[2]

This supposed doctrine of the Pope speaking *ex cathedra* as the "Vicar of Christ on earth" did not even become official church doctrine until 1830 A.D.

Popes, as the so-called "Vicars of Christ," are exalted and venerated by their subjects. Certainly, the appearance of Catholics bowing down to kiss the ring of the Pope strongly suggests an act of worship. This is in marked contrast to Paul's adamant refusal to allow men to worship him (Acts 14:11-15), and with an angel's refusal to allow the apostle John to even bow down before him (Revelation 22:8-9).

But was Peter the first Pope? Much of the Catholic teaching hangs on this highly dubious and disprovable premise. Catholic writers use John 21:15-17 and Matthew 16:13-19 to substantiate their position. However, in the former, Peter was actually being *censured* more than *commissioned*. He had been the blatant denier of Jesus, and now the depth and quality of his love for the Lord was being questioned. He was being reinstated as an apostle, even as the lead apostle given the responsibility to share the keys of the kingdom. But there is nothing here to signal the beginning of the papacy.

Matthew 16 is more important to the Catholic position, especially verses 18-19.

> "And I tell you that you are Peter, and on this rock I will build my church, and the gates of Hades will not overcome it. I will give you the keys of the kingdom of heaven; whatever you bind on earth will be bound in heaven, and whatever you loose on earth will be loosed in heaven."

A common Protestant explanation of this passage is that Jesus is making a word-play with the words "Peter" and "rock." The former, *petros* in the original language, means a small rock. The latter, petra, designates a large rock or a ledge. Thus, Jesus is saying that Peter's name means rock, but that he is going to establish his church on a *real* rock, a quite *solid* rock. Of course, that Rock was Jesus himself, as may be seen in other passages (Romans 9:33; 1 Corinthians 10:4; 1 Peter 2:4-8). 1 Corinthians 3:11 clarifies the issue: "For no one can lay any foundation other than the one already laid, which is Jesus Christ."

The context of Matthew 16 is Peter's confession of Jesus as the Son of God. Men in that society considered Jesus a great spiritual leader, even a prophet, but Peter confessed him as Deity (*Son of God*—see John 5:18). It was on Jesus himself as the Son of God that the church was to be built. To have it built on any man, especially on an individual as human as Peter, would be scary for sure! The entire context undermines the Catholic position; when one understands the exact words used for "rock," that position is without biblical support.

Although the foregoing explanation is the only one I included in the first edition of this book, I must mention that the argument as stated is not the only one possible, and in fact has apparent weaknesses upon closer examination. Making an absolute distinction between *petros* and *petra* is one such weakness. Most experts in the Greek language believe this to be more than questionable. Furthermore, if Jesus were speaking to Peter in Aramaic, as was likely the case, he would have used the term *keypha* both times. It seems best to understand that Peter's role in the establishment of the church is simply expressed in two ways in this verse: a foundational role and an initiation role (with the keys to the kingdom)—both fulfilled in Acts 2 with the Jews and in Acts 10 with the Gentiles. Neither the NT nor the early church writers indicate anything at all about a papacy with a succession of popes tracing back to Peter, and regardless of the interpretation we adopt for Matthew 16:18, it does not teach the Catholic viewpoint.

How much supremacy did Peter really have? He certainly had a great influence among the apostles, and he was the key spokesman when the Jews (and later the Gentiles) were ushered into the kingdom (Acts 2 and 10). He was the leading apostle in the evangelization of the Jews, as Paul was to the Gentiles (Galatians 2:7-9). His authority to bind and loose in Matthew 16:19 was also given to all of the apostles in Matthew 18:18-19. As apostles, they had the authority to enforce God's message which they had been given by direct inspiration. Today, we have the same message in written form, and leaders have the authority to enforce it. But neither then, nor now, do leaders have the authority to originate a new or different message. At issue here is the difference between upholding God's will and man's traditions.

If I were going to pick a "Pope" from the pages of the NT, Paul would easily be the choice rather than Peter. Paul, as the apostle to the Gentiles (Galatians 2:7-9), was over the group which became by far the largest. He was more stable than Peter, having had to rebuke Peter in front of the church on one occasion (Galatians 2:11-16). Paul wrote the letter to Rome, and he also wrote the majority of the NT letters. Peter wrote only two brief books. Furthermore, Paul was single, whereas Peter was married (Matthew 8:14; 1 Corinthians 9:5). In order to dodge the marriage issue, Gibbons amazingly states: "Even St. Peter, after his vocation, did not continue with his wife, as may be inferred from his own words: 'Behold, we have left all things, and followed Thee.'"[3] In other words, Peter, and others like him, either violated the Scriptures by divorcing their wives or by failing to fulfill their marital duties (1 Corinthians 7:3-5)! How anyone could make or accept such unbiblical reasoning is a mystery!

What about the Priesthood?

According to Catholic teaching, their priesthood is the continuation of the apostolic office, complete with infallibility. Gibbons writes: "On the contrary, as the Apostles transmitted to their successors their power to preach, to baptize, to ordain, to confirm, etc., they must also have handed down to them the no less essential gift of infallibility."[4] No biblical proof is offered for this assertion, just human reasoning. Biblically, there is no indication that Jesus intended to inaugurate a continual apostolic line. In Acts 1, Matthias was chosen to take Judas' place, evidently because God did want twelve apostles present at the establishment of the church. Furthermore, the qualifications required there could only be met by two men out of the 120 present. And no one today could possibly meet these qualifications! When James the apostle was killed in Acts 12, nothing is said about choosing a successor for him. Therefore, the concept of a perpetual apostleship in the form of a "popehood" or priesthood is based on mere assertion, and it flatly contradicts the qualifications for an apostle given in Acts 1:21-22.

Another biblical issue regarding the Catholic priesthood is that priests are called "Father" as a religious title, which is expressly forbidden in Matthew 23:9. Matthew 23:8-10 also forbids using "Rabbi" and "Teacher" as religious titles. We must see the difference in *function* and *title* in this connection. Paul was both a father and a teacher in function (1 Corinthians 4:15; 2 Timothy 1:11), but he was called simply Paul rather than Father Paul or Teacher Paul. Leadership in the church is designated by role and function, not by title or position as men think of it. Notice that the very next words Jesus spoke in Matthew 23 were these: "The greatest among you will be your servant. For whoever exalts himself will be humbled, and whoever humbles himself will be exalted" (Matthew 23:11-12). Jesus is not ruling out *leadership* here, but he is ruling out *lordship* as it pertains to human beings. We are to be servant leaders who exalt God and not ourselves. Our greatness in the kingdom is to be measured by how many we *serve*, not by how many we *are served by*.

The NT teaching about the priesthood is quite clear and simple. We have one High Priest, who is Jesus (not the Pope!). The Book of Hebrews calls him our High Priest many times and makes it clear that he functions like no human priest ever did or ever could. Then, the regular priests in the church are Christians and all Christians are priests. The term is not reserved for leaders. Every disciple, no matter how young or immature, is a priest in the kingdom of God (see 1 Peter 2:5, 9). One of the main emphases in Hebrews is that we no longer have to go through humans as intercessors with God, as was the case with the OT priesthood. Now we offer spiritual sacrifices directly to God through our High Priest, Jesus. To bring back an inferior system is to do the very thing Hebrews warns us against (Hebrews 7:18-28), and that is precisely what the Catholic Church has done.

Who Can Be a Saint?

In Catholicism, saints are those who "exhibit a fervent piety and a zeal for religion." The normal technical definition of a saint is reserved for those canonized after their death, after they meet a set of stringent requirements. By their own admission, only a tiny number of people from within their ranks will ever be saints. The double standard of clergy/ laity is nowhere more obvious than in the Catholic Church.

Biblically, all Christians are saints, just as surely as they are disciples. The NT calls Christians "saints" more than 40 times. The Greek word, *hagios*, from which it is translated, simply means consecrated or set apart (for God's service). True Christianity (as defined by the Bible) knows nothing of classes of members, all varying in commitment level. (See Jesus' comments on this point in Luke 9:23-26 and Luke 14:25-33.) There can be no double standard, for our only standard is total commitment to Christ as we make his character *our* character, and his mission *our* mission.

The Exaltation of Mary

The adoration, exaltation and worship of Mary are a cornerstone of the Catholic religion.[5] As the falling away gathered momentum during the first several centuries of the church, the teaching increasingly became a combination of Christianity, Judaism and paganism. Christianity was promoted by making it palatable to nearly anyone.

- The priesthood, incense-burning and other practices from Judaism were brought into Catholicism.
- Catholic holidays were established to accommodate those accustomed to observing certain dates.
- The exaltation and eventual worship of Mary was used to attract those pagans accustomed to worshiping female deities.

Basic Catholic teachings about Mary exalt her to a position far beyond that of a normal human being. She is said to have been conceived without original sin (which is itself an unbiblical doctrine—see page 217), as Gibbons states: "Unlike the rest of the children of Adam, the soul of Mary was never subject to sin, even in the first moment of its infusion into the body."[6] Therefore, the sacrificial blood of Jesus affected her differently than it did everyone else. All other humans had to be *cleansed* by it, but she had only to be *preserved* from the taint of original sin.[7] This teaching led to the official doctrine of the *Immaculate Conception* in 1854 A.D.

Catholics not only believe that Mary was born without *original* sin— they also believe that she never *committed* any sins. Speaking of Mary, Gibbons says, "…who never grieved Almighty God by sin, who never tarnished her white robe of innocence by the least defilement, from the first moment of her existence till she was received by triumphant angels into heaven."[8] This shocking affirmation would have stunned Paul, who thought that *all* humans had sinned, except for Jesus (Romans 3:23)! The truth is that Mary and her other children were, at one point, so deficit in faith that they thought Jesus was out of his mind (Mark 3:20-21). Then, when they came for him, he would not even go to the door and respond to their lack of faith (Mark 3:31-35). Mary wasn't quite perfect here, was she? She definitely qualified for membership in the human race with the rest of us!

Eventually, it was claimed that Mary was a perpetual virgin. In other words, after Jesus was born, she and Joseph never had a sexual relationship. Gibbons thought that it was unimaginable that Mary would be "desecrated and profaned by human use."[9] Profoundly influenced by Gnostic and other Greek thinking, Catholicism has a long history of viewing sexuality, even in marriage, as something distasteful. (Medieval theologian Peter Lombard taught that the Holy Spirit left the room whenever married couples had sexual intercourse[10] because intercourse always contained elements of evil.[11]) In Catholic thinking, Mary would be worthy of adulation only if she abstained from sex throughout her life, and so this became their dogma.

As Mary's position became more exalted, it was taught that she, like God, could receive prayers. "The Church exhorts her children not only to honor the Blessed Virgin, but also to invoke her intercession."[12] This exaltation of Mary raised her nearly to the level of Jesus; within the ranks of Catholicism, she is worshipped on virtually an equal basis with him. After the Council of Ephesus in 431 A.D., she began to be commonly called "Mary, the mother of God." The original intent of this phrase was to emphasize the Deity of Jesus, but with the passage of time, the emphasis changed. Originally, the emphasis was on "Mary, the mother of God," but it came to be "Mary, the Mother of God."

The Second Vatican Council in the 1960s stated its desire to avoid excesses in regard to Mary,[13] but it is remarkable what that council went on to say. Consider several examples:

> Finally, preserved from all guilt of original sin, the Immaculate Virgin was taken up body and soul into heavenly glory upon the completion of her earthly sojourn. She was exalted by the Lord as Queen of all, in order that she might be the more thoroughly conformed to her Son...[14]

The teaching here is that Mary never died, but was bodily assumed into heaven to the position of Queen of the Universe.

> For, taken up to heaven, she did not lay aside this saving role, but by her manifold acts of intercession continues to win for us gifts of eternal salvation...Therefore the Blessed Virgin is invoked by the Church under the titles of Advocate, Auxiliatrix, Adjutrix, and Mediatrix.[15]

While Jesus theoretically is held to be the one mediator between God and man, Mary is declared to be the Mediatrix of All Graces from whom Catholics gain gifts of eternal salvation. But then consider perhaps the most startling statement of all:

> At the same time, it [the Second Vatican Council] admonishes all the sons of the Church that the cult, especially the liturgical cult, of the Blessed Virgin, be generously fostered. It charges that practices and exercises of devotion toward her be treasured...[16]

In other words, the college of bishops working in Vatican II gave the Catholic Church a solemn charge to promote and encourage the cult of Mary.

Granted that Mariolatry is a false doctrine of an apostate religion, what is the proper and biblical view of Mary? After Jesus was born, she and Joseph had a normal marriage, one that included the sexual relationship planned by God. Matthew 1:25 states: "But he had no union with her until she gave birth to a son." The clear implication is that, after she gave birth to her son, she then had a sexual union with her husband. Therefore, we are not surprised to read that she had other children, which would have been half-brothers and half-sisters to Jesus. "Isn't this the carpenter's son? Isn't his mother's name Mary, and aren't his brothers James, Joseph, Simon and Judas" (Matthew 13:55—see also Mark 3:32; 6:3; Galatians 1:19)?

Clearly, she was a very special person chosen for an amazing purpose. A careful reading of Luke 1:26-56 will demonstrate that this young woman was full of love for God and trusted him completely with her life and reputation. She was truly a remarkable woman from these early days until the days she died as a disciple of Jesus Christ. The honor rightly due her should never be lessened in an overreaction to false teaching.

However, having said that, it must also be noted that she was a normal sinner in need of a Savior just like the rest of us. Mary was decidedly a great woman, but not a goddess. Let's respect, admire and honor her in a right way as we reject the idolatrous Catholic view.

QUICK REFERENCE GUIDE: _____

1. **Catholic Claim**: The Pope is the visible head of the Church. **Bible Truth:** Jesus is the only head of the Church, and all Christians are the members of his spiritual body (Ephesians 1:22-23; Colossians 1:18-24).

2. **Catholic Claim:** The Pope is, for all intents and purposes, to be worshipped by his subjects (bowing down, kissing ring, etc.). **Bible Truth:** Paul refused worship (Acts 14:11-15) as did even an angel (Revelation 22:8-9).

3. **Catholic Claim:** Peter, as the Rock upon which the church was built, was the first Pope, establishing a succession of popes tracing back to him. **Bible Truth:** Jesus was the ultimate foundation of the church, although Peter was used by him in the initial establishment of the church, as he preached the gospel of the resurrected Jesus (see 1 Corinthians 3:11; 1 Peter 2:4-8).

4. **Catholic Claim:** Peter was the first Pope. **Bible Truth:** There is not the slightest evidence that Peter was viewed in this way in the first century. The concept of the papacy did not develop for three hundred years. Peter had less influence over the whole church than Paul had, for Paul was the apostle to the Gentiles, which was the larger group (Galatians 2:7-9). Also, Peter wrote only two brief books of the NT, while Paul wrote at least 13, including the one to the Roman church.

5. **Catholic Claim:** The Priesthood is based on apostolic succession. **Bible Truth:** A succession of apostles is impossible because of the qualifications in Acts 1:21-22.

6. **Catholic Claim:** Only special clergymen are priests. **Bible Truth:** All Christians are priests (1 Peter 2:5, 9).

7. **Catholic Claim:** Saints are highly spiritual people, usually canonized after their death. **Bible Truth:** All Christians are saints (Romans 1:7; 15:25-26—note in v. 26 that all Christians in Jerusalem were not poor, but all were saints).

8. **Catholic Claim:** Mary was a perpetual virgin. **Bible Claim:** She had other children (Mark 3:32; 6:3).

9. **Catholic Claim:** She never committed any sins. **Bible Claim:** She was a normal sinner like all humans (Romans 3:23), and at least once, she was very weak in her faith in regard to Jesus and his mission (Mark 3:20-21, 31-35).

Notes _____

[1]James Cardinal Gibbons, *The Faith of Our Fathers* (New York: P. J. Kenedy & Sons, 1917), p. 80.

[2]Gibbons, p. 101.

[3]Gibbons, p. 328.

[4]Gibbons, p. 54.

[5]Gibbons, p. 19.

[6]Gibbons, p. 141.

[7]Gibbons, pp. 140-141.

[8]Gibbons, p. 166.

[9]Gibbons, p. 139.

[10]Quoted in Dwight Hervey Small, *Christian: Celebrate Your Sexuality*, Fleming H. Revell, p. 62.

[11]Small, p. 72.

[12]Gibbons, p. 154.

[13]*The Documents of Vatican II*, Guild Press, New York, 1966, p. 95.

[14]Vatican II, p. 90.

[15]Vatican II, p. 91.

[16]Vatican II, p. 95.

CHAPTER FOUR

RITUALISM VS. FAITH: COMING TO CHRIST

Works, Grace and Faith

While the Catholic Church, especially since the days of Vatican II, officially expresses that salvation is by grace, the idea of meriting, or earning one's salvation, is quite pervasive within the membership of this group. Although their theologians can quote certain writings which seem to support a more biblical position regarding works and grace, the average Catholic has little grasp of the biblical message. The *Catechism* makes this "salvation by works" emphasis quite obvious:

> Since the initiative belongs to God in the order of grace, *no one can merit the initial grace* of forgiveness and justification, at the beginning of conversion. Moved by the Holy Spirit and by charity, *we can then merit* for ourselves and for others the graces needed for our sanctification, for the increase of grace and charity, and for the attainment of eternal life. (Italics are in the original.)[1]

This works' orientation was one of the main motivations behind the Reformation Movement. Men like Luther and Calvin had strong reactions to what they had personally seen and experienced within Catholicism, and they were convinced it was at odds with the message of the gospel, especially as found in Romans and Galatians. In our time, practices such as doing penance for one's sins and praying through rosary beads by repeating "Hail Mary's" and "Our Father's" make it pretty clear that the focus actually is on works. This system teaches, in many ways, that a person is to "work off" his sins and to *earn* the favor of God.

The lack of understanding of salvation based on faith trusting grace is quite obvious in this quote from Gibbons concerning the necessary existence of purgatory: "If this brother of yours dies with some slight stains upon his soul, a sin of impatience, for instance, or an idle word, is he fit to enter heaven with these blemishes upon his soul? No; the sanctity of God forbids it, for 'nothing defiled shall enter the Kingdom of Heaven.'"[2] The question "Is he fit"? just about says it all. Does anyone *deserve* to go to heaven? *No*, a thousand times *no!* We can only enter because Jesus paid the price for us, and with our faith trusting that grace, the price redeems us for God. The idea of merit-based salvation is inherent in the whole Catholic system, but it is completely foreign to the Bible.

The Biblical Message of Grace and Faith

In Ephesians 2:8-10, Paul wrote: "For it is by grace you have been saved, through faith—and this not from yourselves, it is the gift of God—not by works, so that no one can boast. For we are God's workmanship, created in Christ Jesus to do good works, which God prepared in advance for us to do." We are to do good works, but not in order to *earn* salvation. This means that we work *because* we are saved (if, in fact, we really are). We do not put our trust in our performance—we trust the grace of God. Even when our performance is outstanding, we still focus on God's goodness and not our own. As Jesus put it, "So you also, when you have done everything you were told to do, should say, 'We are unworthy servants; we have only done our duty'" (Luke 17:10).

A key passage for our understanding of how grace, faith and works interrelate is found in Romans 4:1-8. This passage is quite to the point. Trust your works, and forgiveness is ruled out; trust God's grace, and you can be a righteous person whose sin the Lord will never count against you! Now, the difference in those two positions is monumental as far as the *effects* are concerned, but the outward *actions* may not be very different. We are talking about heart issues here; about trust issues. Two people can do much the same things outwardly, but one can go to heaven and the other to hell. The type of trust in the heart will either validate or invalidate our actions. As Paul put it in Galatians 3:10: "All who rely on observing the law are under a curse."

In Romans, Paul uses the word "justified" to describe our standing with God. This word is a legal term, literally meaning *just-as-if-I'd-never-sinned*! Biblically, we are either saved (justified) completely, or we are lost. Hebrews 7:25 provides us with this amazing promise: "Therefore he is able to save completely those who come to God through him, because he always lives to intercede for them." We cannot be saved any more than *completely*! Salvation by grace through faith does not mean that God did 50% and now we must do our 50%! It is not faith *plus* grace which equals salvation; it is faith *trusting* grace. Faith is merely our acceptance of Christ's completed work on the cross for us.

David wrote of a man whose sin the Lord would never count against him. Who is that man? He is the one who has been baptized into the death of Christ with a dependence on that death as his only hope (Romans 6:3-4; Galatians 3:27). He is now "in" Christ where all spiritual blessings are (Ephesians 2:10), and where there is no condemnation (Romans 8:1). To remain in Christ, he walks in the light with Jesus and has his sins continually cleansed (1 John 1:7-9). In context, a part of this walk in the light is a continued confession of sin, thereby remaining dependent on the mercy of God. Now that *is* good news! But it is *not* Catholicism. I have talked with many Catholics about these matters, and I have yet to find one who understood much at all about these vital concepts. They were focused on the externals, having been taught to trust in those externals, thereby ruling out faith trusting grace. It should be added that Catholics are not the only ones with this problem. Much religion naturally tends in this direction, and we must all be vigilant about keeping the emphasis in the right place.

The failure to stress grace/faith salvation, combined with a huge emphasis on ritualism and priesthood mediation, helps explain how Catholics are so strongly tied to their religious roots. "I was born a Catholic, and I'll die a Catholic" is a common statement by those who have little Biblical basis for their beliefs. Many, it seems, are afraid to question or examine those beliefs. We must convince Catholic people that only good can come from opening the Bible and hearing its message. Even though they may be initially afraid to look, the Word of God will still do its work. The truth dispels ignorance and thereby eradicates errors.

Infant Baptism

The practice of infant baptism began, at least among some believers, sometime in the third century, and it has continued in the Catholic Church and (as we will see later) in many Protestant churches as well to this day. This practice is fully linked with a belief in the concept of original sin and with the belief that infants need to be baptized to have that sin removed. In *The Eternal Kingdom*, his book on church history, F.W. Mattox traces the development of this doctrine.[3] First, Irenaeus (early third century) taught that Adam's sin took away man's divine likeness. Then, Tertullian (160-220 A.D.) developed the doctrine into more of its present form, and slightly later, Cyprian made a connection with the need to baptize infants. However, infant baptism was not generally practiced until the fifth century.

In an interesting section, Gibbons gives the current Catholic view that many infants and children will miss heaven because they have not been baptized. He presents a questioner who asks, "But is not that a cruel and heartless doctrine which excludes from heaven so many harmless babes that have never committed any actual fault?" And then he says, "To this I reply: Has not God declared that Baptism is necessary for all?"[4] Here Gibbons affirms that infant baptism is taught by God, and that those who do not experience it will lose their eternal blessings.

Let us look first at the biblical view of baptism and then at the doctrine of original sin. In the NT, the act of baptism is always connected with faith and repentance (Acts 2:38, Galatians 3:26-27). Those who were baptized were those who made a conscious decision to turn from sin and make Jesus Lord. To suppose that a mere outward act can somehow benefit someone who is incapable of neither faith nor repentance is to teach "baptismal regeneration" or "water salvation" in its purest form! In an effort to substantiate their position, those who practice infant baptism usually refer to the household baptisms in the Book of Acts. But the nature of these "households" is ambiguous, with a lack of specifics about those who were actually involved. In some cases, as in Acts 18:8, we do know that all of those in the household *believed,* and that does nothing to support the presence of infants or the practice of infant baptism.

In a similar vein, some passages may mention simply that a person believed, while another passage mentions that they *repented* or were *baptized.* To argue that the word believed, by itself in the first case, rules out repentance in the other case, is poor interpretation indeed. We must look at all of the passages on a given subject in order to really understand that subject. On the subject of household baptisms, we cannot look only at those passages and overlook all of the passages which explain the overall requirements for baptism. The requirements for baptism, given in many other passages in the Bible, rule out the possibility of infants in those particular households being baptized.

If a person told me that everyone in their household had graduated from college, or had run a marathon, I would automatically know that no one in that household was a baby! And if a person told me that everyone in their household had been baptized, I would know the very same thing. If a person is too young to believe and repent, they would not be included in a baptized *household.* A key passage in this regard is Colossians 2:12: "...having been buried with him in baptism and raised with him through *your* faith in the power of God, who raised him from the dead." Note that being buried and raised with Christ occurs through your faith in the power of God, not through your parent's faith or your priest's faith. But, the appeal to household baptisms in Acts is not the main basis for teaching infant baptism. That is found in the concept of original sin.

We have dealt with this extensively in Appendix II found on page 217, but in summary, we can say this: babies are not born guilty of Adam's sin or anyone else's sin. They are innocent at birth. Ecclesiastes 7:29 states: "This only have I found: God made mankind upright, but men have gone in search of many schemes." Paul said of himself, "Once I was alive apart from law; but when the commandment came, sin sprang to life and I died" (Romans 7:9). In other words, he was spiritually alive before he reached an age of being accountable before God. Then, when he was old enough to really understand and respond to the commands of God, sin became a reality for him, and at that point, he died spiritually. That seems plain enough, doesn't it? Jesus told us to become like little children, and he talked of them in a way which made it clear that they are right with God (Matthew 18:1-4, 10). Keep in mind that the children about whom he spoke had not been baptized yet, for the doctrine of infant baptism had not yet been invented!

Babies cannot biblically be baptized, nor do they need to be. They do not need forgiveness, for they have nothing to forgive. They do not need to be *saved,* because they are already *safe.*

QUICK REFERENCE GUIDE: _____

1. **Catholic Claim:** Man can and must merit grace and work off sins. **Bible Truth:** We cannot merit grace, and if we try to serve God while relying on performance, we rule out grace (Luke 17:10; Romans 4:1-8; Galatians 3:10; Ephesians 2:8-10).

2. **Catholic Claim:** Salvation is a very insecure thing, and purgatory is necessary to pay for all of your sins. **Bible Truth:** If we are in Christ, there is no condemnation (Romans 8:1), our sins are continually cleansed (1 John 1:7-9) and none of them is even placed on our record (Romans 4:8). Salvation is complete (Romans 7:25).

3. **Catholic Claim:** The sin of Adam is passed on to every person (called original sin). **Bible Truth:** We suffer the consequences of Adam's sin, physical death (Genesis 3:22-24; Romans 5:12; 1 Corinthians 15:21-22). We cannot inherit his guilt (Ezekiel 18:20), for our spirits come directly from God (Zechariah 12:2; Ecclesiastes 12:7; Hebrews 12:9).

4. **Catholic Claim:** Infants need to be baptized because they are guilty of Adam's sin. **Bible Truth:** Baptism is always a response of faith and is accompanied by repentance (Acts 2:38; Colossians 2:12). Babies do not need to be baptized to be saved, because they are already safe (Matthew 18:1-4, 10; Romans 7:9). Also, Psalm 51:5 is a hyperbole (overstatement for emphasis), as are Psalm 22:9; 58:3.

Notes _____

[1]*Catechism*, p. 487.

[2]Gibbons, p. 183.

[3]Mattox, F.W. *The Eternal Kingdom.* Delight, Arkansas: Gospel Light Publishing Company, 1961, pp. 17-119.

[4]Gibbons, p. 223.

CHAPTER FIVE

RITUALISM VS. FAITH: LIVING IN CHRIST

Confirmation

According to Catholic teaching, confirmation is necessary for the completion of the grace received in baptism. Gibbons writes about what supposedly occurs at the point of receiving this sacrament. "Confirmation is a Sacrament in which, through the imposition of the Bishop's hands, unction and prayer, baptized persons receive the Holy Ghost, that they may steadfastly profess their faith and lead upright lives."[1] This doctrine is wrong on two basic points.

One, the laying on of the apostle's hands, to which this action is compared, imparted the *miraculous gifts* of the Holy Spirit. In Acts 8, we find that Philip the evangelist had preached the gospel in Samaria with great results. When the apostles in Jerusalem heard about the number of people being converted, they sent Peter and John to lay their hands on the people, in order to impart the miraculous gifts which were needed in that new church (Acts 8:14-19). In verse 18, it says very specifically, "When Simon saw that the Spirit was given at the laying on of the apostles' hands, he offered them money." Much more will be said in a later chapter about the miraculous gifts when we discuss the Pentecostal Movement. Suffice it to say, at this point, that apostolic succession is one problem for Catholic theology, as we have already shown, and the reception of the Spirit is another problem. Biblically, it had nothing at all to do with what is now called *confirmation*.

Two, the ordinary indwelling of the Spirit is received at baptism, as shown clearly by Acts 2:38; Galatians 4:6; Ephesians 1:13-14. The separation of baptism and the reception of the Spirit by *years* is completely an invention of man. In the Scriptures, there is a major difference between the reception of the Spirit at baptism and the reception of his miraculous gifts, but in Catholicism, they are combined and confused beyond recognition.

Penance

According to the Catholic doctrine of penance, a person's sins can be forgiven only through the priest. Gibbons writes:

> I have said that forgiveness of sins is *ordinarily* to be obtained through the ministry of the Apostles and of their successors, because it may sometimes happen that the services of God's minister cannot be obtained. A merciful Lord will not require in this conjuncture more than a hearty sorrow for sin joined with a desire of having recourse as soon as practicable, to the tribunal of Penance.[2]

Even the exception mentioned here is only temporary, to be followed up with confession and absolution by a Priest.

The supposed basis for this teaching is Matthew 16:19 and Matthew 18:18. In both passages, the apostles are told "whatever you bind on earth will be bound in heaven, and whatever you loose on earth will be loosed in heaven." Another possible translation, given in some editions of the New American Standard Version, reads "shall have been bound in heaven." In other words, the Holy Spirit would guide the apostles, as inspired men, to pass down the decisions that God had already determined in heaven. Both passages are found in the context of authoritative discipline by the apostles, recognizing that as Spirit-inspired men, the apostles would be led to enforce the will of God in the early church. To apply this passage to non-inspired men and make it a requirement for all forgiveness is another issue indeed!

Concerning the practice of church discipline ("excommunication" is their word), the Catholic church misses the fundamental point. Biblically, discipline by the church (or withdrawal of fellowship) is simply man's recognition of where a person's sins have already placed him with God. If a person is in fellowship with God, he is certainly in fellowship with the church. On the other hand, if someone has lost fellowship with God because of unrepentant sin, then the church must recognize that and act accordingly. In the *Catholic Catechism*, they have the doctrine of church discipline exactly reversed. "The words *bind and loose* mean: whomever you exclude from your communion, will be excluded from communion with God; whomever you receive anew into your communion, God will welcome back into his."[3] Thus, they have God obeying church leaders rather than *vice versa*!

James 5:14-16 shows that, although forgiveness comes from God, healing can come from the elders' prayers. The context begins by showing the need for the seriously ill to call for the elders to pray for their physical problems. The sick person could be expected to confess sins to these church leaders, as the end of verse 15 suggests. But the verb tense in verse 16 brings out the idea that we should not wait to confess until we are sick and call for the elders, at which time we feel compelled to do it; we should be in the *habit* of confessing to each other on an ongoing basis! Actually, the Catholics are correct in recognizing the tremendous power of confession to another human being, but they are wrong in limiting the hearing of confession to the clergy and in making that a requirement of forgiveness. (However, if we have sinned against another person, reconciliation would mean that we *would* seek his or her forgiveness.)

Indulgences, Extreme Unction and Purgatory

These three Catholic practices are also issues which logically relate to forgiveness. Of course, Catholics themselves tie together seven Sacraments which they relate directly to salvation. According to their catechism, "The Sacraments are efficacious signs of grace, instituted by Christ and entrusted to the Church, by which divine life is dispensed to us."[4] These seven Sacraments are baptism, confirmation, the Eucharist, penance, anointing of the sick (extreme unction), Holy Orders and Matrimony.

The practice of granting *indulgences*, according to Gibbons, is:

> ...simply a remission in whole or in part, through the superabundant merits of Jesus Christ and His saints, of the temporal punishment due to God on account of sin after the guilt and eternal punishment have been remitted.[5]

However, as Gibbons admits, indulgences were also promoted as a way to cover sins not yet committed, especially during the Middle Ages. By the purchase of indulgences, it was also supposedly possible to lessen the suffering of specific deceased loved ones in purgatory, a practice which produced much opposition during the Reformation period. One of the common sales pitches during this period was reportedly this: "as soon as a coin in the coffer rings, another soul from purgatory springs." The large revenues produced from this practice financed, among other things, the construction of immense cathedrals. The whole issue of indulgences exposes the salvation by works orientation discussed earlier and reveals a long-standing failure to understand the grace of God and the means of salvation which he freely offers us.

The doctrine of *extreme unction* is supposedly based on James 5:14-15, and applies to both physical and spiritual healing. The more common usage is to administer these rites to a person who is most likely about to die. This teaching is an outgrowth of the doctrines of apostolic succession of the priesthood and penance. In their teaching, it is the work of the priest in an act of mysticism, for the person being "blessed" may be in a coma or even dead. To pray for the sick is to do a wonderful thing, but to presume to confer the blessing of forgiveness on a person in a coma is yet another. The Bible knows nothing of one person's prayers securing forgiveness for another person who is not himself seeking God according to God's will. In 1 John 5:16, we find that, in the case of some people, praying for them is not even recommended!

Gibbons describes purgatory as "a middle state of temporary punishment, allotted for those who have died in venial sin, or who have not satisfied the justice of God for sins already forgiven."[6] He further justifies the concept of praying for the dead through the assumption that such an intermediate state exists. Again, at issue is the lack of understanding of salvation based on man's faith accepting God's grace. To live your entire life without a sense of complete forgiveness, all while looking forward to going to purgatory, at *best* must be a miserable experience.

Biblically, death seals our fate forever. At death, we are judged (Hebrews 9:27). Once we are judged, we cannot cross the great chasm that separates the saved from the lost (Luke 16:19-31, especially verse 26). The doctrine of purgatory calls into question the forgiveness of God, who both forgives and forgets our sins (Hebrews 8:12), and who completely wipes them out (Acts 3:19). Finally, the concept of purgatory draws an unbiblical distinction between venial and mortal sins. Biblical distinctions between sins deal with whether they are unmeditated or premeditated, and also with the nature of their impact on self and others. But any manmade classification which causes someone to view any sin lightly is dangerous business, besides just being unbiblical.

Worship: The Mass and the Eucharist

This concept involves the idea of making a sacrifice to God, and is thus called "the Sacrifice of the Mass." Gibbons makes a connection between this practice and the sacrifices of the Jewish period. Actually, much of Catholicism is borrowed from the Jewish system. Paul's comments in Colossians 2:14-17 demonstrate the futility of such borrowing:

> ...having canceled the written code, with its regulations, that was against us and that stood opposed to us; he took it away, nailing it to the cross. And having disarmed the powers and authorities, he made a public spectacle of them, triumphing over them by the cross. Therefore do not let anyone judge you by what you eat or drink, or with regard to a religious festival, a New Moon celebration or a Sabbath day. These are a shadow of the things that were to come; the reality, however, is found in Christ.

The OT system was given to people who had just come out of slavery with little understanding of spirituality. Therefore, God gave them a covenant which was often focused on physical things in order to train them. According to the Letter to the Hebrews, these OT institutions were intended to point forward to greater institutions in the NT, namely spiritual institutions. Hebrews 9 and 10 discuss this OT typology at great length, showing that these former institutions and practices were merely "external regulations applying until the time of the new order" (Hebrews 9:10). For example, the temple in the OT is fulfilled in the NT as the spiritual temple, the church (Ephesians 2:21-22). The animal and grain sacrifices in the OT have given way to spiritual sacrifices now (1 Peter 2:5). The OT High Priest is fulfilled completely in Jesus, and the priests of that former institution have been replaced by Christians, for every Christian is a priest of God. Catholicism has gone back to the physical focus because that is the tendency of natural man.

The Catholic idea of the sacrifice of the Mass maintains a view of the cross which is unbiblical and depressing. Jesus' idea is far better, as Hebrews 7:27 shows: "Unlike the other high priests, he does not need to offer sacrifices day after day, first for his own sins, and then for the sins of the people. He sacrificed for their sins once for all when he offered himself." The victory has been won, and our view of the cross is now one of victory. Feeling the conflict of this passage with his doctrine, Gibbons writes:

> St. Paul says that Jesus was offered once. How, then, can we offer Him daily? I answer, that Jesus was offered once in a bloody manner, and it is of this sacrifice that the Apostle speaks. But in the Sacrifice of the Mass, He is offered up in an unbloody manner.[7]

Of course, we could note that the doctrine of transubstantiation declares that the wine of communion becomes the literal blood of Jesus, and thus their sacrifice is not so "unbloody" after all! In any case, this doctrinal focus explains why church services were changed from the *family reunion* atmosphere described in the NT to a *funeral* atmosphere! And since Protestantism grew out of Catholicism, the deadness of most groups in that movement is likewise explained!

The Eucharist, from a Greek word meaning "to give thanks," is a highly important ritual in Catholicism. In the words of the *Catholic Catechism*, it is "the source and summit of the Christian life."[8] According to their view, (*transubstantiation*), the bread and wine of communion, when officially blessed by the presiding priest, become the literal body and blood of Jesus (called also the *Real Presence*). Gibbons argues that

no dogma of the Catholic Church rests on stronger Scriptural authority, and then bases his case on John 6 with notable dogmatism.[9] For
example, assuming the very point he is trying to prove, that this passage
is talking about communion, he writes: "For His language is not susceptible of any other interpretation."[10]

Gibbons' comments notwithstanding, John 6 is assuredly not talking about communion. The passage under consideration is John 6:53-
60, which reads as follows:

> Jesus said to them, "I tell you the truth, unless you eat the flesh of the Son
> of Man and drink his blood, you have no life in you. [54] Whoever eats my
> flesh and drinks my blood has eternal life, and I will raise him up at the last
> day. [55] For my flesh is real food and my blood is real drink. [56] Whoever
> eats my flesh and drinks my blood remains in me, and I in him. [57] Just as
> the living Father sent me and I live because of the Father, so the one who
> feeds on me will live because of me. [58] This is the bread that came down
> from heaven. Your forefathers ate manna and died, but he who feeds on this
> bread will live forever." [59] He said this while teaching in the synagogue in
> Capernaum. [60] On hearing it, many of his disciples said, "This is a hard
> teaching. Who can accept it?"

The Catholic view invites several challenges. One, this teaching
preceded the establishment of the Lord's Supper by a long time. How
could they have even connected it with what was later to be called communion? Two, the Jews were very open to rituals. Their religion was
full of it. Why would they have struggled with eating a piece of bread
once a week, if that were what Jesus was referring to in this passage?
Three, what challenged the Jews was accepting Jesus as the Messiah and
answering his call to discipleship—that is what this chapter is all about!
John 6 is not talking about communion at all, but about a total acceptance of Jesus and his teachings into our hearts and lives. That was, and
still is, the challenge of Jesus.

In this passage, much emphasis is on the true life which comes by
accepting Jesus and his teachings. In verse 53, life comes from eating
and drinking Jesus. In verse 54, this food gives us eternal life. In verse
56, such eating allows us to remain in Christ. Verse 57 says that we live
by feeding on Jesus. Then, verse 58 says that if we feed on the bread of
Jesus, we will live forever. The emphasis on life through Jesus is quite
obvious. Now look at other statements in the same chapter. Verse 35 says
that if we come to Jesus, we will never go hungry, and if we believe in
him, we will never go thirsty. In verse 40, Jesus says that all who look to
the Son and believe on him will have eternal life. Verses 44-46 teach that
this "coming to Jesus" is accomplished by listening to God and being

taught by him. Then, in verse 47, the result of listening to God is that "he who believes has everlasting life."

The focus of John 6 is the necessity of faith in Jesus as the Son of God. Believing in Jesus is equated with eating him. Three times in the context, a reference is made to the "last day." In verses 39-40, if people look to Jesus and believe in him, they will receive eternal life and be raised up at the last day. In verse 44, those who come to Jesus by allowing the Father to draw them will be raised up at the last day. Then, in verse 54, eating Jesus' flesh and drinking his blood will cause a person to be raised up at the last day. The three passages are worded differently, but the meaning in context is the same in each. As Jesus said in verse 63, "The words I have spoken to you are spirit and they are life." He is discussing believing his words, not taking communion. No passage which is clearly speaking of the Lord's Supper uses the term "flesh"—it is always "body."

In response to Jesus' challenges, many people turned away; Jesus then asked the apostles if they were going to leave as well. Peter's answer tells us exactly what the thrust of Jesus' challenges had been. "Simon Peter answered him, 'Lord, to whom shall we go? You have the words of eternal life. We believe and know that you are the Holy One of God'" (John 6:68-69).

The idea that the elements of communion become the literal flesh and blood of Jesus requires further scrutiny. In Matthew 26:26-29, along with parallels in Mark and Luke, Jesus did say that the bread was his body (not flesh) and that the fruit of the vine was his blood. Here he is speaking figuratively, as he often did. In John 10:7, he called himself a "gate," and in John 15:1, a "vine." By what rule of biblical interpretation should we accept one as literal and not the others? When Jesus instituted the Lord's Supper, he had not yet died. He was standing right there before his apostles. How could bread and wine have somehow become literal? This teaching is an example of the mysticism which is a pervasive part of the Catholic religion.

Asceticism

Ascetic practices in the Catholic Church had their beginning with very early Gnostic tendencies, as we discussed in an earlier chapter. A clear reference to this kind of thinking is found in 1 Timothy 4:1-3, where Paul warns of false teachers who are urging people to abstain from marriage and from certain foods. One of the early Catholic practices was that of *monasticism*. Believing that material things were inherently evil, many people, in and out of the ministry, withdrew from society. Monasteries were established, and the truly "spiritual" avoided the very world they were supposed to influence. Jesus lived out no such example, nor did he leave any such command.

The NT clearly shows that such practices do not help one to avoid sin. Paul addressed this issue very directly in Colossians 2:20-23 as follows:

> Since you died with Christ to the basic principles of this world, why, as though you still belonged to it, do you submit to its rules: 'Do not handle! Do not taste! Do not touch!'? These are all destined to perish with use, because they are based on human commands and teachings. Such regulations indeed have an appearance of wisdom, with their self-imposed worship, their false humility and their harsh treatment of the body, but they lack any value in restraining sensual indulgence.

The entire mission of the kingdom demands that we be a part of society in order to be the salt and the leaven for Jesus. To separate ourselves from those we are supposed to influence, either physically or emotionally, is to oppose the example and commission of our Master. After Paul condemned the ascetics in 1 Timothy 4:4-5, he concluded in this way: "For everything God created is good, and nothing is to be rejected if it is received with thanksgiving, because it is consecrated by the word of God and prayer."

Perhaps the most blatant example of asceticism in the Catholic religion is the celibacy required of priests and nuns. Consider these statements by Gibbons:

> Although celibacy is not expressly enforced by our Savior, it is, however, commended so strongly by Himself and His Apostles, both by word and example, that the Church felt it her duty to lay it down as a law.[11]

In attempting to explain away Peter's marriage, he writes: "Even St. Peter, after his vocation, did not continue with his wife, as may be inferred from his own words: 'Behold, we have left all things, and followed thee.'"[12] Feeling the weight of the 1 Timothy 4 passage, Gibbons wrote that Paul referred to false teachers who taught that marriage itself was sinful, whereas the Catholics do not teach that.[13] However, they do teach that exact thing as it relates to the priesthood! No amount of verbiage can change that one.

Then, in an attempt to also explain away the qualifications of a Bishop in 1 Timothy 3:2, Gibbons writes: "The context certainly cannot mean that a Bishop must be a married man, for the reason already given, that St. Paul himself was never married" (page 332). Note that Gibbons assumes that Paul must certainly have been a Bishop! However, Paul never refers to himself as an elder (or bishop, another term for the same role). Peter, on the other hand, did say that he was an elder (1 Peter 5:1). Not only was Peter married (1 Corinthians 9:5), but he was bound by the teaching of 1 Corinthians 7:1-5 to fulfill his marital duty sexually. Notice the exact wording of 1 Corinthians 9:5: "Don't we have the right to take a believing wife along with us, as do the other apostles and the Lord's brothers and Cephas?" Peter and the other apostles were, *at that time,* living with their wives! The Catholic claim is that those who were married when they came into the church later became a part of the clergy and then quit living with their mates at that point. In light of the plain wording of 1 Corinthians 9:5, this explanation is inconceivable. The Scripture is not open to any other interpretation. We must be dealing with willful deception in this case.

The overall view of Catholicism toward sexuality is thoroughly unbiblical. Sadly, one has only to look at the sexual irregularities among the priesthood which are coming to light in increasing measure to understand the seriousness of the problem in the practical realm. When men pervert biblical teaching, it always results in serious consequences in real life. These issues are not simply academic or doctrinal. They are life issues with both temporal and eternal consequences.

QUICK REFERENCE GUIDE: _____

1. **Catholic Claim:** Confirmation is when those previously baptized receive the Holy by the laying on of the Bishop's hands. **Bible Truth:** The indwelling of the Spirit comes when a disciple is baptized (Acts 2:38; Galatians 4:6). The laying on of apostles' hands imparted the miraculous gifts of the Spirit (Acts 8:14-19).

2. **Catholic Claim:** The doctrine of penance means that a priest must forgive a person's sins. **Bible Truth:** The passages in Matthew 16:19 and Matthew 18:18 did not make the apostles into law-makers; they were law-enforcers. Forgiveness comes from God, but healing comes from our confessing to one another (not priests)—James 5:16.

3. **Catholic Claim:** Indulgences helps the deceased to get out of purgatory quicker. **Bible Truth:** There is no purgatory (Luke 16:19-31; Hebrews 9:27; once people are dead, their eternal fate is sealed.

4. **Catholic Claim:** Jesus is sacrificed in the mass daily. **Bible Truth:** Jesus was sacrificed once for all (Hebrews 7:27).

5. **Catholic Claim:** John 6 refers to the Catholic doctrine of transubstantiation. **Bible Truth:** John 6 refers to accepting Jesus as the Son of God by accepting his teachings (compare the requirements

for being raised up at the last day—verses 39-40, 44, 54). Also, look at the emphasis on the words of Jesus as the means to life (verses 63, 68-69).

6. **Catholic Claim:** Practices of asceticism, such as monasticism and celibacy of the clergy, are spiritual and pleasing to God. **Bible Truth:** Such practices are neither spiritual nor helpful in avoiding sin (Colossians 2:20-23). Requiring celibacy is strictly forbidden (1 Timothy 4:1-5); Peter was married and living with his wife (1 Corinthians 9:5).

Notes _____

[1]Gibbons, p. 230.
[2]Gibbons, p. 282.
[3]Gibbons, p. 363.
[4]Gibbons, p. 293.
[5]Gibbons, p. 307.
[6]Gibbons, p. 173.
[7]Gibbons, p. 258.
[8]Gibbons, p. 334.
[9]Gibbons, pp. 235-244.
[10]Gibbons, p. 236.
[11]Gibbons, p. 328.
[12]Gibbons, p. 328.
[13]Gibbons, p. 333.

SECTION TWO

PROTESTANT
RELIGION

CHAPTER SIX

A LONG HISTORY OF REACTIONS

The Catholic Reaction: Rejection of the Bible

Religious history is filled with reactions of various kinds. For that reason, it is difficult, or even impossible, to understand a specific group without understanding something of the cultural *milieu* from which it arose. The word "reaction" may conjure up a negative image in our minds, but reactions may be very badly needed. Some of the reactions we will consider in this chapter are bad ones, but others are good, at least with respect to original motives. Since the history of Christendom does reflect a long history of reactions, not only must we understand what those reactions were and what they produced, but we also must understand our own human tendency to be reactionary. Even when the reactions are needed against unbiblical ideas, we must guard against going too far and *overreacting*. As has often been said, if we do not learn the lessons of history, we are certain to repeat them.

As we examine the Catholic reaction—the rejection of the Bible in favor of human reasoning and traditions—we will include some information mentioned in previous chapters, but looking at it from only a historical viewpoint without dealing with its biblical inaccuracy. The main errors we encounter in studying with Catholic people have been adequately addressed already. But we do need to see how these changes crept in subtly. What began innocently enough often became perverted over a period of many years. For example, the phrase "Mary the mother of *God*" was originally coined to stress the Deity of Jesus, but was gradually changed into "Mary the *Mother* of God," now stressing the *near-divinity* of Mary.

The amazing range of the changes we will look at happened over decades, and sometimes over *hundreds* of years. Our hindsight may be 20/20 today, but to a person living a religious life on a daily basis, changes were most likely not obvious. And that is a challenge for us all. We must always be determined to be a people of the Book—searching it, discussing our findings, getting input from others, remaining open in our positions and never allowing others to study or think for us.

One of the first departures from the biblical pattern was in the area of leadership and organization. In the NT, the terms elder, bishop (meaning "overseer") and pastor (meaning "shepherd") were all describing the same role or function. All elders had equal authority. Over a period of time, however, the title of bishop was applied to the elder who presided over elders' meetings. By 150 A.D., these men were recognized as monarchical bishops ruling over the other elders, but holding no authority outside of their local congregations. With the passing of more years, the city bishops were exercising authority over bishops from rural areas, and by the end of the third century, the doctrine of apostolic succession was applied to these city bishops. Each of the Roman provinces had one head bishop who had the authority to call councils. The bishops of Rome, Antioch and Alexandria were regarded as the top bishops because of the size of these cities and possibly the early apostolic connections with these churches.

Another serious but seldom mentioned departure was found in the decline and eventual elimination of the role of the evangelist. Prominently mentioned in the NT (Acts 21:8; Ephesians 4:11; 2 Timothy 4:5), evangelists clearly had major leadership responsibilities, in addition to their mission of preaching the word (1 Timothy 4:11; 5:21; Titus 1:5). But after the first century, there is hardly any mention of the term, and certainly the role, as Paul envisioned it, was ignored and discarded.

The development of the priesthood was a noticeable trend by 150 A.D. It began with a distinction between the clergy and the laity patterned after the Jewish priesthood. The bishop was like the high priest, the elders were like the regular priests and the deacons were like the Levites.

Original sin and baptism of infants, as we discussed in Chapter Four, can be traced back to the early third century, with Tertullian being the first to actually espouse the doctrine of original sin. Cyprian, writing from 248-258 A.D., was the first to make the connection between this doctrine and the need to baptize infants. Sprinkling was occasionally practiced in emergency cases, with the first known instance in 251 A.D. by Novatian. Obviously, the exception became the rule at some point. Some instances of infant baptism can be traced back before 325 A.D., but it was not until the fifth century (around 450 A.D.), under the influence of Augustine, that infant baptism was generally practiced. Augustine was a man of great influence during this period, and he is often referred to as the "Father of the (Catholic) Church." His teaching paved the way for the adoption of a number of doctrines, including original sin, infant baptism, celibacy in the clergy and the elevation of church traditions to the level of Scripture. Regarding the latter, he once stated: "I should not believe the Gospel unless I were moved to do so by the authority of the Catholic Church."

The Eucharist (from the Greek word meaning "to give thanks") had its beginnings as a simple memorial observance of the Lord's Supper, but this concept gradually gave way to the idea of "the sacrifice of the mass." Cyril of Jerusalem (315-386 A.D.) was the first to clearly claim that the Eucharist had the power to help the dead. Later, this focus became a common one in Catholicism. Augustine taught that the Communion was a sacrifice, and by the time of Gregory the Great (540-604 A.D.), the sacrifice of the mass was completely accepted in doctrine and practice. The doctrine of transubstantiation was much more slowly developed, with John of Damascus (700-750 A.D.) being the first to argue that the bread and wine become the literal flesh and blood.

These changes are some of the key departures from the teaching of the Bible within early Catholicism. However, some of the later, less significant changes are interesting to note. The following departures and dates of other events are chosen from a longer list in an article by Douglas Jacoby entitled, *Where It All Went Wrong (A Brief Overview of Church History)*. Douglas called his list a "Directory of Departure Dates," footnoting the fact that "many of the doctrines listed actually appear in embryonic form several generations earlier."

Doctrinal Departure Dates	
160 A.D.	EASTER celebrated (Rome)
180 A.D.	Authority of TRADITION upheld
200 A.D.	INFANT BAPTISM tolerated
200 A.D.	PRIESTS
-to-	Communion table becomes ALTAR
300 A.D.	First MONKS
232 A.D.	First CHURCH BUILDING
300 A.D.	CANDLES
-to-	KISSING THE BISHOP'S HAND
400 A.D.	Mystical view of the Lord's Supper
313 A.D.	Christianity becomes legal
325 A.D.	Council of Nicea: Loss of Separation of Church and State

325 A.D.	One bishop per city
	Roman Emperor over bisops
337 A.D.	40-day LENT
c.350 A.D.	Holy Days:
	Christmas, Pentecost, Ascension Day
381 A.D.	Christianity official religion:
	PAGANS (and paganism) flood church;
	church structure patterned after Roman Empire
382 A.D.	Bishops of Rome claiming more and more power
450 A.D.	VESTMENTS for clergy
476 A.D.	Fall of Roman Empire plunges
	church into Dark Ages
606 A.D.	Boniface III, first bishop of Rome to
	claim universal authority as POPE
1000 A.D.	INDULGENCES
1050 A.D.	HAIL MARYS
1054 A.D.	Split between Roman Catholic &
	Eastern Orthodox
1215 A.D.	TRANSUBSTANTIATION affirmed
1546 A.D.	APOCRYPHA canonized as
	scripture by Catholic Church
1854 A.D.	Doctrine of IMMACULATE CONCEPTION
1870 A.D.	INFALLIBILITY OF THE POPE

The Protestant Reaction: A Cry for Reformation

Financial matters in the Catholic Church became, in some ways, more of an issue than the multitude of false doctrines being taught. Church offices were sold for large sums of money, as were other favors. Indulgences (pardons for sins) were sold in a blatant manner. For example, Prince Albert of Brandenburg paid Pope Leo X about $25,000 for a second office, and then around $500,000 for a third! John Tetzel was the master salesman of indulgences in Germany, arousing the ire of Martin Luther, thus igniting the zeal of the most significant figure in the Reformation era.

Prior to Luther, a number of men advocated returning to the authority of the Bible, but none of them exerted a major influence on the *status quo.* Luther, however, brought the major issues to the public's attention. He was born in Eisleben, Saxony in 1483. After obtaining a Master's Degree, he entered a monastery, where he remained a somewhat tormented soul. A superior suggested he read the writings of the apostle Paul. As a result, Luther came to the conclusion, by the year 1508, that the Catholic doctrine of works righteousness was clearly in opposition to the teaching of the New Testament. His theme became that of the book of Romans—"the just shall live by faith."

On October 31st, 1517, Martin Luther nailed his ninety-five theses to the door of his church in Wittenburg. In this document, he stated his opposition to the sale of indulgences and offered to debate anyone who disagreed. He did debate John Eck, a professor of theology; ultimately, the Catholic Church issued a papal bull against Luther, which he publicly burned. This act of defiance led to a long battle with the powers of the church. He developed a movement which first was called "Protestant" in 1526 because of its protests against the Catholic Church. Although he expressed no desire to start a church named for him, his movement became known as the Lutheran church, and it soon spread from Germany into other countries. Obviously, this "Church of *Luther*" was a direct violation of 1 Corinthians 1:10-13.

A number of other figures in the Reformation Movement had substantial followings and influence. Huldreich Zwingli (1484-1531 A.D.) from Switzerland was also a Catholic priest. In 1522, he prepared sixty-seven theses outlining his differences with the church, and two years later was married in defiance of the church. Like Luther, he appealed to the Scriptures as the ultimate authority; he stressed many of the same teachings that Luther did. John Calvin (1509-1564 A.D.), also Swiss, became the most systematic organizer of Protestant doctrine, carefully defining a system which has influenced most of the Protestant movement down to our present day. His system, appropriately called *Calvinism*, became the basis for the Presbyterian Church and a variety of other denominations in the "reformed" tradition. (His system will be examined in our next chapter in some detail.) Later, John Wesley and his brother Charles did much to spread the Reformation in England, ultimately leading to the establishment of the Methodist Church. Their focus was on personal spirituality, with specific, carefully observed devotional approaches. Their critics dubbed them *"Methodists"* because of these specific "methods" and their "methodical" prayer life and Bible study.

Appreciation should be expressed for the courage and convictions of these leaders, and many more like them, who were willing to stand against the religious corruption of their day. Many noble and biblically accurate positions were espoused, and the doors were opened for further examination of spiritual beliefs which had been traditionally held.

However, the Reformation did not really deal with the heart of the problem. The whole idea of reformation is to reform something, which in this case was the Catholic Church. But the exact area to be reformed varied with different leaders. Some wanted change in one area and others wanted change in different areas. Ultimately, they simply did not go deep enough to uproot the whole system. In their reaction against the monolithic structure of the Catholic Church, they ended up in a myriad of factions and sects. By the 1700s, Protestantism was divided into nearly 150 opposing groups. This sad state of affairs set the stage for the beginning of the next major reaction movement.

One Reaction against Protestantism:
The Restoration Movement

This reaction against Protestantism was primarily *doctrinally* focused, whereas a second reaction which we will discuss, the Holiness Movement, was primarily *emotionally* focused. In America, denominationalism flourished under the banner of religious freedom. The divisions between (and among) different groups caused major concern to biblically-sensitive leaders, some of whom began to call for an end to denominationalism and division. Eventually, the term *restoration* became popular, for these people decided the need was not to *reform* any existing church, but rather to *restore* the original church of the Bible.

Key leaders came from many different religious backgrounds. James O'Kelley, who began preaching in 1775 as a lay preacher in the Episcopal Church, pled for the Bible to be the only rule of faith and practice, and for people to be satisfied to be known as "Christians only." Abner Jones, a Baptist doctor in Vermont, became convinced that sectarian names and creeds should be abandoned. Elias Smith, a Baptist preacher, joined his efforts, and they began establishing what they called "Christian churches" across New England. Barton W. Stone, a Presbyterian minister, was one of the most influential in the development of this new movement. His teaching led to the formulation of the Last Will and Testament of the Springfield Presbytery in the summer of 1804. This document, which became famous within the movement, dissolved their denominational basis and appealed for all followers of Jesus to be simply Christians and take the Bible as the only sure guide to heaven.

Thomas Campbell and his son, Alexander, also Presbyterians, had come to America from Scotland as ministers. Alexander was one of the nation's brightest minds and most influential Restorationists. He wrote prolifically and spoke all over his new country with great impact. His conclusions on subjects like baptism became the basis for the Restoration plea. The younger Campbell conducted some public debates which gained national attention and had major impact. Most were on the subject of baptism and were in opposition to the practices of sprinkling and infant baptism. The great statesman, Henry Clay, actually moderated one of these debates, showing what national attention Campbell drew during the formation of this movement.[1]

Walter Scott was a very popular speaker who did much to spread the movement. He devised a five-step "plan of salvation" which culminated in baptism and the reception of the Holy Spirit. His preaching led to thousands being baptized. Then, as now, the teaching that biblical baptism was immersion and was necessary for forgiveness of sins led to much controversy and persecution from other religious groups. However, the movement enjoyed great growth for many years, becoming (during the late 19th and early 20th centuries) the fastest growing indigenous religious movement in America.

Some of their goals were excellent, as they originally sought *unity* rather than simply *union*—to be *non-denominational* rather than *inter-denominational*. Two basic failures, however, led to a dwindling impact by this group. One, the doctrinal focus produced much "Pharisaism" and division as the group began to major in the minors and minor in the majors. Two, the lack of one-another relationships and discipling produced spiritual lethargy and the death of their sense of mission. Not only did their growth decline markedly, but those who came into the group from an increasingly sinful society were not matured in the spiritual life. Without discipleship (*teaching them to obey everything*—Matthew 28:20), maturity of the individual and subsequent growth of the group cannot occur. (Much more attention will be given to these weaknesses in Chapter 9, as Restoration churches are addressed.)

Another Reaction against Protestantism: The Holiness Movement

This emotionally-based movement began around the beginning of the twentieth century as a reaction to Protestant coldness, intellectualism and spiritual deadness. Some of the heirs of this movement, such as the Pentecostal Church, the Church of God and Assemblies of God, are now well-defined and distinct denominations. Others are less organized, but focus on the same basic doctrines of healing, tongue speaking and other related miracles. (In a later chapter, we will deal with the key doctrines of these groups.)

For a number of years, the phenomena associated with these groups were contained within them. The earliest growth of this movement took place mainly in rural areas, and the members tended to be less educated than those in more established churches. They were most likely alarmed by society's growing secularism and humanism rather than the formalism of the typical Protestant church. The value systems in the big cities were changing rapidly, and many people in the common man's world were looking for something stable to hold on to. Having a personal experience with God—manifested by tongue speaking and other activities of the Holy Spirit—looked very appealing. As a result, these churches began to make inroads into the established churches.

The atmosphere of these early groups was noticeably emotional. The more emotional a person was, the more readily he seemed to be able to "get the Spirit." Some of the activities in their excited services brought about such designations as "Holy Rollers." For 50 years or more, these groups were viewed with suspicion and with humorous disdain as they conducted their controversial meetings.

However, with the passage of time, their impact began to be felt on a broader plane. The *Full Gospel Businessmen's Fellowship International* did much to spread their doctrines into settings which were neither rural nor uneducated. Some of the holiness churches became more sophisticated and began appealing to a broader audience, while others kept much the same clientele. But the influence of the overall movement was destined to spread in a totally unexpected way. Members of mainline Protestant and Catholic groups began experimenting with charismatic practices, which became the identifying mark of the "truly spiritual." Spiritual gifts became much more important than the denomination to which one belonged.

Thus was launched the Neo-Pentecostal movement. Without a doubt, the motivation for this movement was dissatisfaction with the emotional coldness and deadness of mainline denominations. Few churches were exempt from this phenomenon, especially in the decades of the 1960s and 1970s. Tongue speaking even found its way into the staid Church of Christ, mainly in small and sometimes secretive groups. When Pat Boone (a famous singer and actor at that time) left the Churches of Christ to join a holiness group, it set off a flurry of sermons and writings against Pentecostal practices by Church of Christ leaders. Interestingly, the Churches of Christ with predominately black memberships did not have this same experience with their members— evidently because, in these churches, more emotional needs were being met through more exciting services and audience participation.

The Reaction against a Failed Restoration:
The Discipleship Movement

By the 1950s, many diverse mindsets characterized the divided movement of the Churches of Christ. Just about all of the attitudes and approaches of the first-century Jewish sects could be observed. Most apparent was a Pharisaical group, with its legalism. A liberal, Sadducee group was growing in both number and in outspokenness, calling into question not only legalistic interpretations of Scripture, but even the inspiration of the Scriptures. There were the Herodians, who wanted to be seen as politically correct (in the view of other religious groups). As was the case in the first century, these various influences were mainly felt in the ranks of leadership. The average member was probably more oblivious to all of the debates about doctrines than most of these leaders would have ever imagined.

However, there were those who had not *bought in* to the religiosity just described, and these individuals longed for a better day—a day when Christianity really counted in one's daily life and their religion was changing the world around them. Out of this confusing and confused *milieu*, a movement of some "radicals" (as they were viewed by the mainline group) arose within the ranks of those involved, particularly in campus ministry. "Campus Evangelism" was a significant but short-lived organization based in a large Lubbock, Texas congregation. This group mobilized college students from around the country and stirred evangelistic zeal. It quickly caught the attention of "the Pharisees" and was driven to disband. However, one of the ministers of this campus-focused group was not deterred by the opposition.

Chuck Lucas led the campus ministry in Gainesville, Florida during the late 1960s and through the 1970s, at what would become known as the Crossroads Church of Christ. It was a volatile time in American history. The Vietnam War, the Civil Rights Movement and the assassination of the Kennedys and Martin Luther King, Jr., the shame of Watergate, the sexual revolution and the continuing tensions between races had not only eaten away at the moral fiber of the nation, but had exacted a terrible toll on the idealism of our youth. In response came the Hippie movement, the organized protest movement and the rejection of many values held by the Establishment. Without doubt, the youth of our nation were looking for something different—even radically different, and God used this trying time to start moving powerfully.

God used the Crossroads congregation, and Chuck Lucas especially, to reach some zealous young leaders. He converted, or strongly influenced, a number of key leaders within our movement of churches, including current well-known leaders such as Bruce Williams, Sam Laing, Wyndham Shaw, Sam Powell, Randy McKean and many others. Such men were trained and sent out to existing Churches of Christ as campus ministers. The traditional mindsets and lukewarmness of many of these groups almost always led to resistance and ultimate expulsion of the campus groups which were started. Before these groups arrived at these churches, the spirituality of the members in mainline churches was measured in terms of attendance, giving and perhaps teaching Sunday school. But the focus and terminology started to change. The talk shifted to Quiet Times, prayer partners, sharing your faith and bearing much fruit. Explosions and divisions were a foregone conclusion. Oil and water do not mix. Old wineskins cannot hold new wine.

In retrospect, it seems obvious that pride was not absent from the young campus leaders or from the older leaders in those existing churches. In my estimation, as an outsider and a minister in the mainline setting in those days, the fault on both sides was about equal. However, I would still place the greater blame on the side of the older leaders, simply because they should have had a greater maturity and broader perspective about working more patiently with young zealots. Jesus' group of twelve disciples were likely young men, perhaps very young. Two of them wanted to burn down a city (Luke 9:51-56) when its citizens didn't welcome Jesus with open arms. You have to admit that this would be defined as a new brand of harshness! Jesus did not let it pass, and he rebuked them, but he continued working with them as young zealots who needed more training. One of them became the first apostle martyred (James) and the other became the great "apostle of love" (John). In spite of the Campus Ministry Movement appearing to create some serious upheavals, it also produced some rather amazing results—on either end of the spectrum of good and bad.

The work at Crossroads constituted a *renewal* movement within the Churches of Christ, and helped pave the way for a more complete return to the vital and long neglected doctrines of evangelism and discipleship. However, this Campus Ministry Movement was not destined to last because it was not broad enough. In most churches hosting these ministries, there was not the expectation that every member—young and old alike—had to make the same commitment as a disciple. While much progress had been made in the direction of biblical relationships, there was an insufficient commitment to unity and to dealing decisively with sin in the ranks. Finally, while it was a "radical" movement within the Church of Christ, it was still saddled with many of the traditions of that group (like the issue of "autonomy" that we will examine in Chapter 9). Today, the Crossroads Church (with a different name) is a dwindling group, as are most of the other churches associated with them. However, this congregation did not meet its demise as a growing evangelistic church until God had accomplished his work of converting some world-impacting leaders in that very location.

The next phase of the movement characterized by evangelism and discipleship came to be called the "Boston Movement." Kip and Elena McKean went to Boston in 1979, and in Kip's better days, he was used powerfully to help restart and unify a movement of churches that ended up planting similar churches in well over 100 nations, some of which had memberships numbering into the thousands. Much could be said about this movement during those early years, and much has been said—good and bad. This group of churches, in time, came to be called the ICOC (International Churches of Christ) because of their emphasis on planting churches in other countries. As stated in the Introduction of this book, my own description of our movement is that it has been like a barbell, with equally large weights at either end—one end representing the amazing accomplishments and the other end representing the bad things. But a fair amount of the bad was comprised of good things done in wrong ways, a fact that must always be remembered.

Our movement has a history that goes far back before 1979 in Boston. We are built upon the foundation of what we now call the Mainline Church of Christ, or by a broader and more descriptive term, the Restoration Movement. The early days of this group were actually pretty glorious. Ministers from many different denominations banded together with the lofty intent of rejecting creeds in favor of following the Bible only. Surely, we would all agree that this was, and remains, a noble goal. Many stories could be recounted from the 1800s that are impressive and thrilling. Thousands of people were baptized at the preaching of men who were sold out for their cause, to the point that some of them actually gave their lives for it as martyrs.

We have another part of our historical root system that is in many ways more important to us as a movement than the mainline background. Of course, I refer to the Campus Ministry segment of our history, which we often call the Crossroads Movement (although I prefer the term "Campus Ministry Movement" because other campus groups were striving for the same goals). They, of course, were not the only group trying to really restore the Christianity of the Bible. I think that this era was glorious in many, many ways, and the claim that we have had a revisionist history regarding the Crossroads' days is unquestionably true. The contribution of that era is larger than many realize or admit. We are indebted to those pioneers who sought to return to the commitment and impact of first-century Christianity. The movement tracing back to the later Boston days had a huge impact, but the campus ministry movement that preceded it blazed some glorious trails, without which none of us would be what we now are. Anything bordering on disdain toward that era on the part of any of us who sit upon that foundation is nothing short of sinful.

I have plenty of sins of which to repent, but being critical of the earlier campus ministry days is not one of them. I first visited the Crossroads Church in 1981, and my life was radically changed as a result of that one week visit and the later trips to speak at the Florida Evangelism Seminar. How that group was spawned out of the tradition-bound

Mainline Church of Christ of that day still amazes and thrills me. We may have built upon that foundation (in good and bad ways, to be candid), but their coming out of their labyrinth is, in my opinion, about as remarkable as what we have done since. My purpose is not to create some kind of prideful and competitive comparison, but only to cause us to look back at all segments of our history in a way that is both realistic and spiritual.

I glory in the many positive qualities and achievements of the Mainline Church of Christ, although my frustration with its shortcomings led to my leaving it, burning bridges in a way that necessarily left scars in my soul. I cannot defend everything I did in that process, to be sure. I am grateful to be where I am today, and during those many years since I came into our present movement, I have never wished to be back in that old root system. But I appreciate my history as I searched for that "more excellent way." Similarly, I glory in the many positive contributions of the Campus Ministry Movement, for without it, we would certainly not be where we are today. Yes, they did some things wrong, but they did far more right than wrong. I am grateful that we have all been delivered from that "church within a church" setting that was the case with many former campus ministry congregations, but I do not make light of all that we learned from it, especially the campus ministry part of it, which was not significantly different from what we do today—unless it be noted that their growth in campus baptisms often eclipsed our present growth on most campuses.

As to the specific contributions of the Campus Ministry Movement, many could be noted with but little thought, even by an "outsider" such as me. The insistence of total commitment as an essential component of repentance preceding baptism was a novel idea and sorely needed. The viewing the Bible as an absolute standard for the attitudes and behavior of Christians, instead of simply being an idealistic standard, was likewise needed. This mindset led to the kind of straightforward and authoritative preaching that was all but absent from the pulpits of traditional churches. Discipleship, in both its vertical aspect (commitment to Christ) and horizontal aspect (close, open spiritual relationships), was admirably stressed. The later focus on "discipleship partners" at all levels, rather than the "prayer partner" arrangement of those days, initially looked much better in theory than the practice ended up, mostly because of the tendency of over/under relationships that were mishandled. The emphasis on relational evangelism, with ample, practical teaching about how to develop such relationships, stood out like a beacon for those not thus trained in other settings. Last, but certainly not least, an impressively large percentage of elders and evangelists in the most influential leadership roles in the ICOC movement today trace their roots back to

Crossroads or to campus ministries led by those who were trained at the Crossroads Church of Christ.

One mistake I often made in generalizing about the Campus Ministry Movement was failing to distinguish between the different "commitment levels" of churches which had campus ministries. The "church within a church" weakness often noted was generally true, in that the demands of discipleship were not equally applied to members of all ages. However, some churches were much more even-handed in calling for and expecting such commitment from its membership, with congregations like Crossroads and San Diego (Poway) being among this number. The amount of persecution each received is a pretty good testimony to that fact. The handling of said persecution by such churches paved the way for responding to later persecution after 1979, for many lessons were learned (both positively and negatively). I do not believe that the commitment levels in congregations like these was where it should have been overall, but it should be noted that they were quite advanced beyond where they had formerly been. I appreciate their determination and advances as they strove to emerge out of the denominational darkness from whence they came. They came further in many ways from their root system than we have since; for philosophically and practically, they had further to go. I would not want to return to where the better Campus Ministry churches were, with the older members not at the same place as the younger ones, but I am both amazed and grateful for the progress that has enabled us to build upon their earlier foundation.

While this movement was a reaction against something that deserved being reacted against, it became over-reactionary and went to some unfortunate extremes. However, the real test of any person or group comes when mistakes have been made and sins committed. As I write this, I am proud of the repentance I have seen and the progress in better directions that has been made. We have been tested by fire, owned our sins publicly and have striven to separate the wheat from the chaff as we move forward. After a period (too long a period in my estimation) of self-examination and repentance, we are once again moving forward by resuming our emphases on discipling, evangelism and church planting.

The firestorm we faced was a purifying one, either caused or allowed by God (the only two options), to help us be refined into something better. I have never seen nor experienced any church or group of churches that has the strengths that we have, and I would never consider leaving the group that routinely practices the kinds of relationships and focuses that are deeply grounded in the principles Jesus lived out and taught. He never called us to simply be church members or religious folks, but rather to be radical followers of his who would change the world and change eternity. Whatever weaknesses we may yet have, we have not forgotten that the very foundation of Christianity is self-denial, taking up a cross daily and following him. Although our reactionary pendulum admittedly swung too far, thank God it is settling in a place that I believe he endorses.

I close this section with the recommendation of two books about the ICOC movement that come from much different perspectives, yet have very complementary perspectives. Several years back, Foster Stanback wrote *Into All Nations: A History of the International Churches of Christ*.[2] Foster became a Christian while a college student in San Diego back in the early to mid 1980s, shortly before I became the congregational evangelist there. He writes in his book of a time when our movement of churches was in its better early days. Near the end of his book, however, he recounts some of the events that led to a developing upheaval in the early part of this decade. The other book is a later book written by Tom Jones, and is entitled, *In Search of a City*.[3] Tom's early work in campus ministry was separate from the Crossroad's movement, but he often had contact with it while also maintaining relationships with the Mainline Churches of Christ and Bible Chair Movement. This book is an intriguing one, from the standpoint of all of the ways that his life and ministry developed and overlapped with so many other individuals and ministries. You will find information here that cannot be found elsewhere. Both of these men are dear friends of mine, and their books will fill in many historical gaps for those not too familiar with the development of what we now call the ICOC.

QUICK REFERENCE GUIDE: _____

Reaction #1—Catholicism

1. Characterized by gradual departures from the biblical pattern in doctrine and life.

2. Eventually, this religion became a mixture of Christianity, Judaism and Paganism.

3. The ultimate excesses financially and morally led to a strong reaction among many Catholic leaders who could no longer turn their eyes away from these sins.

Reaction #2—Protestant Reformation

1. Key figures: Martin Luther, Huldreich Zwingli, John Calvin.

2. Main accomplishments: Stood up against the existing religious corruption and advocated a return to biblical authority.

3. Weaknesses: Did not go far enough, for more was needed than a mere reformation of the existing church.

Reaction #3—Restoration Movement

1. Key figures: Thomas and Alexander Campbell, Barton W. Stone, Walter Scott.

2. Main accomplishments: Rejection of human creeds in favor of the Bible alone. Plea was for restoration of the original church rather than reformation of an existing one. Doctrinal positives were a much more accurate understanding of baptism, and a rejection of the Calvinistic underpinnings of mainline Protestantism.

3. Weaknesses: Allowed the mission to become sidetracked due to a doctrinal focus at the expense of personal discipleship. Legalism became rampant, and a true understanding of biblical repentance was lost.

Reaction #4—Holiness Movement

1. Underlying causes of this movement: Breakdown of morals in society, and formalism and deadness of existing churches.

2. Strengths: Having the desire to have a meaningful, personal relationship with God, to live more holy lives and to allow the Spirit to work in their churches.

3. Weaknesses: Going after good ends by using unbiblical means. The doctrines regarding the miraculous gifts of the Holy Spirit are misunderstood and misapplied.

Reaction #5—Discipleship Movement (Intl. Churches of Christ)

1. Early contributing influences: Chuck Lucas and the Crossroads Church of Christ in Gainesville, Florida.

2. Strengths: Commitment to, and insistence on, every member being a true disciple, determined to maintain a close and personal relationship with God while making other disciples; every church being totally dedicated to carrying the gospel to every nation; caring for the poor and needy in a significant way, both worldwide and in their own communities.

3. Challenges: Keeping every member zealous in his walk with God and in his evangelism; taking it much higher in financial sacrifices to support the need for world evangelism; every church staying "on the edge," thus avoiding the spiritual plague of a lukewarm fringe. Avoiding the extremes that developed among us, including an authoritarian leadership style and judgmental spirits.

Notes _____

[1]The original Restoration Movement eventually led to three distinct groups—those we will refer to as the "mainline" Church of Christ, the Independent Christian Church and the Disciples of Christ denomination. The latter group ultimately rejected the absolute authority of the Scriptures, gave up the idea of restoration and gladly took its place among other mainline denominations like the Methodist and Presbyterian Churches. Those in the Christian Church held to the authority of the Bible and the concept of restoration. A different view of interpreting Scripture led those in the Churches of Christ and the Christian Churches to different conclusions, with the latter group feeling that something was permitted (instrumental music, for example) as long as Scripture did not expressly forbid it. In general, the Churches of Christ focused more on the Restoration Movement's goal of doctrinal purity and the Christian Church more on the movement's unity plea.

[2]C. Foster Stanback, *Into All Nations: A History of the International Churches of Christ* (Spring, Texas: Illumination Publishers International, 2005).

[3]Thomas A. Jones, *In Search of a City* (Spring Hill, Tennessee: DPI Books, 2007).

CHAPTER SEVEN

CALVINISM: THE DOCTRINAL BASIS OF PROTESTANTISM

The TULIP System Explained

The Reformed system of theology developed by John Calvin, which influences the majority of evangelical Protestant churches today, was just that—an effort to reform the Catholic system with which Calvin had much agreement. Calvin advocated a return to the Bible, but he was particularly influenced by the writings of Augustine. As a reformer, he was at times in agreement and at times at odds with traditional Catholic theology. With his keen mind, he developed a systematic and seemingly rational explanation of the nature of man and the nature of salvation needed by such a man. Once the first presupposition of Calvin's systematic theology (which he clearly learned from Augustine) is accepted, the whole system seems to fall into place. On the other hand, if this first tenet is rejected, the whole system collapses. A "pure" Calvinist will readily admit that the entire system stands or falls together.

Calvinism is known by its five major points of emphasis, and the first letter of the key words in these points spells out the word "tulip."

> **T**—*total depravity*
> **U**—*unconditional election*
> **L**—*limited atonement*
> **I** —*irresistible grace*
> **P**—*perseverance of the saints*

Total depravity means that every person is born in a totally depraved state, incapable of choosing anything good. Therefore, if they are to be saved, God will have to elect them unconditionally, for a totally depraved man cannot choose to meet any conditions whatsoever. If he is one of the elect, Jesus has atoned for his sins, because Jesus death was not for everyone but only for the elect. Furthermore, if God has elected a person and Jesus has died for him, that person will become a Christian, for God's grace is irresistible. Finally, if this totally depraved person has been unconditionally elected by God and has felt the grace of that limited atonement, he will persevere in his faith and will never fall from grace. Once he has been saved, he can never become unsaved.

The first thing that we will do is to quote from the Calvinists themselves as they argue for each of these five points, and then we will examine these points in light of Scripture. The quotes are quite necessary in a study of Calvinistic theology, for at least two reasons. One, if I simply stated these views, some readers would think I was painting a worst-case scenario and exaggerating their position. But since the Calvinists are not bashful about presenting their own case, there is no temptation to create a straw man. Two, people in Calvinistic churches are not in touch with what true Calvinism really is, and you might be able to help them by showing them actual quotes that would seem very extreme to any average Bible reader.

Total Depravity

Professor Herman Hanko, a leading advocate of Calvin's system, first writes of his understanding of the non-Calvinist position (or the "Semi-pelagian View" as he calls it):

> God on His part, said the Semi-pelagians, has prepared salvation for all men. He has prepared the cure for this malady which afflicts mankind. And God is also prepared to give this healing balm to all men. In fact, God even goes one step farther than this, and offers this balm to all men to be accepted or rejected by them...The whole matter of his cure therefore, of his salvation, turns upon the choice of his own will.[1]

The average person who has studied the Bible without the guidance of a man-made creed would find nothing alarming about the above quote regarding God's offers and man's free will choices. But the Calvinists consider such concepts to be absolute heresy!

Hanko argues that totally depraved man is completely incapable of responding to God's offer. In his words: "This means that his nature is so thoroughly corrupted by sin that it is incapable of producing anything good. There is nothing which the sinner can do which is pleasing in the sight of God...Man cannot even will the good."[2] The importance of this first point of Calvinism is paramount, says Hanko, as he continues his argument:

It is on this foundation that the Catechism erects the whole structure of the truth. The truth of total depravity is part of the whole truth of Scripture. If this truth is denied, softened, vitiated in any respect, it becomes impossible to preserve any of the truth of God's Word...To the extent that he is not totally depraved, he is capable of doing good. And to that extent he is capable of participating in the work of salvation. And to that extent grace is not sovereign at all. The two truths stand or fall together. And so it is with the whole of the truth.[3]

Unconditional Election

On the subject of the freedom of man's will, two main schools of thought have existed for many years. Against the idea of man's ability to choose good are (of course) the Calvinists. The opposing position is usually called "Arminianism," after Jacob Armenius (1560-1609 A.D.), a Dutch theologian who was convinced that man does have a choice to accept or reject the merciful offers of God. The Calvinists reject such concepts, as the following quote demonstrates:

They wanted to preserve in man the freedom of his will—the power of man's will to choose for the good, to accept the offer of the gospel. It was their contention that God on His part loved all men, that hatred and wrath were foreign to God's nature; that it was God's intention and desire to save all men; that, therefore, God made salvation available and obtainable to all men through the universal atonement—a universal cross on which Christ died for the sins of every man. But it is clear that in such a system as that proposed by the Arminians, there is no room at all for unconditional election.[4]

Hanko then describes his view of unconditional election:

He did not base His choice on man in any way. Not on man's goodness, works, faith, holiness; not on man's faithfulness to the gospel. There could not be found in man any good thing. It was a free choice, a sovereign choice of God. He made it without any consideration of man whatsoever.[5]

Such positions raise a very important question as we examine this dogma of Calvinism: if God unconditionally elected certain individuals to be saved, would he not also have had to unconditionally predestine all other individuals to be lost? That is a good question, and one from which true Calvinists do not shrink back. This latter "election" to the ranks of the damned is called by them "reprobation," and Hanko says that "it must be emphasized that the truth of election and reprobation stand or fall together . . . There is no compromise at this point."[6]

Therefore, the total picture of unconditional election is that God chooses certain people to be eternally saved and certain people to be eternally condemned, without any of them having anything to do with it at all. *Their own desires or choices have absolutely nothing to do with where they spend eternity.* God is the only player in this game, and man is totally a puppet with no ability or opportunity to affect the outcome of his own destiny. This definition of true Calvinism is not in the least bit exaggerated. Real Calvinists do not try to smooth off rough edges or dodge tough issues. As unbiblical as some of their statements may seem to the *uninitiated*, they are part and parcel of the system.

Limited Atonement

Homer Hoeksema, another advocate of Calvinism, writing in the same book with Hanko, describes the general idea of atonement accurately, but then inaccurately limits its scope.

> We say, on the basis of Scripture: the death of Christ was **atonement,** that is, payment for sin and purchase of righteousness and eternal life. Still more: we say that it was **vicarious** atonement. It was substitution. Christ atoned not for Himself, but as a substitute for others (whoever those others may be). Christ was a substitute for others. Still more: the Reformed faith maintains, on the basis of Scripture, that the death of Christ was **limited** vicarious atonement. That is, Christ atoned as a substitute not for all and every man, but for His elect people alone.[7]

Again, to make it perfectly clear that I am not overstating Mr. Hoeksema's case, consider the following: "I do not say the truth, I do not present Christ crucified, therefore, if I merely say, 'Christ died for sinners.' And I certainly do not present the gospel of Christ crucified when I say, 'Christ died for all men.'"[8] In his closing remarks on this subject, he says: "For remember: a Christ for all is really a Christ for none!"[9]

Obviously, this position flies in the face of a number of clear scriptures, and we will note those in the examination section of this chapter. But this position does show the lengths to which even scholarly people can go when they strain everything through the eyes of a creed. If a person was building a fence and noticed that one fence post had been set up out of line with all of the others, he then would have a choice to make, if he wanted a straight fence. He could do the logical (and easiest) thing and set that one post back in line with the others. Or, he could set all of the others in line with the one misaligned post. Dealing with denominational doctrines often presents a similar choice—you must reject the erroneous doctrine and get it back in line with the Scripture; or, you must force the Scriptures to fit in with your doctrine. We can be sure that God does not recognize such a "fence building" system!

Irresistible Grace

The third contributor to *The Five Points of Calvinism*, Gise J. Van Baren, describes this point of their theology with these words:

> Do not think that irresistible grace is some sort of blind force which simply drags the struggling, rebellious sinner into heaven against his will...The grace of God is not such a power that compels to enter into heaven those who would not. That God's grace is irresistible emphasizes the idea that not only does grace bring His people to glory, but it *prepares* them for this glory and works within them the desire to enter into glory. Grace is irresistible in the sense that by it the knee is bent which otherwise would not bend; the heart is softened that otherwise is hard as stone. Nor is there anything which can prevent the accomplishment of that purpose of God to save His people by His grace.[10]

Van Baren goes on to say: "But also, were His grace resistible, it would mean that all assurance would be gone concerning my salvation...If I *can* resist, I *will* resist."[11]

This view puts man in the universe as a robot. He is predetermined to accept or reject God, and unless God basically *makes* him accept, he will not and cannot. One wonders just what satisfaction God derives from a relationship with a robot? If my wife could not have chosen me of her own volition, seeing her walk down the aisle would not have been so special. But such is the view of the Calvinists.

Perseverance of the Saints

The same writer, in describing Calvinism as an integrated whole, again disagrees with the Arminian on the nature of a Christian's security.

> The Arminian would be ready to say that there is and must be perseverance—and there will be if we remain steadfast to the

end. If we continue to maintain the truth of God's Word, then we will persevere to the end. It is we who have the strength to persevere if we want to; but also we can lose that which we have and be lost. So the Arminian would also urge the saint to persevere. But he teaches then that it is really possible, and does happen, that a saint can finally be lost. We deny that such is ever possible. The saint cannot fall because his preservation rests not on his own act, but on the power of the almighty God.[12]

This doctrine is also called "security of the believer," and is more popularly expressed as "once saved, always saved." Practical experience has shown many examples of those who seemed to be on fire for God for a long time, perhaps decades, and then later went in the opposite direction. Will they still go to heaven? That is a question with which the Calvinist must deal. He answers with 1 John 2:19: "They went out from us, but they did not really belong to us. For if they had belonged to us, they would have remained with us; but their going showed that none of them belonged to us." While this passage does describe those whose hearts were never involved with Jesus in the right way, many other passages do show that a true, saved believer can turn from God and once again be in a lost condition.

Because the Calvinist denies that point, he must, therefore, deny some very clear passages. One of those is Hebrews 6:4-6, to which Van Baren replies: "Were these regenerated sons of God? No; in this particular instance the text speaks of one unconverted or unregenerated."[13] To be a Calvinist, you must believe that those described as *once enlightened, tasters of the heavenly gift, sharers in the Holy Spirit, tasters of the goodness of the word of God and the powers of the coming age* had never become Christians! Buy it if you will, but I cannot possibly swallow that one. In the next part of the chapter, we will see just why the whole system rests on false interpretations.

Calvinism: The TULIP System Examined

Totally Depraved?

The concept of total depravity rests on the assumption that original sin is true. However, many groups accept the doctrine of original sin without accepting the doctrine of total depravity. Refer back to Chapter Four under the topic of *infant baptism* (and to Appendix II) for a full discussion of Adamic sin. In this present chapter, we will confine our remarks to the depravity issue, for this issue is the foundation of the TULIP system of theology. Is a human being a creature of choice in spiritual matters or not? Does he have a free will or does he not? Those questions go to the heart of the Calvinistic doctrine, and they must be answered biblically.

Several passages should be sufficient to clearly demonstrate that men are not born totally depraved. In Luke 8:11-15, Jesus gave the interpretation of the Parable of the Soils. Four kinds of hearts are described, along with the different responses to the gospel. But if all hearts are totally depraved unless and until God changes them, why would Jesus even bother to discuss differences in hearts and responses if, in fact, man has no choice in the matter anyway? As he talked of the four kinds of hearts, he made this statement in verse 15: "But the seed on good soil stands for those with a noble and good heart, who hear the word, retain it, and by persevering produce a crop." According to Calvinism, all hearts are totally depraved. Jesus obviously had not read Calvin.

The case of Cornelius, the Roman centurion, reveals more biblical evidence that refutes "total depravity." Consider this passage from Acts 10:1-4:

> At Caesarea there was a man named Cornelius, a centurion in what was known as the Italian Regiment. He and all his family were devout and God-fearing; he gave generously to those in need and prayed to God regularly. One day at about three in the afternoon he had a vision. He distinctly saw an angel of God, who came to him and said, "Cornelius!" Cornelius stared at him in fear. "What is it, Lord?" he asked. The angel answered, "Your prayers and gifts to the poor have come up as a memorial offering before God."

Here we find a man, according to the Calvinists, totally incapable of making any good choices or doing any good acts, and yet God seemed to be quite impressed with him. Because of this man's heart and life, God went to a great deal of trouble to make sure that he did hear the gospel and become a Christian. Before he became a disciple, he was that "good soil" that Jesus had described.

Another interesting passage in view of Calvin's teaching is 2 Timothy 3:13: "...while evil men and impostors will go from bad to worse, deceiving and being deceived." If a person is already as bad as he can possibly be, how can he go from "bad to worse"? If Calvinism is true, how can the radical differences in people's hearts and behavior be explained?

Scripture is full of appeals on the part of God for man to turn and to come to him. Consider this one in Ezekiel 33:11:

> "Say to them, 'As surely as I live, declares the Sovereign LORD, I take no pleasure in the death of the wicked, but rather that they turn from their ways and live. Turn! Turn from your evil ways! Why will you die, O house of Israel?'"

Why would God possibly issue such an urgent appeal if man was so totally depraved that he had no possibility of responding? And why would God give universal commands if these commands could not be obeyed by all of those being commanded? Acts 17:30 says: "In the past God overlooked such ignorance, but now he commands all people everywhere to repent." If Calvinism is true, God's offer in Revelation 22:17 is nothing short of a cruel joke. "The Spirit and the bride say, 'Come!' And let him who hears say, 'Come!' Whoever is thirsty, let him come; and whoever wishes, let him take the free gift of the water of life."

Is Election *Unconditional?*

The *fact* of election by God is quite true, but what is the *nature* of that election? There is an election for spiritual *purposes*, one that does not guarantee spiritual salvation to those elected. The greatest example of this kind of election was God's election of the nation of Israel. Clearly, being in that nation, and even being used by God, did not equate with being right with him on an individual basis. The Jews had difficulty comprehending that difference, as evidenced by John the Baptist's statement in Matthew 3:7-10. They trusted in the fact that they were physical children of Abraham, and John informed them that they were about to be cut down and cast into the fire unless they repented. As a nation, they had been elected, but that election was anything but *unconditional*. In 1 Kings 9:6-7, God said:

> But if you or your sons turn away from me and do not observe the commands and decrees I have given you and go off to serve other gods and worship them, then I will cut off Israel from the land I have given them and will reject this temple I have consecrated for my Name. Israel will then become a byword and an object of ridicule among all peoples.

If Calvinistic predestination and reprobation (also called *double predestination*) were true, God would be a respecter of persons. But a number of verses say that he is not. Peter stated this in Acts 10:34-35: "I now realize how true it is that God does not show favoritism but accepts men from every nation who fear him and do what is right." God accepts those who make the *choice* to accept him (see also Romans 2:11 and Colossians 3:25). His election is conditional, based on people accepting him—which they most certainly are *able* to do if they *want* to. In Romans 1:21-26, we find that God gave people over to sin because of their *hearts,* not because they were excluded from the unconditionally elected. Ezekiel 33:11 (quoted earlier on page 91) shows which choice God wants the wicked to make and the one he offers them the opportunity to make.

Romans 9 is a often-used chapter by the Calvinists in their attempt
to show unconditional election. The focus of that chapter is that God
has the total right to make a choice. He had always made choices in his
dealings with the Jews. Their lineage showed God's choices, and none
of them would have argued that the choices were poor ones. It had never
been simply an issue of physical descendancy. Abraham had two sons,
but only one was chosen. Isaac also had two sons, and only one of them
was chosen. Jacob was loved and Esau hated—a quote from Malachi
1:2-3, referring to the nations of Israel and Edom respectively, and one
showing that the term "hate" applies primarily to a nation. God chose
Jacob, who had his own character flaws, but who ended up as a man of
faith after he responded to the discipline of the Lord. Sometimes, writers
describe Jacob in as negative of terms as his brother, which suggests that
God's choice had no moral basis at all. In this case, the passage of time
showed that Jacob had the more righteous heart. However, the point of
Paul's argument is that God had the *right* to make these choices.

God's deliverance of the people from Egypt showed other choices
made by God. Moses was especially blessed by God to catch a glimpse
of God which no one else was privileged to see (Exodus 33:18-23). Pharaoh was hardened by God. This one is a favorite with the Calvinists, but
what does it really mean? God "hardened" Pharaoh through his commands and Pharaoh's free will to choose. In Exodus, the text says a number of times that God hardened Pharaoh's heart and a number of times
that Pharaoh hardened his own heart. *God's word hardens some hearts and
softens others, depending on the type of heart which is responding to that word.*
The same sun hardens clay and melts butter. The thrust of Romans 9 is
that God has the right to do what he pleases. Thankfully, he pleases to
always do the righteous thing and the thing which allows men to make
their own moral choices.

The potter and clay illustration is likewise a favorite one of those
trying to prove unconditional election. The clay has nothing to do with
how the potter chooses to shape it. However, similar potter and clay passages show that, while God has the right to do what he wants, the clay
has a choice in the outcome of the shaping. For example, in Jeremiah
18:1-10 we find this account:

> This is the word that came to Jeremiah from the LORD: "Go down to the
> potter's house, and there I will give you my message." So I went down
> to the potter's house, and I saw him working at the wheel. But the pot he
> was shaping from the clay was marred in his hands; so the potter formed
> it into another pot, shaping it as seemed best to him. Then the word of
> the LORD came to me: "O house of Israel, can I not do with you as this
> potter does?" declares the LORD. "Like clay in the hand of the potter,

so are you in my hand, O house of Israel. If at any time I announce that a nation or kingdom is to be uprooted, torn down and destroyed, and if that nation I warned repents of its evil, then I will relent and not inflict on it the disaster I had planned. And if at another time I announce that a nation or kingdom is to be built up and planted, and if it does evil in my sight and does not obey me, then I will reconsider the good I had intended to do for it."

An important New Testament passage is 2 Timothy 2:20-21:

In a large house there are articles not only of gold and silver, but also of wood and clay; some are for noble purposes and some for ignoble. If a man cleanses himself from the latter, he will be an instrument for noble purposes, made holy, useful to the Master and prepared to do any good work.

The sovereignty of God and the free choice of man run concurrently all through Scripture. As difficult as it may be for our minds to harmonize the two, we cannot throw out either part of the equation. Acts 2:23 is a classic example showing both sides of the issue, as it reads:

"This man was handed over to you by God's set purpose and foreknowledge; and you, with the help of wicked men, put him to death by nailing him to the cross."

God's foreknowledge and man's choices, complete with total responsibility, are not mutually exclusive. And just because God knows in advance what someone will do, it in no way rules out their free moral agency nor causes them to do it. Even in the case of a human illustration, we can accept that point. A person on top of a building may see two cars traveling at a high rate of speed toward each other at the same corner and *know* that their speed and direction will insure a crash, but his knowledge from "on high" in no way would *cause* the accident.

In Romans 8:30, we find that we have been predestined, called, justified and glorified. Predestination means that God laid out a plan to offer up Christ and then bless everyone who would respond to this plan with faith. It means that God determined the plan and not the man (as an individual). In other words, God did not arbitrarily choose certain individuals to be saved and others to be lost. But what exactly is predestination?

This illustration should help our understanding: A school teacher prepares a syllabus, or plan, which predetermines that some students will make "As," others will make "Bs," and so forth, even *before* he meets his students. Depending on how these students *respond* to these plans, they are in that sense *predestined* to make specific grades. Similarly, God predetermined that all who are "in Christ" by believing and accepting the gospel will receive glory (all "As"!). Read Ephesians 1:3-14 carefully to see how this concept is developed.

God calls us by the gospel (2 Thessalonians 2:13-14), to which we must respond in order to be chosen. The parable in Matthew 22:1-14 teaches us a vital truth about election, about being chosen. The background of this parable is that all invited guests were given a garment to wear when they arrived at the wedding feast. Therefore, the person without the garment had no one to blame but himself for not accepting it. Similarly, God offers us the *opportunity* to be clothed with Christ (Galatians 3:27; Romans 13:14), and if we do not accept his provisions, we have no one to blame but ourselves! Simply stated, God votes for us, Satan votes *against* us, but we have the deciding vote—the *choice* to be *chosen* is ours! Keep in mind that God loves every person desperately, and he deeply desires their repentance (2 Peter 3:9) and their salvation (1 Timothy 2:4).

The Atonement *Limited?*

This part of Calvin's equation—a logical consequence of his basic teaching—has little to commend it, for it is so blatantly contrary to Biblical teaching that any Scriptures thus used are obviously twisted to fit their presuppositions. The Calvinists' argument is that if Jesus really died for everyone, and yet everyone does not accept him, then God would have failed. That sort of human reasoning might appeal to some, but just why I am not even sure. I am more than a little impressed that God loved the world enough to give his Son, knowing that most would not accept him. God has given the world millions of blessings that go unappreciated, simply because he is love and his nature is to give. His election may not be unconditional, but his love certainly is!

Reasoning is not needed in answering this false teaching. A few passages will more than answer it—they will *destroy* it for anyone who is willing to listen.

- **Luke 2:10:** "But the angel said to them, 'Do not be afraid. I bring you good news of great joy that will be for all the people.'"
- **John 1:29:** "The next day John saw Jesus coming toward him and said, 'Look, the Lamb of God, who takes away the sin of the world!'"
- **John 3:16-17:** "For God so loved the world that he gave his one and only Son, that whoever believes in him shall not perish but

have eternal life. For God did not send his Son into the world to condemn the world, but to save the world through him."

- **2 Corinthians 5:14-15:** "For Christ's love compels us, because we are convinced that one died for all, and therefore all died. And he died for all, that those who live should no longer live for themselves but for him who died for them and was raised again."
- **1 Timothy 2:5-6:** "For there is one God and one mediator between God and men, the man Christ Jesus, who gave himself as a ransom for all men—the testimony given in its proper time."
- **Hebrews 2:9:** "But we see Jesus, who was made a little lower than the angels, now crowned with glory and honor because he suffered death, so that by the grace of God he might taste death for everyone."
- **1 John 2:2:** "And he is the propitiation for our sins: and not for ours only, but also for the sins of the whole world."
- **1 John 4:14:** "And we have seen and testify that the Father has sent his Son to be the Savior of the world."

Surely nothing else need be said on this issue. Jesus died for *all*, the elect and the non-elect. And he did it gladly for the joy that was set before him (Hebrews 12:2). This joy was in seeing those who do accept him, thus claiming his death in their behalf. He tasted death for every man (Hebrews 2:9), but he is the source of eternal salvation to all who obey him (Hebrews 5:9). For him and the Father who sent him, our loving acceptance of his love makes it all worthwhile. Who can describe such love?

Grace That Is *Irresistible?*

If grace is irresistible, then exhortations in the Scripture are meaningless. On the day of Pentecost, Peter first preached the gospel of Jesus and then told people how to respond to the message. In fact, he said that "every one of you" should repent and be baptized (Acts 2:38). Then, Acts 2:40 states this: "With many other words he warned them; and he pleaded with them, 'Save yourselves from this corrupt generation.'" If grace was really unavoidable for the elect, why did Peter exhort all of them so passionately?

The passages which use the word "if" to show conditionality demonstrate that unconditional election cannot be true, and they also show that grace is resistible. Consider a few of these passages.

- **Luke 9:23:** Then he said to them all: "If anyone would come after me, he must deny himself and take up his cross daily and follow me." Why say a person must meet these conditions if he cannot do otherwise?

- **John 7:17:** "If anyone chooses to do God's will, he will find out whether my teaching comes from God or whether I speak on my own." In other words, any person has the choice to do God's will or not.
- **John 8:24:** "I told you that you would die in your sins; if you do not believe that I am the one I claim to be, you will indeed die in your sins." If these people had no choice in whether or not they believed, it would seem that Jesus would have been more sympathetic and less demanding.

Then, in Romans 2:6-11, Paul follows a line of argument which makes absolutely no sense unless the people could make a choice to accept or reject God's grace.

> God "will give to each person according to what he has done." To those who by persistence in doing good seek glory, honor and immortality, he will give eternal life. But for those who are self-seeking and who reject the truth and follow evil, there will be wrath and anger. There will be trouble and distress for every human being who does evil: first for the Jew, then for the Gentile; but glory, honor and peace for everyone who does good: first for the Jew, then for the Gentile. For God does not show favoritism.

We can resist grace, for Hebrews 3:15 says: "Today, if you hear his voice, do not harden your hearts as you did in the rebellion." We can accept or reject; resist or repent. Hebrews 12:25 makes this quite clear:

> See to it that you do not refuse him who speaks. If they did not escape when they refused him who warned them on earth, how much less will we, if we turn away from him who warns us from heaven?

Will All Saints *Persevere?*

In an example of inconsistency, this doctrine is about the only part of the Calvinistic system that remains in many denominational groups which once accepted the entire system. As one Baptist scholar has observed: "Let it be remembered that, less than a hundred years ago, all five cardinal points of Calvin's system of theology generally prevailed among Baptists, as theological textbooks of the times will confirm. Today, only one point remains to any appreciable extent among Baptists—inevitable perseverance, and there is growing evidence that Baptists are increasingly questioning this last vestige of the central core of Calvin's system of theology."[14]

In 1960, Robert Shank wrote a book entitled, *Life in the Son: A Study of the Doctrine of Perseverance.*[15] He planned on writing a book to support the Calvinistic position, the accepted one within his denomination. However, as he looked carefully at all of the supposed Calvinistic prooftexts, they did not support the position. With a careful analysis of the Greek verb tenses used in relevant NT passages, he showed that the security of the believer is completely tied to a perseverance of faith. The idea of the security of the believer is a beautiful biblical concept. But the truth is that a believer can become an unbeliever, and at that point, there is no security at all. While many denominations have now rejected the first four Calvinistic tenets, the "once saved, always saved" doctrine is still held tenaciously by the majority of evangelical Protestant groups. But what does the Bible have to say on the subject?

In teaching those who are not really entrenched in this doctrine, pointing out a few passages often solves their problem. The entire book of Hebrews is dealing with the possibility of apostasy (see especially 2:1-3; 3:7-13; 6:4-6; 10:26-31; 12:25). James told *brothers* (1:2) that sin can become full-grown and bring about spiritual death once again (1:13-15). Paul clearly stated that if we deny Christ, he will also deny us (2 Timothy 2:12). He wrote in Romans 6:16, "Don't you know that when you offer yourselves to someone to obey him as slaves, you are slaves to the one whom you obey—whether you are slaves to sin, which leads to death, or to obedience, which leads to righteousness?" In 1 Corinthians 10:1-12, the disobedient of the OT are presented as examples, imploring NT people to "be careful that you don't fall!" An unbiased person should be able to grasp this point readily, for the NT is absolutely full of such passages.

However, some are so rooted in this error that time and patience must be expended with them before they are willing to give it up. With such people, we suggest approaching the subject from a slightly different angle. Admit that the NT does teach the "security of the believer." The key to the whole misunderstanding is found in the term *believer.* A believer is one who has become a Christian through an obedient faith and who then continues to exercise the same obedient faith. This does not imply perfect obedience, but a heartfelt consistent obedience. Once one stops exercising this faith, he ceases to be a believer. A believer can become an *unbeliever.* It is just that simple.

Notice carefully the wording of Hebrews 3:12: "See to it, brothers, that none of you has a sinful, unbelieving heart that turns away from the living God." Therefore, a *brother* can become an unbeliever and, as such, *fall away.* In John 5:24, we are told this by Jesus: "I tell you the truth, whoever hears my word and believes him who sent me has eternal life and *will not* be condemned; he has crossed over from death to life."

Then, in John 3:36, we find these words: "Whoever believes in the Son has eternal life, but whoever rejects the Son *will not* see life, for God's wrath remains on him." Now, which *will not* is stronger? Why should either of these statements be irreversible? If an unbeliever can become a believer and escape the wrath of God, a believer can turn back to the state of unbelief and thereby be under condemnation again.

At this point, a trained Calvinist will usually say something like this: "Well, if they fall away, they never really were saved in the first place." If they resort to this, even after we have studied how believers can become unbelievers, their minds may be closed. In this case, about all that we can do is turn to a passage like 2 Peter. 2:20-22 and *camp* there until they either deny the passage or deny their error. Do not be sidetracked. Stay with *this passage* until they accept it or deny that Peter was correct when he wrote:

> If they have escaped the corruption of the world by knowing our Lord and Savior Jesus Christ and are again entangled in it and overcome, they are worse off at the end than they were at the beginning. It would have been better for them not to have known the way of righteousness, than to have known it and then to turn their backs on the sacred command that was passed on to them. Of them the proverbs are true: "A dog returns to its vomit," and, "A sow that is washed goes back to her wallowing in the mud."

For further study of perseverance, see John 15:5-6 which shows that a branch in Christ can be cut off and burned. In 1 Corinthians 9:27, Paul states: "No, I beat my body and make it my slave so that after I have preached to others, I myself will not be disqualified for the prize." 1 Corinthians 10:5-12 uses the OT people in the wilderness-wandering period as examples of those who sinned and lost the grace of God. Can a Christian fall from grace? If we wanted to prove it beyond any doubt in words that are precisely to the point, no better statement could be penned that the one in Galatians 5:4: "You who are trying to be justified by law have been alienated from Christ; you have fallen away from grace." With those passages, we conclude the examination of the doctrine of perseverance and of the entire TULIP system. It has been examined in the light of the Bible, and it has come up short. Let God be true and every man a liar.

QUICK REFERENCE GUIDE: _____

1. **Calvinistic Claim:** Every person is born guilty of Adamic sin, and, in fact, is totally depraved. **Bible Truth:** Jesus spoke of those with "good and honest" hearts, who could thus choose to obey God (Luke 8:11-15). Cornelius had impressed God with his heart, even as a non-Christian (Acts 10:1-4). Deceivers were said to go from "bad to worse," which makes no sense if they were already totally depraved (2 Timothy 3:13).

2. **Calvinistic Claim:** Due to man's supposed total depravity, God's election of man must be unconditional. **Bible Truth:** God does not show favoritism, but accepts those who choose to do right (Acts 10:34-35). God does not want the wicked to die, but rather to repent (Ezekiel 33:11). The potter and clay illustration of Romans 9 does not mean that the clay has nothing to do with how it is shaped (2 Timothy 2:20-21). God calls us by the gospel (2 Thessalonians 2:13-14), and he wants all to receive this call (Mark 16:15), but we have the responsibility to accept the "clothing" offered to us as we choose to be chosen (Matthew 22:1-14).

3. **Calvinistic Claim:** The atonement was limited, hence Christ died only for the elect. **Bible Truth:** Jesus clearly died for everyone, although everyone will not accept him. See Luke 2:10; John 1:29; John 3:16; 2 Corinthians 5:14-15; 1 Timothy 2:5-6; Hebrews 2:9; 1 John 2:2.

4. **Calvinistic Claim:** God's grace is irresistible to the ones whom he has elected. **Bible Truth:** All of the choices given by God in his Word would make no sense at all unless they are indeed genuine choices (Luke 9:23; Acts 2:40; Romans 2:6-11; Hebrews 3:25; 12:25). Jesus says very pointedly that we can choose to do God's will (John 7:17).

5. **Calvinistic Claim:** If a person is one of the elect, he will become a Christian, and he will persevere (cannot fall away). **Bible Truth:** Hebrews is an entire book warning about this possibility (Hebrews 2:1-3; 3:7-13: 6:4-6; 10:26-31; 12:25). Compare the will not's in John 3:36 and John 5:24. Why would one be reversible and the other irreversible? An unbeliever can become a believer, and a believer can become an unbeliever (Hebrews 3:12). See John 15:5-6; 1 Corinthians 9:27; Galatians 5:4; and 2 Peter 2:20-22 for similar passages.

Notes _____

[1]Herman Hanko, Hoeksema, Homer C.; Van Baren, Gise J. *The Five Points of Calvinism,* Grand Rapids: Reformed Free Publishing Association, 1976, pages 12-13..

[2]Hanko, p. 18.

[3]Hanko, p. 23.

[4]Hanko, p. 30.

[5]Hanko, p. 35.

[6]Hanko, p. 36.

[7]Hoeksema, p. 48.

[8]Hoeksema, p. 62.

[9]Hoeksema, p. 65.

[10]Van Baren, p. 73.

[11]Van Baren, p. 79.

[12]Van Baren, p. 90.

[13]Van Baren, p. 88.

[14]William Adams quoted in Robert Shank, *Elect in the Son,* Bethany House, p. 16.

[15]Robert Shank, *Life in the Son,* Bethany House, 1960.

CHAPTER EIGHT

PROTESTANT DOCTRINES OF SALVATION

The Relationship between Faith and Baptism

Within Protestant denominations, one will find several different teachings regarding conversion and baptism, but they all fail to see baptism as something intimately connected to the forgiveness of sins, the new birth or the beginning of a life in Christ.

Infant Baptism: No Relationship

Since infants cannot have faith, this type of baptism (as practiced in such groups as the Methodists, Presbyterians, Anglicans or Episcopalians) bears no relationship to faith at all—unless the faith of the parents or priests was considered. However, Colossians 2:12 makes it clear that baptism requires the *personal* faith of the one being baptized. The main reason that infant baptism ever became a practice is that the doctrine of original sin was developed and the baptism of infants seemed a necessary corollary of that doctrine. That issue was discussed at length in Chapter Four and the related Appendix.

However, another argument often used to justify infant baptism comes from the attempt to make it parallel to circumcision in the OT. The passage often used to support this comparison is Colossians 2:11-13.

> In him you were also circumcised, in the putting off of the sinful nature, not with a circumcision done by the hands of men but with the circumcision done by Christ, having been buried with him in baptism and raised with him through your faith in the power of God, who raised him from the dead. When you were dead in your sins and in the uncircumcision of your sinful nature, God made you alive with Christ. He forgave us all our sins.

The passage is making a contrast between the two types of circumcision; it is not making the parallel suggested by those who practice infant baptism. Verse 12 militates against infant baptism in at least two ways. Baptism is said to be a burial, which is used by almost no church which baptizes infants. Also, personal faith is tied inseparably to the act of baptism in the passage.

However, aside from that text, a number of compelling facts demonstrate the invalidity of the attempted parallel:

- Circumcision was for the Jews, but baptism is for all nations (Matthew 28:19).
- Circumcision was for Jews eight days old, but baptism is for those old enough to believe and repent.
- Circumcision was for males only, but baptism is for males and females.
- Circumcision was for those already born into the covenant, but baptism puts us into the covenant under Christ (Galatians 3:26-29).
- Circumcision placed the one circumcised under the obligation of the Law, but baptism frees us from the Law (Galatians 3:24-29).
- Circumcision bore no relationship to the cross, but baptism is into the death, burial and resurrection of Christ (Romans 6:3-4).
- Circumcision had no connection to forgiveness of sin, but baptism is expressly for the forgiveness of sin (Acts 2:38; 22:16).
- Circumcision was not connected to the reception of the Holy Spirit, but baptism is followed by our reception of the Spirit (Acts 2:38).
- Circumcision caused those circumcised to go on their way weeping, but baptism causes those baptized to go on their way *rejoicing* (Acts 8:36-39)!

The timing of teaching and entering the covenant is altogether different in the NT and OT. Note this difference in Hebrews 8:11 as the writer contrasts the OT and the NT: "No longer will a man teach his neighbor, or a man his brother, saying, 'know the Lord,' because they will all know me, from the least of them to the greatest." Under the old covenant, the people were born into the covenant and then taught about God. The overall failure of that system was that many who wore the name of God did not really know him. They had *not* been taught about God. Under the new covenant, people must first be taught before they can be born (born again, the new birth). In summary, in the OT, people were born and then taught; in the NT, they are taught and then born.

Therefore, attempting to justify infant baptism by trying to compare it to circumcision falls very far short!

Evangelical Adult Baptism: The Wrong Relationship

The standard approach of Protestant churches that do immerse adults is to teach that a person is saved at the point of faith (their definition of faith) and then baptized at some later point. Baptism is viewed as "an outward sign of an inward grace" or as a "demonstration to others of what has already occurred between a person and God." In other words, baptism is much like observing the Lord's Supper—it is an act of one who is already a Christian.

The definition of faith being used here is incomplete and highly dangerous to the souls of men. The passages used to supposedly prove salvation by faith without baptism are the ones which mention only the words "faith" or "belief." This approach necessitates the ignoring of other passages which do mention baptism. A common line of argument is that since many more passages mention *faith* than mention *baptism*, faith must be the *essential* ingredient while baptism is important but *not* essential. The ultimate result of such reasoning is that baptism passages have to be explained away, and even faith passages have to be twisted.

In the former case, Acts 2:38 is interpreted to mean that baptism is to be done *because* sins are already forgiven. The explanation is based on the use of the Greek preposition *eis* in the passage and compared to the translation of the same preposition in Matthew 12:41, which reads: "The men of Nineveh will stand up at the judgment with this generation and condemn it; for they repented *at* the preaching of Jonah." The meaning of the word "eis" is literally "into," "for" or "looking forward to." In Matthew 12:41, the word should not be translated "because." The people repented "into" the preaching of Jonah; they repented "looking forward to" the deliverance that he preached if they did repent. Matthew 26:28 is a critical passage for this discussion, for it has exactly the same Greek construction as Acts 2:38. Here Jesus says, "This is my blood of the covenant, which is poured out for many for the forgiveness of sins." Surely Jesus did not go to the cross because our sins were *already* forgiven! It is interesting to note that no major translation of the NT has ever translated Acts 2:38 with the word "because," even though the actual beliefs and practices of many of the translators are exactly in keeping with the doctrine we are questioning. In this case, they are much better *translators* than *theologians*!

Romans 10:9-10 is often quoted as *proof* that we are saved without baptism. However, a *proof-text* out of *context* is a *pretext*! Verses 9-10 cannot be used to exclude baptism from the salvation process—for several reasons: One, chapter 10 follows chapter 6, and in that chapter, baptism is clearly taught to be a part of dying to sin and being raised to begin a new life; and two, "trust" in verse 11 and "call on him" in verse 12 go *farther* than simply believing and confessing. The progression in verses 14-15 is preaching, hearing, believing and calling. Calling on the name of the Lord *includes* baptism, as may be readily seen in Acts 2:21, 38, and also in Acts 22:16. In Acts 2:21, Peter quotes from Joel 2:32 which states: "And everyone who calls on the name of the Lord will be saved." Then, when the people ask, in essence, just how to do that, Peter tells them to repent and be baptized (Acts 2:37-38). Acts 22:16 is even clearer, as Paul is told to "Get up, be baptized and wash your sins away, calling on his name."

In Romans 10:9-10, Paul is talking about the Jews who had failed to accept Christ, and he is addressing the reasons for that rejection. He was making the point, beginning in verse 5, that the righteousness which comes by faith is not a complex issue, nor an unreachable goal. God has already done the difficult work by sending his Son to the cross. Now, in response to what he has done, we need to accept him as Lord and Messiah. That was the challenge to the Jew. Being baptized was not a hard concept for them. It had been a part of John's ministry, and large numbers of Jews had received it from his hands. Matthew 3:5-6 says that: "People went out to him from Jerusalem and all Judea and the whole region of the Jordan. Confessing their sins, they were baptized by him in the Jordan River." Proselytes to Judaism were customarily baptized as an initiation rite into Judaism. Therefore, Paul had no reason to mention baptism again in this chapter. That was not their stumbling block.

The problem that the Jew did have was to accept Jesus as the Messiah and to then make this crucified Jew from despised Nazareth their Lord and King. Now *that* was a challenge! This background focus explains why the passage was worded as it was. Similarly, the problem with Gentile acceptance of the gospel was repentance. Therefore, Luke focused on that need all through the Book of Luke. In fact, his account of the Great Commission only mentions repentance: "He told them, 'This is what is written: The Christ will suffer and rise from the dead on the third day, and repentance and forgiveness of sins will be preached in his name to all nations, beginning at Jerusalem'" (Luke 24:46-47). Luke's failure to specifically name faith in this account does not mean that he was excluding it from the conversion process. He was simply focusing on their greatest challenge. And Luke's approach follows exactly the same principle used by Paul in Romans 10.

But what about those individuals who are immersed as adults, but merely as an "outward sign of an inward grace"? How should we view their baptisms? More importantly, how does God view them? The understanding and convictions with which we respond to God's teaching either validate or invalidate the response. Christianity is a religion of motive and purpose. Outward acts, without proper understanding and heart, have never been acceptable to God. Under the old law, even the sacrifices were to be offered with a clear grasp of the *purposes* behind them. The statutes in the Pentateuch spell out these purposes in no uncertain terms. Likewise, the NT defines the purposes of baptism very plainly. Baptism is for the forgiveness of sins (Acts 2:38; 22:16), the point at which one is born again (John 3:3-5), the means of entering Christ where salvation is (Galatians 3:27; 2 Timothy 2:10) and the act which places us into the one body where God promised to save (1 Corinthians 12:13; Ephesians 4:4; 5:23).

Now the real question is this: can one be taught *incorrectly* and baptized *correctly*? Our answer is no! Certainly a person could sing, pray, give and partake of the Lord's Supper in a wrong manner. This being true (and surely no one would disagree on these matters), one can also be baptized in a wrong manner, even if the person is sincere. For the sake of illustration, let us consider a hypothetical case involving the Lord's Supper. Someone could be taught to partake every Sunday, but be taught incorrectly concerning the purpose. He could be told that, in partaking, he is to remember Christ as the agent in creation (and he was—John 1:1-3), rather than as our sacrifice. The person involved would be observing the Supper regularly for a sincere religious motive, but for the wrong purpose. Would God be pleased with this worship based on an incorrect understanding? In the case of baptism, a person being baptized would not have to have a comprehensive understanding of *everything* which takes place at baptism, but he would have to understand the basics. However, there is a major difference in having a somewhat *incomplete* understanding and having an *incorrect* understanding.

Sincere and even "religious" purposes in the act of baptism can be unacceptable to God. The evangelical denominations who teach that baptism is "an outward sign of an inward grace" teach those being baptized that they are baptized *after* they are saved, and not *in order to be* saved. This is totally unscriptural. Consider Colossians 2:12: "Having been buried with him in baptism and raised with him through your faith in the power of God..." We are raised to walk a new life (as Romans 6:4 also mentions) through our personal faith in the power of God in the act of baptism itself. How can our "faith in the power of God" be transferred to another act (belief alone), and another time (before baptism), and still be acceptable?

Some are opposed to "re-baptism," but Paul was not (Acts 19:1-5). These whom Paul baptized had previously been immersed according to John the Baptist's teaching, but they needed to be immersed according to

Christ's teaching of the Great Commission baptism. Also bear in mind that Jesus even administered the baptism of John at one time (through his disciples—John 4:1-2). However, after the cross, only *one* baptism was acceptable (Ephesians 4:5), and that was the baptism of the new covenant. Although other baptisms are mentioned in the NT, by the time Ephesians was written, only one remained as a necessary part of our response to God.

A few years later, Peter wrote that "this water symbolizes baptism that now saves you also—not the removal of dirt from the body but the pledge of a good conscience toward God. It saves you by the resurrection of Jesus Christ" (1 Peter 3:21). Thus, this one baptism was water baptism, and it was clearly connected to salvation. Any variation of this baptism was not acceptable to Paul, and it should not be to those of us today who are seriously trying to follow the Bible. No one can be taught incorrectly and then baptized correctly. The logical and biblical route to take should be obvious, and certainly God would not be displeased with any person who was doing all that he could to conform to accurate teaching. I have never found an honest and sincere person who was satisfied for long with a *questionable* baptism once they were taught accurately.

Bible Baptism: A Faith Relationship

A Response of Faith

Properly understood, baptism is a response of faith to the cross. Romans 6:3-4 says that "all of us who were baptized into Christ Jesus were baptized into his death. We were therefore buried with him through baptism into death in order that, just as Christ was raised from the dead through the glory of the Father, we too may live a new life." Far from being a "work," as some claim, baptism is an honest recognition that we are hopelessly lost in sin without the death of Jesus, and a commitment of our hearts to him and the cross. Biblically, baptism is inseparably connected to faith in the substitutionary death of Christ on the cross.

However, many who are taught incorrectly hold the belief that a person is saved by *faith only*, without a further response. This view is a popular one held by a majority of people in the religious world today. One of the reasons for this wrong belief is perhaps because the Bible so often just mentions faith in connection with salvation. Of course, a lesser number of passages tie repentance, confession and baptism just as clearly to salvation. Some people are prone to line up the majority passages against the minority passages, claiming that faith is *essential* while the commands in the other categories are *optional*. This pits Scripture against itself and is therefore erroneous. Several answers can be given to this misconception of *faith only*.

One approach is to explain that biblical faith is a common figure of speech (synecdoche) where the part is used for the whole. Usually *faith* is mentioned, since it is the beginning point out of which all other conditions grow and also the most central quality needed for continuing in the Christian life. However, other terms are used in other passages in this same way. For example, Luke's version of the Great Commission (24:44-49) mentions that "repentance and forgiveness of sins should be preached." Since faith is *not* mentioned, it is obvious that *repentance* is mentioned as a part of the whole process of salvation, which would certainly *include* faith. Obviously, when the term "faith" is used in this manner, it is meant to include all other aspects of the salvation process, including both repentance and baptism.

Another approach to clarifying the steps of salvation is to compare the passages containing these steps of obedience to a *recipe*. All items must be included which pertain to the end product. A cake recipe may place sugar and shortening on the top of the list, but these alone would not make a cake. The Bible recipe for salvation may place faith by itself in some passages, but the recipe is not *complete* without the rest of the list. In this manner, the Bible forms a pattern, and therefore all parts must be considered before the recipe is complete and salvation secured.

A third approach can be well demonstrated with examples of conversions in Acts. In three such cases, the teaching sounds like it differs, but it simply corresponded with the people's position and need. A man traveling from Texas to New York may ask what the distance is while still in Texas. The answer he receives will be *different* from the answer to the same question asked when he is halfway to New York. In both cases, the answer is based on his present position. Similarly, the Philippian jailer was told to believe (Acts 16:31) because he was just beginning his trip to salvation. The audience on Pentecost had already believed, so they were told to "repent and be baptized" (Acts 2:38). Saul was already a repentant believer when he was told to "get up and be baptized" (Acts 22:16). In each case, the command was based on the position and need of those being addressed.

Restricted Faith and Comprehensive Faith

The last approach that we will mention is more detailed, but possibly the most effective when trying to help a person who is really grounded in the *faith only* doctrine. In this approach, we show that the Bible uses the term "faith" in both a *restricted* sense and in a general *comprehensive* sense. Many passages use belief as a type of mental assent, which would be the narrow or restricted sense. For example, Acts 18:8 states that "many of the Corinthians who heard him believed and were baptized." Something besides faith is mentioned, so faith here is used in the narrow sense. Other similar passages are Acts 11:21; Mark 16:16; John 12:42; and James 2:19.

The general or comprehensive use of faith is seen in passages like John 3:16; John 20:30-31; Romans 1:16; and Acts 4:4. The familiar statement in John 3:16 that "whoever believes in him should not perish" actually *includes* baptism rather than *excluding* it. This point may be demonstrated by considering such passages as John 3:36, which states: "Whoever believes in the Son has eternal life, but whoever rejects the Son will not see life..." The NASV provides a more literal translation as it contrasts faith and obedience in these words: "He who *believes* in the Son has eternal life; but he who does not *obey* the Son shall not see life..."

Notice that belief and obedience are used interchangeably in the two phrases. Here, belief is used in the broader, general sense and is synonymous with obedience (see Acts 14:1-2; 16:30-34; 19:1-3; and Hebrews 3:18-19 for further illustrations of the same principle). In both of the Acts accounts, it is obvious that the phrases "when you believed" and "he had come to believe" included the act of baptism. Understood correctly, these passages will show that faith is often used in a manner that includes all obedience to the gospel, of which baptism is a part.

Other Illustrations and Analogies

Several additional approaches also should prove helpful in establishing the proper relationship of faith to baptism. *The fall of Jericho illustration* is one such approach. In Joshua 6:2, God said that *he had* given (past tense) the city into the hands of the Israelites. Surely, no one can doubt that the promised victory was a *gift* from God and not earned by *works*! However, God then places specific *conditions* on the reception of the gift (such as walking around the city a number of times). But when the conditions were met, the promises were received, and they were received by faith. Hebrews 11:30 reads: "By faith the walls of Jericho fell, *after* the people had marched around them for seven days." Bottom line, faith receives the promises of God when the conditions (if any are specified) are met! Faith does save us, but *when* does it save? That is the issue. In the NT setting, our faith saves *when* we obey the conditions which God has given us.

Another illustration derives from a *marriage analogy*. In the OT, a beautiful lesson may be learned by showing that God married the nation of Israel at Mount Sinai, and, through her, had a son named Jesus. Many Scriptures fit into this analogy. As with all marriages (except arranged ones!), the beginning point of the relationship is an attraction to one another. In the NT analogy, Jesus becomes the suitor who was attracted to us enough to leave heaven in order to win us over. When we became aware of his love, his miracles and his teaching, then the attraction became *mutual*! However, it must be kept in mind that a mutual attraction does not mean that we are married yet. For example, I was strongly attracted to my wife, Theresa, well over 40 years ago when we were both in high school. Amazingly, she was also strongly attracted to me (there is a God)! But when we were merely high school sweethearts, no one would have called her Mrs. Ferguson. A few years later, they started doing that, but only after we were married.

How does this apply to our relationship to Jesus? How does this attraction develop into a marriage relationship? Actually, much like it develops between a man and a woman! After the attraction stage, we then move to the *going steady* stage. Others are ruled out in favor of this special one. The Bible calls this stage *repentance*! Then this stage leads to an engagement—in biblical terms, we are now really *counting the cost*! Finally, we go through the procedures which are required in order to be officially married. In the spiritual realm, this *ceremony* (the entrance into the covenant) is described simply and beautifully with these words: "...for all of you who were baptized into Christ have clothed yourselves with Christ" (Galatians 3:27). At this point, we are now married to the Lord according to the official requirement of God himself (as revealed in the Bible)!

Another explanation has to do with getting *into* Christ. The blessings of being "in Christ" (in a relationship with him) are mentioned in such passages as 2 Timothy 2:10; Romans 8:1; and Ephesians 1:3. Only three passages in the NT tell us specifically how to get "into" Christ: Romans 6:3; 1 Corinthians 12:13; and Galatians 3:27. Interestingly enough, all are baptism passages. Thus, baptism is the culminating act of faith through which we enter that precious relationship with Jesus.

Furthermore, note that, in John 8:31-32, *holding to the teaching* indicates more than faith. Here the people were listening to Jesus and "even as he spoke, many put their faith in him" (verse 30). Yet, in verses 31-32, Jesus makes it clear that much more was demanded. Similarly, in John 12:42, many "believed in him" but would not confess it. Therefore, their faith was not biblical saving faith at all (see Mark 8:38)!

A Frequently Asked Question

Another issue often arises with those who are confused about the relationship of faith and baptism. That issue is usually raised with this question: "But what about the thief on the cross—he wasn't baptized?" Whether or not he was baptized, no one knows. Since huge numbers of people had been baptized by John (Matthew 3:5-6), he might well have been. However, this is not the main consideration. This issue is a covenant issue. Jesus himself lived and died under the Judaic covenant. The Great Commission baptism was not required nor preached until the day of Pentecost as described in Acts 2. No one could have experienced this baptism before then, because it was a baptism into the death, burial and resurrection of Jesus. It was not possible, then, until Jesus had accomplished those things, nor could it have been required until the new covenant went into effect. Read Hebrews 9:15-17 with this principle in mind.

> For this reason Christ is the mediator of a new covenant, that those who are called may receive the promised eternal inheritance—now that he has died as a ransom to set them free from the sins committed under the first covenant. In the case of a will, it is necessary to prove the death of the one who made it, because a will is in force only when somebody has died; it never takes effect while the one who made it is living.

Therefore, what the thief did or did not do has little to do with us. We live in the time of the new covenant and are thus under its requirements. And one of those requirements is the one baptism of the Great Commission, which was given after the death, burial and resurrection of Jesus.

A Helpful Exercise

One final approach may prove helpful in trying to move a resistant person who is blocked in their understanding of baptism by their denominational background. Take out a sheet of paper and write down these two opposite statements:

> **Baptism that now saves you also.**
> **Baptism that now does *not* save you also.**

Then hand them a pen and ask them to mark out the statement that is not true. If they mark out the first one, they mark out 1 Peter 3:21! If they mark out the second one, they admit that their doctrine is wrong. Forcing the issue in this way is not the place to start, but in some cases, it can move a person to a new conviction. Everyone needs to see and accept what the Bible says about this important salvation issue.

Not Faith Plus Baptism

In conclusion, faith is man's response to God. Hebrews 11:6 provides us with an excellent definition of a saving faith. "And without faith it is impossible to please God, because anyone who comes to him must believe that he exists and that he rewards those who earnestly seek him." This passage identifies three aspects of such a faith: belief, trust and obedience. The faithful person *believes* the *facts* in the Bible; he *trusts* the *promises* in the Bible; and he *obeys* the *commands* in the Bible. Therefore, faith which pleases God is the appropriate response to his Word. We cannot obey a fact, nor can we simply believe a command. We must match our response to the form of teaching found, thereby taking God at his word. Since we are commanded to be baptized, our obedience to that command is not faith *plus* baptism. It is simply faith in the cross when being baptized into Jesus. As the British scholar G.R. Beasley-Murray once said in commenting on Galatians 3:26-27: "Faith and baptism are the inside and the outside of the same thing."[1] Together they form the inside and outside of the same conversion experience. Whenever and wherever people turn to Jesus Christ with the faith and heart of a disciple, and then humbly submit to baptism in his name, they are born again and clothed with Christ. This is God's simple plan.

QUICK REFERENCE GUIDE: _____

1. **Protestant Infant Baptism Doctrine:** Infant baptism takes the place of circumcision in the OT. **Bible Truth:** The passage often used to support the above claim (Colossians 2:11-12) actually teaches the opposite, for it shows personal faith of the one being baptized (impossible for an infant). In Hebrews 8:11, we find that the basic difference in entering the OT and NT covenants was that, in the former, you were born and then taught, whereas in the latter, you are first taught and then born (re-born spiritually). This order now rules out infants experiencing the new birth, for they must be old enough to be taught first.

2. **Evangelical Adult Baptism Doctrine:** A person is saved at the point of faith and then baptized later as "an outward sign of an inward grace." **Bible Truth:** Baptism is the culminating act of becoming a Christian (Acts 2:38; Acts 22:16; Romans 6:2-4; Galatians 3:26-27; 1 Peter 3:21). Romans 10:9-10 does not teach faith only because calling on the name of the Lord in verse 12 includes baptism (Compare Acts 2:21 with Acts 2:37-38; then Acts 22:16). Salvation is "in Christ" (2 Timothy 2:10), and only three passages tell us how to get "into" Christ (1 Corinthians 12:13; Romans 6:3-4; Galatians 3:26-27). The word "faith" may be used in a narrow way (John 12:42; Acts 11:21) or in a broad way (Romans 1:16; Acts 4:4). In the latter case, faith includes baptism (Acts16:30-34). Furthermore,

in that broad usage, faith and obedience are used interchangeably (John 3:36; Acts 14:1-2; 19:1-3; Hebrews 3:18-19). The city of Jericho was a gift, with conditions attached (Joshua 6), and when the walls fell, it was faith that caused it. But, faith caused the walls of Jericho to fall after the conditions had been met (Hebrews 11:30). Faith saves us, after we have obeyed Jesus in baptism (Romans 6:17-18).

Notes _____

[1]Statement made in symposium on "Baptism in the New Testament," Houston, Texas, 1974. For further treatment see G.R. Beasley-Murray, *Baptism in the New Testament,* Wm. B. Erdmans, 1973, pp. 146-151.

CHAPTER NINE

RESTORATION CHURCHES

Definitions and History

Writing this chapter is very difficult for me, because it concerns my own root system and the many cherished friends in the Mainline Church of Christ, a part of what we call the Restoration Movement. In the first edition of this book, I entitled this chapter "The Mainline Church of Christ." I still have the concerns expressed then about this group, but I am saddened by the fact that I expressed those concerns in a poor way at times. And for that, I sincerely apologize. My experiences since then have demonstrated that my concerns affect a broader fellowship of churches, and so I am entitling this chapter, "Restoration Churches" —which include the Mainline Church of Christ and also the Christian Churches, with whom we share a common early history. To be perfectly candid, I almost left this chapter out of the second edition of the book. The tendency to be sentimental is very real with me. However, something like a "prophet's spirit" in me moves me beyond sentimentality, and so I would ask that this material be read with the understanding that I wish I didn't have to say what I am going to say. But I believe it is needed, and the concerns are broader than for my former fellowship of churches. They clearly extend toward many other churches within the broader restoration fellowship.

The first two concerns expressed in the material to follow are the ones that caused me to leave that fellowship of churches in favor of a group that was very serious about both of these issues. Nothing I have seen nor experienced in the past 24 years after leaving has caused me to feel substantially different. However, without question, we owe much to the Restoration Movement conceptually, just as the first-century church owed much to the Jewish movement. Frankly, due to their persecution by the Jews, it was not easy for our first-century brothers to fully appreciate

113

the good things from Judaism. Similarly, due to the persecution by some in Mainline Churches of Christ, it has not been easy to appreciate the foundational backdrop which we have received from them. Those of us who have received this persecution in the past need to grow in the area of forgiving those who have sinned against us, and we need to genuinely appreciate all of the correct things which we have learned from this group and from any other group. We also need to recognize our own sins in the past in regard to our views and reactions, and then repent of those things. Pride and self-righteousness have no place in a true disciple's life.

Back in Chapter Six, the Restoration Movement was introduced briefly. It began with some noble ideas and made a significant impact for decades. The concept of going back to the Bible, striving to be "Christians only" and forsaking denominational and unbiblical traditions was entirely admirable. The focus on *restoration* rather than *reformation* was likewise insightful and powerful. Many biblical doctrines were in fact restored, and Bible study was greatly encouraged. The doctrine of infant baptism was challenged, as was the idea of becoming a Christian simply by "faith alone." It was shown that baptism is the immersion of adults for the forgiveness of sins. Many books have been written that describe in detail the history of this movement, which dates back to the close of the 18th century. The impact made on the American frontier was nothing short of amazing. People were baptized by the thousands as denominational dogmas were forsaken in favor of a more pure form of Christianity.

However, with the passage of time, some very unfortunate events occurred. The genesis of these events traced back to issues that had been developing for decades, as seeds were planted which would work at cross purposes with the stated goal of unity. Alexander Campbell, the most influential thinker in the movement, had been deeply influenced by rational philosophers of the Enlightenment, like John Locke, who believed everything could be reduced to a set of facts. Applying Lockean philosophy to the Bible, Campbell viewed the NT as a *pattern*, comparing it to the pattern which God gave to the Jews for the construction of the tabernacle. He stated that all that Christians had to do was observe the elements of the pattern and then follow them in order to be the NT Church. Alexander and his father, Thomas, gave the movement several ideas that would shape it profoundly for many years:

(1) Early on, Thomas coined the phrase: "Where the Bible speaks, we speak. Where the Bible is silent, we are silent." This would become the movement's most well-known slogan.

(2) Alexander taught that disciples could follow the NT pattern by recognizing that two things were binding on the church: one, specific commands found in the Bible (e.g. "repent and be baptized") and two,

approved apostolic examples (e.g. taking the Lord's Supper on the first day of the week). Later, a third element—necessary inferences—would be added to the list.

(3) The elder Campbell had also taken an older saying and popularized it in these words: "In matters of faith—unity, in matters of opinion—liberty, in all things—charity."

But what sounded like a formula for success, (which it might have been with the right spirit), became a recipe for even greater division. First, there was disagreement over the expression, "Where the Bible speaks, we speak, and where the Bible is silent, we are silent." For some, this meant what the Bible did not expressly allow, Christians should not do. For others, it meant what the Bible did not prohibit, God allowed. Various elements of the movement agreed that there must be a distinction drawn between matters of faith (essentials) and matters of opinion (non-essentials), but because of their different approaches, they could not agree on what those were, and often, very little of the third element—charity—was demonstrated! For some, the silence of the Scriptures meant there was no problem with instrumental music, a paid local minister or a missionary society to help evangelize the world. For others, that same silence meant that none of those things were approved by God, and would in fact be sinful to practice.

These differences led, in 1906, to the U.S. Religious Census listing the Churches of Christ and the Disciples of Christ as separate groups for the first time. The most obvious distinction between the two groups was the rejection of using instrumental music for worship in the Churches of Christ. The controversy over instrumental music dated back to around 1860 when some congregations introduced organs into their services. After the division, Disciples of Christ eventually called themselves Christian Churches, but in the middle of the 20th century, the Disciples of Christ term came to be used as an official designation for the more liberal part of the Christian Church, who declared they were a denomination within denominations. With that declaration came the rejection of the once popular plea for restoration of the original brand of Christianity as described in the NT.

Because of the narrow approach to interpreting the Bible, those churches known as the Church of Christ splintered and splintered again, with each new sect often being convinced it comprised the only true church. The mentality thus produced was that of spiritual insecurity, legalism and distrust of leaders outside their specific group ("they might miss the pattern, you know"), while gnats were carefully strained out and camels were swallowed whole (Matthew 23:24)! Some years ago, I read one church bulletin which harshly condemned the idea of *youth ministers* because it was not a biblical term, and yet in the same bulletin talked of the church *nursery* and *educational director* (which NT letter do you find those in?)!

In all fairness, no religious group can be defined in a one-size-fits-all manner. Because of a lack of central organizational structure, no two churches are alike, especially among the Churches of Christ. After no longer being a member of that group for almost 25 years, I cannot claim to understand just where they are now as a movement. My associations with various leaders among them, along with reading their literature, would lead me to believe that some of the larger, urban churches have become much more progressive, whereas the majority of congregations are much the same in perspective and practice as when I left that movement. It is also my judgment that many of those who are more progressive in more practical areas are also more progressive in doctrinal areas, to a degree that I likely could not be comfortable with personally.

One fact seems sure: at the beginning of this century, the Mainline Church of Christ is in the midst of an identity crisis. This crisis appears to be founded on two basic issues: loss of membership and a growing rift between the more progressive congregations and the more traditional ones. In the most current issue (February 2009) of a popular Mainline Church of Christ publication, the *Christian Chronicle*, both of these issues are chronicled. (Note that I often use the term *Mainline Church of Christ* simply to distinguish it from our own movement, popularly called the *International Church of Christ*.) Under the heading on the front page, "Church in America marked by decline," an official study identified 12,629 non-instrumental churches with 1,578,281 members. Those figures are said to represent 526 fewer churches and 78,436 fewer members than six years earlier.

The article reminded me of a comment I heard several years ago at a lectureship hosted by Abilene Christian University, one of the better known universities with Church of Christ origins. I was one of four panelists from the ICOC, along with five panelists from the mainline churches, sharing in a forum about our differences. It was a time of healing, to be sure, as those of us on the ICOC side of the panel tried to be vulnerable about our own mistakes of the past and apologize for the hurts we had caused. I was gratified by the graceful spirit of the mainline panelists and the audience. It was a very positive experience. But the comment to which I referred was made by the oldest panelist on the mainline side, who had a wonderful spirit about him. He stated at least twice that we were in the last days of a dying movement, referring to his own group. Some of his fellow panelists took exception to his comment, but he made it again in the public forum at least once.

The *Christian Chronicle* article went on to mention that some Churches of Christ were omitted from the statistics because of starting to use instrumental music in worship for at least one of their multiple services. However, it was admitted that this omission of 21 congregations did not provide sufficient explanation for the decline in congregations and membership. It should also be noted that the pages of the *Christian Chronicle* have contained many articles in the past couple of years arguing both sides of the instrumental music issue. Most of these churches now beginning to use instrumental music are doing so in only one of two or more Sunday services. They are trying to please those on both sides of that issue, and as would be expected, the instrumental service attracts an audience that is generally younger, and the non-instrumental service attracts an older audience. Either way, another division reminiscent of 1906 seems imminent, while decreasing membership is occurring at the same time.

I am not nearly as familiar with the Christian Churches, but I do know that some are growing significantly in attempts to become "Mega-Churches" (which will be discussed in a later chapter on 21st-century evangelicalism). On the other hand, others are maintaining less progressive approaches (and likely more biblical ones) and are more concerned about their larger counterparts becoming doctrinally compromised. Although such different perspectives are not absent in most Protestant groups, it does seem that churches who share the history as restoration churches have a greater propensity to differ and divide.

Doctrinal Concerns

Biblical Repentance

One of my doctrinal concerns for restoration churches is shared by both the Mainline Church of Christ and the Christian Church. Again, it is important to state that all generalizations have exceptions, and I pray that there are many exceptions to the concern addressed here. This concern has to do with the biblical process of conversion, which is surely a most important and fundamental issue. A careful study of the writings produced by the restoration movement reveals that there has been little emphasis on responding to the gospel in baptism with a radical commitment to discipleship. What is so central to Jesus' message shows up in precious few places in the sermons and articles which influenced this movement. From research and from personal experience, I believe that the key failure in teaching about the new birth is a failure to properly emphasize the doctrine of repentance. Nearly all restoration churches will affirm that baptism is an immersion in water by someone old enough to have faith—for the forgiveness of sins. To substantiate that affirmation, passages like Acts 2:38 are quoted. However, the main focus is on baptism for the forgiveness of sins (in stark contrast to what most evan-gelical churches teach, by the way), and not on the repentance that is to precede baptism.

This lack of emphasis produces a view of conversion that approxi-mates something like fire insurance for the Judgment Day, rather than the understanding that baptism is the total commitment of one's life to the Lordship of Christ. And there is a huge difference between the two viewpoints! My own experience in the mainline group was that repen-tance was viewed mainly as the avoidance of evil (sins of *commission*), rather than vowing to follow Jesus' example and mission, thereby for-saking sins of *omission* as well. Some questions must be asked: one, is halfway repentance really repentance at all? Two, if repentance isn't bib-lical repentance, is the baptism that follows valid before God? Those are probing questions to contemplate, and while only God can fully answer them, we at least ought to wrestle with them.

Perhaps some examples will illustrate the reality of the potential problems in this realm. Decades ago in my home congregation (main-line group), the preacher's wife had the practice of going up to fairly young children (at least as young as 10 years old) and asking if they had been baptized yet. If they said no, she then told them that they should seriously consider it. A week or so later, these same children were often seen in the baptistery being baptized. At their ages, and through this process, I would certainly have to question what they understood about repentance. If they understood the subject much at all, it is likely that they only understood the need to forsake the bad things (sins of commis-sion) and not the sins of omission (not taking up the mantle of Christ in the world).

After entering the ministry, one of my first roles was holding per-sonal evangelism workshops in mainline congregations. Once, during an afternoon session on door knocking and setting up studies, a hippy (this was back in the early 70s) walked in off the street and asked if he could be baptized. The men present said, "sure," and proceeded to take him back to the baptistery; and in a matter of minutes, he was baptized "for the forgiveness of sins." After the baptism, he dried off, got dressed, said goodbye and left. Whatever he knew about baptism was not increased in that particular setting. As far as I know, he was never heard of again by the group that baptized him. Even back then, I was left in shock by what I had witnessed. That is why the term "fire insurance" comes to mind when thinking about baptisms where repentance seems to be all but ab-sent. Baptism is not simply about getting saved; it is primarily about accepting Jesus as both Lord (Master) of our lives and as Savior. And as the old saying goes, if he is not Lord *of all* (in our lives), he is not Lord *at all*.

Very recently, a member of my present congregation attended a service at a very large Christian Church in our area. It would qualify as a Mega-Church, and as such had a professional quality music service and an effective speaker delivering the lesson. According to my friend in attendance, the following events occurred. Near the end of the service, the minister made the comment that last year (2008), 600 people were baptized and that anyone who wanted to come up to be baptized was welcome. He wanted to make it as inviting as possible from a physical perspective, explaining that robes, towels and baptismal clothes to wear were all available and plentiful. About 60 people of all ages came forward and were baptized. The youngest appeared to be in the 10-12 year-old age category. My friend said that when people came up from their immersion, they shook hands with the one who baptized them, but showed little excitement or exuberance about finding the Pearl of Great Price or experiencing a life-changing event. That sort of practice is different from the conversion stories one reads about in the Book of Acts.

Toward the end of my ministry among the mainline fellowship, I began teaching and preaching much more about discipleship and evangelism, as I was learning it from those in discipling churches. The puzzle to me was that this teaching that I was trying to pass on met with so much resistance. After all, it was a *biblical* emphasis, although one which was generally missing from those churches. Finally, it dawned on me that the people in that group had been baptized with a different concept of Christianity—one that did not involve a total commitment to the mission of Christ. They evidently had been baptized for the forgiveness of sins in order to avoid hell and go to heaven after they died. The emphasis seemed to me to be much more about preparing for death rather than preparing for the new life in Christ, representing him before a lost world and carrying on the mission that he began two centuries ago of seeking and saving the lost.

A preacher friend of mine in a nearby church at the time had much the same experience in the mainline church for which he preached. As he was teaching about discipleship in a Sunday morning Bible class, one young married man commented that if he had known what it meant to really be a disciple, he would never have been baptized. That rather blatant comment does get to the heart of the issue, and it explains why a minority of members in those churches are seriously committed to changing the world for Christ. It also helps explain why most of the ones they do baptize are not brought to spiritual maturity, because Christ's plan for producing both numerical and spiritual growth is discipleship (Matthew 28:18-20). Being baptized is the new birth, but being taught to obey all things that Jesus commanded the disciples is a lifelong process that demonstrates true repentance.

Biblical Discipleship

Having just mentioned the call to discipleship found in Matthew 28:18-20, it is a good time to deal with another doctrinal concern that applies to both the Mainline Churches of Christ and the Christian Church. This concern is tied to the previous one regarding a failure to teach biblical repentance prior to baptism, but that failure is compounded by failing to teach a continuing repentance from that point forward. The idea of teaching a continuing repentance is simply another way of describing biblical discipleship. Matthew 28:19 addresses the conversion process; Matthew 28:20 addresses discipleship, or what I prefer to call discipling—the maturing process. In family terms, having a baby is the easy part (though a woman in labor would at least temporarily dispute that!). Raising the child to maturity is definitely the more demanding part. Jesus said that after someone is baptized, they are to be taught "to obey everything I have commanded you." Thankfully, he follows that command up with the promise to be with us as we do this!

Note that Jesus does not say simply to *teach* them all he had commanded, but rather to teach them to obey all that he had commanded. Therein lies the challenge, as any parent will readily attest. The Greek text in Matthew 28:19 literally says, *"going, therefore, disciple* (a verb) *all the nations."* The rest of the verse makes it clear that "teaching them to obey everything I have commanded you" is a part of the discipling process. Thus, a "discipling" relationship is one in which a disciple helps another person to become more obedient to Jesus in attitude, life-style and mission. The primary reason I left the mainline church to become a part of the group now commonly called the ICOC was because my own ministry experiences proved to me that discipling was the forgotten art, the missing ingredient, in so many efforts to build churches and practice what is commonly known as Christianity.

It is difficult to put into words why this practice is so important to me, but I will try to explain. Hebrews 3:13 says: "But encourage one another daily, as long as it is called Today, so that none of you may be hardened by sin's deceitfulness" (Hebrews 3:13). Back when I first was visiting churches that practiced discipling, I met a man who was writing a book defending the practice in a controversial congregation. He gave me a copy of the manuscript, which I took back home with me. A few days later, I started reading it and was shaken to my roots. I honestly don't remember too many details in the material, but I do remember what he said about discipling's potential to stop sin at the temptation level. For three days, I read the manuscript, and literally could not sleep! My mind would not quit racing and my heart would not stop pounding.

I thought of friends and family members whose lives had been devastated by sin and realized what being discipled could have done to stem the awful tide. One religious relative of mine had become close to a friend at church and had become immoral with the person. They both ended up divorcing their mates and marrying each other, leaving mates and children to wash up on the shores of pain and devastation. I kept thinking, "What if they had been in a group following the Bible's admonitions about discipling? What if they had been open at the temptation level?" I knew in my heart of hearts that the damage could have been averted and their lives spared some of the worst pain possible. I could not get the horrors out of my mind, and I could not quit thinking about what might have been if biblical discipling had been part of their lives.

I cried all my tears out in those three sleepless nights. And I vowed to God that I would begin obeying his teaching about discipleship, and learn as much about it as possible. I knew that in order to do these two things, I would have to accept the controversial nature of the subject and follow God rather than men. I made the decision to follow the Bible and its clear teaching about discipleship and discipling and let the chips fall where they may. Praise God, for my life has never been the same since. Only God knows how much sin and pain has been averted in my family by me learning how to deal with sin at the temptation level. In my judgment and experience, those who are not being open with their temptations are playing with spiritual dynamite. Every time I am open with another person with my sins and temptations to sin, my heart breathes a sigh of relief. Delivered again—praise Jesus! Satan then has to retreat into his vile darkness and look for other souls to deceive. But he will be back, tempting me to cover up the garbage in my heart. If I listen to him, he will have the opportunity to get a foothold in my soul. If I listen to God and obey his directives for discipleship, victory is assured. The whole issue is really quite simple, although not always easy. But I would not trade anything for the light flooding into my life through discipling. It is God's plan.

The term discipleship includes both vertical and horizontal aspects. The vertical is about our relationship to Christ, being totally committed to him and his plans for our lives. This aspect of discipleship will be severely hampered if the initial making of a disciple does not include biblical repentance, but it will also be difficult, if not nearly impossible, to maintain without the horizontal aspect being implemented. That aspect, of course, is what Matthew 28:20 is all about. Actually, either aspect without the other doesn't work. My commitment to Christ makes me want to get all the help I can to become more like Jesus. My commitment to his plan of discipling helps me grow in my relationship to him. It is a package deal consisting of two parts. And that is not simply a good idea—it is precisely what Jesus commanded in the Great Commission.

Of course, it is easy to say that it doesn't have to be done in the way I've just described, and many say just that. Well then, please tell me how you have made it work in making followers of Jesus who are totally committed to him and continually growing into his image throughout their entire lives. Frankly, I have heard and read many discussions on ideas of how it *should* work; I've just never actually observed it working without a serious practice of this thing called discipling. In the ICOC, our own practice of it all but disappeared for a while after the upheaval we experienced beginning in 2003. Those of us in this group can attest to the fact that our commitment level as a whole has suffered, and sins of a nature and an amount we would never have anticipated entered into our fellowship. Thankfully, most leaders and members have realized that the missing ingredient for us is in fact discipling, and we are returning to a biblical practice of it (without the abuses of the past that were too often present). My shorter of two books on the subject, *The Power of Discipling*, has sold out and a new edition is in the process of being prepared for the printer as I write this.

Speaking of abuses or potential abuses in discipling, challenges are always inherent in such relationships. But is that so shocking? The same is true of all relationships, isn't it? It is especially true of the closer ones, and relationships in the kingdom of God are to be close. After forty-four years of marriage, I can tell you that my wife and I have some relational challenges periodically. We misunderstand one another and even hurt each other. But we both treasure the relationship and would die before we would give it up. The issue is not "Could I be hurt?" in a discipling relationship. Growth in character will never be painless, and truthfully, it seldom occurs in quantity without someone else lovingly administering challenges (that feel painful). Did not the writer of Proverbs state that "Better is open rebuke is than hidden love. Wounds from a friend can be trusted, but an enemy multiplies kisses" (Proverbs 27:5-6)? Looking back, the teachers I had in school whom I most appreciate now were the hard ones, the ones who challenged me to be my best. Relationships which don't help us to "take it higher" end up as the ones least appreciated (if we have much in the way of goals or ambition to better ourselves).

Then there is the issue of "Will someone make mistakes in a discipling relationship?" Of course they will! Have you been free of mistakes in all of your relationships? Have you never given bad advice or hurt someone, even with the best of intentions? Sure you have, if you have real relationships. Relationships will always have challenges and problems because they involve humans. But a life without deep relationships is empty, and a life without deep spiritual relationships will be stagnant at best. With the kinds of relationships described in Scripture, life is more joyful than most can imagine, and the resultant growth keeps us "on the edge" as disciples whose commitment and zeal are not dimmed by the passing of the years. And that phenomenon, you will have to admit, is a rarity in a religious world most often characterized by lukewarmness and downright indifference.

On a very practical note, how is someone best taught to become a disciple in the first place—in a group setting or one-on-one? Easy answer, don't you think? Sitting down with someone and studying the Bible with them in the privacy of their home or yours is far more effective than having them simply listen to a lesson in an audience of hundreds or thousands. If the personalized approach is the most effect way to help someone become a disciple (and it is), then the same approach is going to be the most effective way to help them grow and mature as a disciple. Beyond that, it will also help them to deal with the temptations Satan brings their way. The manuscript I mentioned earlier described discipling as God's way of helping us deal with sin at the temptation level before it comes into our lives and causes severe damage. That observation is far more profound than most realize when first hearing it.

Without some type of functional discipling relationship, many passages in the NT will never be obeyed. There are more than 60 passages that use the term "one another" or "each other" in ways that only discipling can effectively address. Of course, there are far more passages that deal with our God-given duty to be our brother's keeper besides these, but just look for a moment at some of the ones using the terminology.

John 13:34-35: A new command I give you: Love **one another**. As I have loved you, so you must love **one another**. By this all men will know that you are my disciples, if you love **one another**.

Romans 12:10: Be devoted to **one another** in brotherly love. Honor **one another** above yourselves.

Romans 15:14: I myself am convinced, my brothers, that you yourselves are full of goodness, complete in knowledge and competent to instruct **one another**.

Hebrews 3:12-13: See to it, brothers, that none of you has a sinful, unbelieving heart that turns away from the living God. But encourage **one another** daily, as long as it is called Today, so that none of you may be hardened by sin's deceitfulness.

Hebrews 10:24-25: And let us consider how we may spur **one another** on toward love and good deeds. Let us not give up meeting together, as some are in the habit of doing, but let us encourage **one another**—and all the more as you see the Day approaching.

James 5:16: Therefore confess your sins to **each other** and pray for **each other** so that you may be healed. The prayer of a righteous man is powerful and effective.

After reading this list, some questions are in order. How did Jesus love his disciples? It was up close and personal, not from a distance. It was not a hearty handshake after a synagogue service, wishing them to be warm and well fed. He poured his life into theirs and then told them to go and do the same with others. How can you be devoted to one another unless you are in each other's lives enough to show that devotion consistently? Being devoted to marriage or to parenting exacts a price. Are you paying it with fellow Christians? In what ways are we instructing one another, instead of just receiving instruction from a minister? How is the daily encouragement being practiced in your life and in your church? Who is spurring you on toward love and good deeds? (The Greek term for *spur* is used only in one other place, where it is translated "sharp disagreement." Who is involved in your life to the point that they are willing to rebuke you if you need that?) And then, of course, who are you confessing your temptations and sins to besides God? The Greek construction used here means literally to "be in the habit of confessing your sins to one another"—not just waiting until you are sick or with the elders of the church (as the previous context mentions).

Last year, after our neighbors first attended church with us, they immediately noticed some real differences in what they experienced with us and in what they had experienced in their Mega-Church (with restoration roots). They said that no one knew their name in the other church, whereas people in our church either quickly learned their names or showed evidence of really wanting to learn them. Until I became a part of a church movement that practiced discipling, I simply did not experience the kind of Christianity that I read about in the New Testament. Discipling was the missing ingredient that I discovered, and it is to me a very important and valuable part of finding the Pearl of Great Price (Jesus and his teaching).

Interestingly, some former ICOC members have gone to worship at large Christian Churches, and their stories typically follow a certain pattern. At first, they rave about the services, especially the music. Knowing that their friends in the church they left have the same doctrinal concerns expressed in this chapter, they are quick to assure them that their new church teaches the same things about baptism and discipling. However, teaching that baptism is an immersion of adults for the forgiveness of sins doesn't equate with teaching NT conversion, which must include real repentance. It was one of these churches in our area that had the baptismal service I described earlier. Saying that discipling is practiced often means that former ICOC members meet occasionally with each other in small groups, but that doesn't necessarily equate with discipling (although it could). A bigger question is not what those in that church do who have learned about discipleship while a part of the ICOC, it is what the main body of members in that church (without that background) are doing. The answer to this question is not generally an encouraging one.

Although the restoration movement started out nobly, it all too often became legalistic or lukewarm, and thus lost its moorings. While doctrinal questions had to be addressed (as they are being addressed in this book), especially because of the 19th-century context of greater religiosity, the emphasis of the movement came to be much more on intellectual issues than on issues of heart and attitude. As the years passed and society's views changed, people changed in some significant ways, and therefore, the approach to meeting their needs should have changed. But those churches who did not adapt to the society and become all things to all men in order to save some (1 Corinthians 9:22) were certain to end up where many congregations have landed. They retained a turn-of-the-century mindset and lost touch with the hearts of people. As a result, many congregations crystallized into stagnant and dying groups. Others have compromised doctrinally, and two such compromises are seen in the lack of real teaching about repentance as the yielding of one's total life to Christ and his purposes on earth for us, and the practice of discipling to help us follow through with that repentance.

Church Autonomy

The next three concerns are mainly concerns involving the Mainline Church of Christ. Not being as familiar with the Christian Church, I don't know exactly what their beliefs and practices are regarding congregational autonomy. However, I do know historically that the early restoration movement held this teaching as one of their major foundational tenets. In arguing for local church autonomy, the early Restoration leaders were more mistaken than evil in intent. They were coming out of religious denominations where complex hierarchies had developed who lorded it over the members and, in their view, forced upon them compliance with unbiblical traditions. They saw their teaching about local church autonomy as a return to a more biblical pattern where there would be "liberty" to follow the Scriptures as they read them, and not as they were interpreted by some cleric caught up in ecclesiastical politics.

But what started out of sincere motivation ended up becoming one of the most damaging, unbiblical traditions of the Mainline Church of Christ. This doctrine has received much emphasis, most often with a spirit of certainty and even smugness. It has been a part of the Church of Christ creed for so long that no one in their group bothers to question it. I can remember personally preaching about how congregational autonomy was God's plan to keep one bad apple from spoiling the whole bunch! Even if one church went liberal, that departure would not hurt the entire brotherhood, we argued. In this way, we could supposedly never become like the Catholics! However, looking more closely, the *fact* of universal unity in the Catholic Church is not their problem. It is their *means* of gaining and keeping that unity. They do it through *positional only* authority, and with edicts passed down by the Pope and his Cardinals. The unity in the NT was based on leader relationships, as the Book of Acts demonstrates.

Even if the kind of congregational autonomy practiced by the mainline group kept at least some of them away from doctrinal heresy, much more is at stake. Sound doctrine in and of itself is not the point. Evangelizing the world is the point, and that cannot be done under the stifling umbrella of congregational autonomy! The mainline church has surely proved that one. But God desperately wants the world to be reached with the gospel of his Son. All of *leading* is either directly or indirectly related to evangelism. In order for the world to be reached, brotherhood unity is an absolute must. John 17:20-23, along with other similar passages, makes this necessity unmistakably clear. Unity based on *agape* love (John 13:34-35) demonstrates to the world that we are genuine disciples. The great mystery of the gospel is that God can unite all kinds of people into one loving group, all over the world (Ephesians 3:1-11). Not only does true unity demonstrate that we are of God, hence attracting people to him, it also is necessary on a practical level to accomplish God's purpose. Unless we are "perfectly united in mind and thought" (1 Corinthians 1:10), we cannot work together in the evangelization of the world. But with this kind of unity, nothing is impossible within God's will.

Although each congregation obviously has responsibilities on a local level, we are still one body. The idea of a non-cooperative, and often prideful, separation from each other as congregations is absolutely nonbiblical. *It guarantees that the world will never be evangelized.* It is therefore contrary to the very purpose of God and is sinful. The early church knew nothing of such isolation. Each member was a part of one body on a brotherhood basis. They worked together with an amazing lack of sinful competitiveness. They cooperated in the prime mission which God has given the church, and as a result, they reached the entire world as they knew it with the message of Christ in about 30 years (Colossians 1:23)! Such marvelous unity was based on a united leadership, brotherhood-wide. Leaders are the ones who produce unity and they are the ones who promote disunity.

After Paul wrote that there was one body (Ephesians 4:4, a universal church), he went on to describe the leaders whom God has placed within that one church (Ephesians 4:11-16). Notice that these leaders were given by God to build up, unite and mature the body. This "body" is no different in verse 12 than the "body" in verse 4—it is the church as a whole rather than one congregation. In other words, the church in the first century considered leaders to be brotherhood leaders rather than simply congregational leaders. A careful study of Acts will demonstrate that key leaders had a striking non-attachment to any one congregation. They went where they were most needed at any one time. They were sent to the places where they could best serve. The example of congregational independence, produced by leadership independence, is absent from the pages of Scripture. The "church autonomy" of the Mainline Churches of Christ, no matter how sincerely conceived, is a most harmful tradition.

The early church was united because leaders viewed themselves as belonging to the body as a whole. They were in fact the key "supporting ligaments" which joined the "whole body" together, making growth a reality rather than an unreachable dream (Ephesians 4:16). One of the most significant ways that these leaders became united was in their training. From the inception of Christ's discipling of leaders, he never left any impression that they would be limited in influence or presence to one location on a permanent or semi-permanent basis. They were taught to be "movers and shakers!" This approach of Jesus in his personal ministry was predictably followed by the apostles in their training of leaders. The importance of building this mindset in our training cannot be overestimated! It produced a brotherhood unity which in turn produced an evangelized world. We must return to the approach used by the early church. Nothing else has worked!

Jesus called men to be with him and then to be sent out to preach (Mark 3:14). The apostles followed the pattern. After Philip had been with them, he was sent out to preach (Acts 8). After Barnabas had been with them, he was sent to Antioch (Acts 11:22). He, in turn, went for Saul, a man of great potential, in order to disciple him in practical ministry; and jointly, Barnabas and Saul discipled many other leaders in Antioch (Acts 13:1; 15:35). Then they were once more sent out to preach in other places. Paul continually called men to be with him for further training. Sometimes, these disciples were simply called his "companions" (Acts 13:13). Sometimes, their names were mentioned. Timothy, a young leader who had influence in two cities, was called to be with Paul for further training (Acts 16:13). Later, he and Erastus would be sent out to preach in Macedonia (Acts 19:22). Still later, he would be sent out to preach in Ephesus (1 Timothy 1:3). Paul was always looking for leaders and potential leaders to be with him and then be sent out. He pulled in Gaius and Aristarchus from Macedonia (Acts 19:30), perhaps leaving Timothy and Erastus in their place. Acts 20:4 mentions a number of other such "companions" (disciples): Sopater, Aristarchus, Secundus, Gaius, Tychicus and Trophimus. A united approach to training this mindset into disciples produced a united brotherhood!

These men were leaders for the brotherhood of believers. They were *world* Christians, not simply Philippian Christians or Ephesian Christians! Leaders with less training were "pulled out" and later "plugged in" by more fully-trained leaders as the need dictated. Additionally, the world-Christian concept was not reserved for full-time supported ministry people; other leaders espoused the same view. They, too, were discipled to think just like the apostles (Matthew 28:19-20). We are first introduced to Aquila and Priscilla in Corinth. They are later sent to Ephesus, then to Rome, and then back to Ephesus (Acts 18:2, 18-19; Romans 16:3; 2 Timothy 4:19). Leaders in the early church were indeed movement leaders—they moved and led a movement! Their main focus in life was the mission of Jesus to seek and save the lost. These principles were once practiced widely within the discipling movement, and still are, but on a more limited basis than in the past. This is one point where the ICOC needs some reexamination, in my opinion.

It must be stated that our own early form of unity in the ICOC, while it has produced some wonderful results in world evangelism, has also produced some very damaging results. In earlier days, we had a type of *forced* or dictated unity through using too much of a military style leadership model. Now that we have repented of that, we are in the process of developing a *forged* unity—which implies that some tensions will be produced and demand resolution. I think we are doing well with that process at this juncture in our history. While we recognize that congregations should not be independent from one another (the wrong kind of autonomy), neither should we be dependent in wrong ways. Interdependence is the better word to describe biblical unity between congregations. New churches planted will require much more direction from the planting church than when they are older and more mature, after having developed their own leadership group. But regardless of maturity level, all congregations need close connections to sister churches for input and help, in order to avoid inbreeding and closed circles of thinking.

Just as individuals need others in their lives to help them continue growing, congregations need similar relationships with other congregations for similar reasons. My favorite analogy to illustrate how this should work is with the family. Children become less and less dependent on their parents as they mature, but they never become independent to the point of not needing the relationship. The nature of the relationship changes, but the need for it will always continue.

I have often told leaders of churches planted by the church I was in that, as they matured, I viewed them in much the same way that I view my grown children. I want a close relationship with them; I want to be able to give input as an older person with more life experience; but their decisions are their decisions. There are going to be differences in the relationships between different congregations, depending on maturity and resources, but there should never be a time when we don't seek input and help from one another. The writer of Proverbs stated this principle in many ways and in many verses—one of which is this classic: "Plans fail for lack of counsel, but with many advisers they succeed" (Proverbs 15:22). The concept of an independent, congregational autonomy simply will not stand up under biblical or practical examination.

Instrumental Music

Distinct from others in the Restoration Movement, Mainline Churches of Christ have been known for years for their stand against the use of instruments as accompaniment to spiritual songs. Historically, this position has not been held as a matter of preference or judgment. It has been a stated doctrinal position, and most of the leaders stating it have made it a test of fellowship—a matter of heaven and hell! The key argument against the use of instruments has been the argument on the basis of "silence" in the NT. Only the word "sing" is found there, and no reference is made to "playing." Therefore, as those using this interpretation say, it is strictly forbidden, and to use it is to go beyond the Scriptures (1 Corinthians 4:6). What does the Bible actually teach on this subject?

Although we are not under the Mosaic covenant, the OT setting can teach us some valuable lessons. Read the following passages to get a feel for the approved use of instruments in that period of time:

> David told the leaders of the Levites to appoint their brothers as singers to sing joyful songs, accompanied by musical instruments: lyres, harps and cymbals (**1 Chronicles 15:16**).

> When David was old and full of years, he made his son Solomon king over Israel. He also gathered together all the leaders of Israel, as well as the priests and Levites. The Levites thirty years old or more were counted, and the total number of men was thirty-eight thousand. David said, 'Of these, twenty-four thousand are to supervise the work of the temple of the LORD and six thousand are to be officials and judges. Four thousand are to be gatekeepers and four thousand are to praise the LORD with the musical instruments I have provided for that purpose'" (**1 Chronicles 23:1-5**).

> At the dedication of the wall of Jerusalem, the Levites were sought out from where they lived and were brought to Jerusalem to celebrate joyfully the dedication with songs of thanksgiving and with the music of cymbals, harps and lyres (**Nehemiah 12:27**).

The most notable thing to realize from these settings is that the use of instruments was *not* a part of the Law of Moses (the original Law given at Mount Sinai). They were actually *introduced* by David. Yet, 2 Chronicles 29:25 states that God commanded their use! "He stationed the Levites in the temple of the LORD with cymbals, harps and lyres in the way prescribed by David and Gad the king's seer and Nathan the prophet; this was commanded by the LORD through his prophets." To say the least, God allowed the OT people a fair amount of latitude in deciding how to worship (even under a system which tended much more in the direction of a legal exactness than does the New Testament).

According to the traditional Church of Christ interpretation, the mention of "sing" is claimed to rule out "play." A favorite illustration involves the building of the ark by Noah. He was instructed to build the ark out of cypress wood (Genesis 6:14, NIV). If he had built it with another type of wood, or in combination with another type of wood, that would have been disobedience, since a specific type of wood was commanded. Hence, the argument goes that the specific rules out something different or in addition to what was specified. While that argument can be made, and made to sound valid, does the Bible itself rule out "playing" in addition to "singing"?

In the OT setting, this distinction does not prove the point which is often asserted. The use of the word "sing" did not preclude the use of instruments. 1 Samuel 21:11 says, "But the servants of Achish said to him, 'Isn't this David, the king of the land? Isn't he the one they *sing* about in their dances: Saul has slain his thousands, and David his tens of thousands'?" Note that only "sing" is mentioned in this context. However, in 1 Samuel 18:6-7, a parallel passage, we read: "When the men were returning home after David had killed the Philistine, the women came out from all the towns of Israel to meet King Saul with singing and dancing, with joyful songs and with tambourines and lutes. As they danced, they sang: 'Saul has slain his thousands, and David his tens of thousands.'" In this biblical example, the use of "sing" did not preclude the accompaniment of musical instruments.

Another very important consideration concerns the original church described in Acts, which was totally Jewish for a number of years. From the establishment of the church in Acts 2 until Ephesians 5:19 (with its specific command to "sing"), more than 20 years had passed. How did those Jews, who were quite accustomed to worshipping with an instrument, know that "sing" ruled out the use of instruments? Other Jewish practices continued for quite some time, with at least God's tacit approval. For example, Paul took a vow and shaved his head as a part of that vow (Acts 18:18). At James's insistence, Paul entered the temple with four brothers who had taken vows and were observing the rites of purification (Acts 21:20-24). Are we to conclude that these early disciples with Jewish backgrounds could, for at least this period of time, observe these Jewish ordinances as a matter of custom, and yet be guilty of sin if they continued to use instrumental music in worship?

What are the key principles of hermeneutics (interpretation) which can help to determine the truth on this subject? Although the OT was much more a code of specific commands than is the NT, even then men *added* some far-reaching practices which were never disapproved of by God. The entire synagogue system was introduced by men during the captivity period. Yet, Jesus went into the synagogue every Sabbath as was his *custom* (Luke 4:16). The Feast of Purim was added during the time of Esther, and it became a regular feast of the Jews. The same is true regarding the establishment of the Feast of Dedication mentioned in John 10:22. Yet, none of these practices were mentioned in the Law itself.

The whole issue likely is a very simple one. Singing is the vital aspect of worship that God wanted us to enjoy, but instrumental music is a matter of *expediency*—it is a choice. If God had *commanded* the use of instrumental music, worship would have been much less flexible as far as the physical setting was concerned. Jesus said that the *place* of worship was to be unimportant in the church (John 4:21-24). In other words, worshipping in the outdoors or in a cave during a time of persecution would be a simple, convenient matter. If instrumental music had been *bound*, then the *place* of assembling would have been more important and more difficult to arrange.

God evidently did not have the NT writers mention the use of instruments in worship in order to make sure that we did not *bind* their use. To say that the lack of mention *forbids* their use is another thing entirely. It would seem that the use of instruments is simply a matter of *expediency or choice*. God is far more concerned about our hearts in worship than about the physical trappings one way or another. A worshipper can sing or sing and play with his heart far removed from the worship of God. Thankfully, a worshipper can sing or sing and play with his heart stirred to greater love as he worships God. The presence or absence of an instrument will not invalidate true heart worship, for that is worship in spirit and in truth.

In most discussions on the subject of instrumental music, pro or con, much is made of the exact words in the NT used for singing. Ephesians 5:19 and Colossians 3:16 are the focal point of such discussions. They read as follows: "Speak to one another with psalms, hymns and spiritual songs. Sing and make music in your heart to the Lord" (Ephesians 5:19). "Let the word of Christ dwell in you richly as you teach and admonish one another with all wisdom, and as you sing psalms, hymns and spiritual songs with gratitude in your hearts to God" (Colossians 3:16).

The Greek word for *sing*, "Psalmos" (from "Psallo"), is the word which is often discussed most in this connection. The evolution of the meaning of this word is a matter of importance. In ancient Greek, the word meant "to pluck" or something similar. It did not originally imply plucking a stringed instrument, but with the passage of time and the development of the Greek language, it did come to imply the use of a musical instrument. As the language further evolved, the idea of plucking an instrument was no longer inherent in the word itself. In the modern Greek language, "psallo" means "to sing" and carries no idea of playing an instrument.

The question at hand is just where this evolution of the term was at the time when the NT was written (during the Koine Greek period). Actually, different writers come out on both sides of the coin in their study of authorities on this matter. In reading the writings of these men, and the sources which they quote as their authorities, I am not convinced either way. I do not believe that the Greek either demands an instrument or excludes it. The focus in the NT passages is that we are to sing thankfully and sincerely from the heart. Whether we do this type of singing with instrumental accompaniment or without it seems not to be the focus of God. If he intended to make the use of instrumental music an *incidental* issue, as I think he did, how could he have done it any better than the way he had the NT actually worded?

It must be admitted that this particular issue is a very emotional one for many people, and the issue of conscience certainly comes into play. Having already admitted that some elements within the more progressive mainline churches are difficult for me to accept, it would be inconsistent and insensitive for me not to recognize the real challenge some have in accepting even the possibility of using instrumental music in worship. However, I think the issue of conscience needs more examination. I was raised in a very conservative (legalistic) part of the mainline group. We were known as the "one cup, no Bible class" group, which would be difficult to even explain in brief to those not from a mainline background. Thus, there were many issues of conscience for me to deal with in becoming a part of the more normal part of the mainline group. I had to deal with those issues, along with issues like instrumental music and a host of other related topics, to end up where I have ended up today.

So how did I end up being comfortable with the differences between my early experiences and training and where I am today? Let me assure you it was not without considerable difficulty. I had to realize that conscience was not an infallible guide—only the Bible was. I was willing to reexamine my previously held beliefs and look afresh at the Scriptures.

While the Bible is clear that we must not violate our consciences, it is also clear that we have the responsibility to see if our consciences are based on biblical principles and are not just an emotional reaction based on our backgrounds. If they are, we have the responsibility to re-train them, as we often ask those with other religious backgrounds to do on many subjects (such as conversion). I have included an appendix that I wrote some time back that explains how I worked through issues that were not easy for me to embrace, and I think it offers some very valuable direction to those currently struggling with matters of conscience in areas like the use of instrumental music in worship to God. I would urge you to read and study that particular article. I believe it will help you, as the principles in it have helped me. I understand your struggle. Hopefully, you coming to understand my struggles in the past will help you struggle with yours more effectively in the present.

The Role of Women

Churches of Christ historically have taken the position that women are to be *seen and not heard* in worship assemblies, except for their singing as a part of the audience. Therefore, the idea that a woman would give a testimony or something similar in such a setting seems totally heretical to many (not all) in this group. The growing women's rights focus in our society has heightened the problem for them, and heightened the awareness of the issues for all of us. Obviously, what society does or does not do cannot be the sole basis for what we do. The Bible must always be the ultimate authority. On the other hand, more is involved in this issue than first meets the eye.

We must be concerned about being our most effective for God in *every age* and in *every cultural setting*. 1 Corinthians 9:19-22 clearly teaches that we should change with our culture as much as the Bible allows such changes in order not to limit the effectiveness of the gospel and its spread. Practices which were once effective can gradually become non-productive traditions. For example, the practice of having two services on Sunday in traditional churches traces back to a rural setting when farmers had to work during all daylight hours at certain times of the year. Thus were Sunday night services begun to allow these men to attend an assembly during harvest times. One hundred years later, in urban settings, church members are still following a totally outmoded practice, or at least were when I was still a part of that fellowship of churches!

Since over half of the membership of most churches is comprised of women, their role is a vital issue for consideration, both in the realm of effectiveness and in the realm of *brotherhood unity*. Paul's description of unity in 1 Corinthians 1:10 is quite exacting, and then in 1 Corinthians

11:16, he demands that this unity be reached in the area of the women's role in the churches. While unity does not always demand uniformity, the spread of the gospel is aided by a fair amount of uniformity.

In Appendix III on pages 222, we have included a detailed discussion of this topic for those readers (and there will be several!) who are interested in a more in-depth study of the biblical teaching on the subject of the women's role.

While a superficial reading of certain NT texts (1 Timothy 2:8-15, 1 Corinthians 14:34-35, 1Corinthians 11:3-16) can lead to the conclusion that they drastically limit the role of women, a closer study without the baggage of tradition can reveal a different view from that which many have held. Yes, we will find that a woman may not have authority over a man, but she can do teaching in a private setting, with a submissive spirit, even when men are involved. While a woman is not to take the authoritative role in preaching to mixed assemblies, sharing her faith in front of an assembly in a submissive manner or participating in a group prayer with men is a different matter altogether. And when we come to what is for some the most controversial issue of all—women baptizing other women—there is not one thing in Scripture to forbid this practice, and much to commend it.

My recent experiences with more progressive congregations in the Mainline Church indicate that their practices have changed quite a bit with regard to the women's role. They likely would agree with most of what I wrote in this section and in the more detailed Appendix. However, if my guess is at all accurate, most congregations in this fellowship are not nearly as progressive and would do well to carefully study out what I have written in the Appendix. Undue limitation of what women can contribute to the church is just as wrong as undue removal of biblical limitations. Open Bibles and minds are meant to coexist. Let's strive to make sure that they do regarding the concerns expressed in this chapter.

QUICK REFERENCE GUIDE: _____

1. **Restoration Churches:** Baptism for the forgiveness of sins is emphasized, but repentance is often defined mainly as turning away from sins of commission, without the proper focus on repenting of sins of omission and taking up the mantle of Christ in this world to carry out his mission on earth. **Bible Truth:** Repentance prior to baptism is not simply preparation for Judgment Day, but is a total commitment of one's life to represent Jesus to a lost world.

2. **Restoration Churches:** Growing in our relationship with Christ is primarily a "do it yourself" project, neglecting the "one another/ each other" commands that demand having others in our lives to

help us grow more and more into the image of Christ. **Bible Truth:** Discipleship has both a vertical aspect (our commitment to Christ as Lord) and a horizontal aspect (our commitment to his plan of maturing us through the discipling process).

3. **Mainline Church of Christ**: Can only do what is specifically authorized. Must be "silent"—that is, not authorize or allow anything—where the Bible is silent. **Bible Truth:** Can do what is not specifically forbidden. For example, the Jews established an elaborate synagogue system, which was acceptable to God. The "pattern" view of Christianity has produced legalistic attitudes, spiritual insecurity and gross division.

4. **Mainline Church of Christ:** Church autonomy is God's plan for each congregation. **Bible Truth:** Such autonomy is neither biblical nor practical, as the extremely divided state of the Mainline Church of Christ amply demonstrates. The "one church" of Ephesians 4:4 is the same universal church in which Christ appointed leaders for the purpose of maturing and uniting this one church (Ephesians 4:11-16). The first-century church evangelized the world through their unity and cooperation, brought about by the "world Christian" concept of leaders and members. The leaders were linked together in their training and in their mission. Discipleship is a vital ingredient for this kind of success.

5. **Mainline Church of Christ:** The use of instrumental music in worship to God is sinful because only singing is mentioned in the NT. **Bible Truth:** Singing is required because it is mentioned, but playing is optional because it is not mentioned. The Jewish Christians continued to practice a number of Jewish customs, and it would be difficult to imagine that taking vows and shaving your head was acceptable, but playing music was not.

6. **Mainline Church of Christ:** Woman cannot share personal testimonies or anything similar in worship assemblies; they can only sing. **Bible Truth:** The focus of 1 Timothy 2:8-15 is that a woman's demeanor is to be quiet (not silent), not teaching men or assuming authority over men. The women who were to remain "silent" in 1 Corinthians 14:34-35 were evidently wives of inspired speakers who were interrupting their husbands and disrupting assemblies. If "silent" applies to all women, they could not even sing in services, because the word means absolute silence. 1 Corinthians 11:3-16 shows that women prayed and prophesied in the early church, during the miraculous days of the miraculous gifts. To say that our women cannot even share is to take a bold leap of opinion (not faith).

CHAPTER TEN

PENTECOSTALISM

Pentecostals (or "charismatics") are the modern heirs of the Holiness Movement and are most known for their teachings concerning alleged "miraculous gifts of the Holy Spirit." This chapter will focus exclusively on these teachings, because other beliefs held by many within these groups are covered elsewhere in this book. (Specifically, two doctrines of many charismatics are discussed in the next chapter that deals with the Jehovah's Witnesses.[1]) But now, let's focus on the main issues with the Holiness groups, which we will break down into two different, but inseparably related, areas—the miraculous gifts of the Holy Spirit and the baptism of the Holy Spirit.

A Study of Miraculous Gifts

Without question, miraculous gifts of the Holy Spirit were very common in the early church as described in the New Testament. To the casual reader, the question would readily arise as to why these gifts would not be available and beneficial for today as well.

Purpose of Miraculous Gifts

In a word, the purpose of these gifts was to reveal and to confirm that the message of the early preachers and teachers was from God, and that these preachers and teachers were also God-sent. Just imagine yourself among those audiences of Jewish listeners described in the early chapters of Acts. Your Jewish training would have caused you to respect the written Word of God, the Scriptures, and to settle all issues of your life by it. Now you are listening to these early apostles and other preachers teaching that this controversial figure, Jesus Christ, has *fulfilled* the OT Scriptures, so you are no longer under their authority. However, these preachers have no written word from God containing this new message. In fact, no book of what we now call the NT will be written for about 20 years! Therefore, the challenge of leaving a written, time-tested covenant, to accept one which was only verbal at that point, would have been *staggering* for a Jew! That is, unless these new preachers could validate their claims with miracles.

In Mark 16:15-20, Jesus spoke of these miracles which were to confirm his message and messengers.

> He said to them, "Go into all the world and preach the good news to all creation. Whoever believes and is baptized will be saved, but whoever does not believe will be condemned. And these signs will accompany those who believe: In my name they will drive out demons; they will speak in new tongues; they will pick up snakes with their hands; and when they drink deadly poison, it will not hurt them at all; they will place their hands on sick people, and they will get well." After the Lord Jesus had spoken to them, he was taken up into heaven and he sat at the right hand of God. Then the disciples went out and preached everywhere, and the Lord worked with them and confirmed his word by the signs that accompanied it.[2]

Hebrews 2:1-4 speaks clearly of the signs and wonders that were needed to confirm the word that was originally preached.

> We must pay more careful attention, therefore, to what we have heard, so that we do not drift away. For if the message spoken by angels was binding, and every violation and disobedience received its just punishment, how shall we escape if we ignore such a great salvation? This salvation, which was first announced by the Lord, was confirmed to us by those who heard him. God also testified to it by signs, wonders and various miracles, and gifts of the Holy Spirit distributed according to his will.

It is vital to remember the background of the Jewish audiences (and later the Gentiles), and how it would have been difficult for them to accept the gospel (as yet unwritten) without these confirming miracles. Also, without the miraculous gifts, there would not even have been a *message,* for "prophecy" (speaking by inspiration from God) was one of these gifts. Some of the gifts were *revelatory* (they revealed God's message) types, and some were *confirmatory* (they confirmed God's message). When Paul mentioned in 1 Corinthians 12-14 that the gifts were to be used to build up the body of Christ, he was referring primarily to the *revelatory* type of gifts. Since God's revelation is now completed in written form, we can enjoy the same strengthening when this message is spoken by those with non-miraculous gifts of teaching and preaching.

For the gifts to have their desired effect, they would need to be obvious, even to unbelievers: and they clearly were, according to Acts 4:15-16 and Acts 8:9-13. These were not the kind of alleged "miracles" which were attributable to other causes. Even the enemies of the early church could not deny that the miracles were real and totally amazing.

Furthermore, if the "tongues" were merely *ecstatic utterances* (unintelligible vocal sounds, as with modern claims), they would not have convinced anyone of anything, because ecstatic utterances were widely practiced in pagan religions long before the church was established. This fact is easily documented, and therefore such "tongues" would have done nothing to impress unbelievers with the truth of these messengers and their messages.

How the Gifts Were Received

The position that I have taken here is that the miraculous gifts in the NT times could only be passed on through the laying on of apostles' hands. They had received a special measure of the Holy Spirit, which enabled them not only to possess these gifts, but to spread them to other Christians as the needs in the church dictated. A careful examination of the applicable passages will yield evidence that is quite compelling.

In Acts 2, although 120 believers may have been present, only the apostles spoke in tongues which were actually *languages* or *dialects* (*glossa* and *dialekto* in Greek). Note the following reasons: (1) in verse 1, "they" goes back to the nearest antecedent "the apostles" in 1:26; (2) in verse 7, all of the speakers were said to be *Galileans*. (Although the apostles were all chosen in Galilee, the setting for this occasion was in Judea, quite a distance away. Certainly, not all of the 120 would have been from Galilee.) (3) in verse 14, it specifically says that Peter stood up with "the Eleven"; (4) the question raised by those in the audience was addressed to Peter and the other *apostles*; (5) after baptism, those early disciples devoted themselves to the *apostles'* teaching; and lastly, (6) verse 43 tells us that the ongoing wonders and miraculous signs were done by the *apostles*.

Acts 2 also demonstrates that the "tongues" were understandable languages, not simply some kind of ecstatic utterances. In verse 6, the audience heard them speaking in their "own language." The Greek word here is actually the word for *dialect*, which is even more specific. The same word indicating dialect is found in verse 8, where it is translated "own native language." Then, in verse 11, it says that "they were declaring the wonders of God in our own tongues." The Greek word for "tongues" here is *glossa*, the basic word for a language.

Between Acts 2 and Acts 6, all miracles were performed by apostles only. Then, in Acts 6:1-6, seven spiritual men were chosen to help with the distribution of food to widows, after which the apostles' hands were laid on them (verse 6). Immediately afterwards, Stephen, one of the seven, did miracles (verse 8). *This is the first mention in the Book of Acts of anyone besides the apostles doing any miracles.* And it occurred right after the seven men received the laying on of the apostle's hands! Philip, another of the seven, is the next person to perform miracles (Acts 8, beginning in verse 5). Although Philip could do powerful miracles, he *could not* pass on this gift to others, as verses 14-19 make clear.

> When the apostles in Jerusalem heard that Samaria had accepted the word of God, they sent Peter and John to them. When they arrived, they prayed for them that they might receive the Holy Spirit, because the Holy Spirit had not yet come upon any of them; they had simply been baptized into the name of the Lord Jesus. Then Peter and John placed their hands on them, and they received the Holy Spirit. When Simon saw that the Spirit was given at the laying on of the apostles' hands, he offered them money and said, "Give me also this ability so that everyone on whom I lay my hands may receive the Holy Spirit."

Notice that Simon tried to buy this ability from the apostles, rather than from Philip, although Philip could do the miracles.

The apostle Paul also laid hands on those who then received miraculous abilities (Acts 19:1-7). When writing to the church at Rome, Paul mentioned that he wanted to impart some additional gift (Romans 1:11) by which the Roman Christians might be strengthened. When Romans 12 is compared with a very similar chapter discussing gifts in the church at Corinth (1 Corinthians 12), the difference in the nature of these gifts is striking. Notice in Romans 12 that the gifts in the body are all non-miraculous, except for prophecy. The parallel in 1 Corinthians 12 names *many* miraculous gifts. Paul planted the church at Corinth, and laid hands on many of the disciples; but when Romans was written, no apostle had yet been there. Therefore, one church had many who could do miraculous gifts, while the other church had very few (if any). Those few evidently had moved to Rome from other churches that had been planted by apostles.

How Long Were the Gifts to Last?

If the miraculous gifts came only through the laying on of apostles' hands, they would cease when the apostles, and those on whom the apostles had laid their hands, had all died. Also, if the reason for the gifts was to reveal and confirm the message and the messengers, then when the message was delivered in written form, the need would have been met. By the time Paul had written his last inspired letter, he must have known that the Scriptures (which now included his own writing) would soon be completed, as the NT joined the OT in God's complete revelation. These Scriptures would equip Timothy and all disciples for every good work (2 Timothy 3:16-17).

An important point to mention at this juncture is that the miraculous gifts accompanied *new* revelation. If the miracles are occurring today, as the Pentecostals claim, where and what is the new revelation? The Mormons actually claim that their additional books are confirmed by their practice of miraculous gifts. The proponents of the Holiness Movement, then, should not reject the Mormon writings, but they do. Now that the message has been revealed and confirmed and committed to writing (the NT), the written descriptions of the miracles do for us today what the actual miracles did for them in that day (John 20:30-31):

> Jesus did many other miraculous signs in the presence of his disciples, which are not recorded in this book. But these are written that you may believe that Jesus is the Christ, the Son of God, and that by believing you may have life in his name.

If the written descriptions of the miracles are sufficient to produce faith in man, which leads to salvation, just what else would we need? Actually, Jesus recognized a *greater* degree of faith in us who have not seen these things personally but have accepted the Word's testimony:

> Then he said to Thomas, "Put your finger here; see my hands. Reach out your hand and put it into my side. Stop doubting and believe." Thomas said to him, "My Lord and my God!" Then Jesus told him, "Because you have seen me, you have believed; blessed are those who have not seen and yet have believed" (**John 20:27-29**).

Some claim that miracles are still needed today in order to confirm the Scriptures for us. This overlooks the fact that the Scriptures have already been confirmed and can now produce saving faith in us (John 20:31; Romans 10:17; 2 Timothy 3:16-17; Ephesians 3:3-5). Also, according to Romans 1:4, Jesus was confirmed to be God's Son by the resurrection. If miracles are needed in each generation to reconfirm the Scriptures, then every generation would also need another resurrection of Jesus to reconfirm him as God's Son! Certainly, the Scriptures have been confirmed adequately, and they carry within themselves their own self-authenticating miracles. Besides these obvious and necessary logical conclusions, 1 Corinthians 13:10 (which we will explore later in this chapter) predicted the ending of the miraculous gifts.

Miraculous Gifts in 1 Corinthians 12-14

Enumeration. The church at Corinth had problems with their attitudes toward, and use of, spiritual gifts. A particular problem was their pride in exercising the somewhat "showy" gift of tongues. Paul corrected their problems by demonstrating the proper way to view and use these gifts. In chapter 12, he gave the *enumeration* (listing) of the gifts; in chapter 13, the *duration* of the gifts; and in chapter 14, the *regulation* of these gifts for as long as they *were* to be in effect. Importantly, the church at Corinth provides conclusive evidence that the presence of the gifts, even in abundance, was no guarantee that the Christians would be spiritual. In fact, this church seemed to have more gifts than any other mentioned in the NT, and yet these disciples were about the least spiritual of any mentioned! The modern claim that the truly spiritual people get the gifts flatly contradicts what we see in the NT.

The *enumeration* of the gifts is found in 12:8-10. They were as follows:

- the message of wisdom
- the message of knowledge
- faith (evidently of a miraculous type)
- gifts of healing
- miraculous powers
- prophecy
- distinguishing between spirits
- tongues
- the interpretation of tongues

In verses 29-30, Paul asks some rhetorical questions: "Are all apostles? Are all prophets? Are all teachers? Do all work miracles? Do all have gifts of healing? Do all speak in tongues? Do all interpret?" Clearly, not everyone had the same gifts. Specifically, *all* did not speak with tongues, contrary to charismatic teaching. Furthermore, verse 30 shows that a non-miraculous gift is *greater* than the miraculous. Thus, Paul leads in to chapter 13 with the call for *every* person, above all else, to exhibit love.

Duration. The *duration* of the gifts is described in chapter 13, in a context which depicts the superiority of love. Tongues, without love, were worthless. Prophecy, without love, was and is worthless. Knowledge, without love, was and is worthless. Faith, without love, was and is worthless. Giving, without love, was and is worthless. Even a sacrificial death without love is worthless (1 Corinthians 13:1-3). Notice that tongues, prophecy, knowledge and faith, in the context of the preceding chapter, are all miraculous gifts. Then, in chapter 13 verses 4-7, Paul describes real love (the "agape" type), as contrasted with their spiritual immaturity and erroneous use of gifts.

Next, in verses 8-10, Paul shows that love will continue when the gifts have fulfilled their purpose and ceased.

> Love never fails. But where there are prophecies, they will cease; where there are tongues, they will be stilled; where there is knowledge, it will pass away. For we know in part and we prophesy in part, but when perfection comes, the imperfect disappears.

This passage says plainly that prophecy, tongues and knowledge were going to cease. Furthermore, they were only *partial* in their effects (verse 9). For example, a prophet could give only a partial message at any one time (see 14:29-32). He could not state all aspects of a subject, as we can today, through the use of a completed Word—the OT and NT.

Then, in verse 10, the partial gifts were said to last until *perfection* came. Just what was the "perfection"? It is not *Christ*, for the Greek term is neuter in gender, whereas it would be masculine if it were referring to him. It is not *love*, because love is feminine in gender. Notice that the "perfection" will take the place of the "partial." Since the partial gifts mentioned here are all *revelatory* gifts, then the *perfection* must have to do with revelation. Otherwise, it could not replace the partial. Therefore, the *perfection* (or *complete,* from "telios" in Greek) must at least include a completed revelation, which would end the need for miraculous gifts. Our earlier study has shown this to be a logical conclusion of a completed revelation, and now this passage has demonstrated the validity of such a conclusion.

We now can turn to a written and "perfect" law of liberty (according to James 1:25) which employs the same Greek word as that in 1 Corinthians 13:10. Paul's argument is a warning against being so enamored with gifts that are temporary anyway. He urges concentration on *love*, for it will always be with us. While it is tempting to say that the *perfect* in verse 10 is simply the completed NT revelation, the text doesn't demand such a limitation; the context suggests that more may be involved and logic would say that more must be involved. The real purpose of these three chapters in 1 Corinthians, as already noted, was to deal with worldly pride and immaturity in their view and the use of miraculous gifts. Having a completed revelation does not rule out pride and immaturity, although it surely would help in their case. What does rule it out is maturity and spirituality. Thus, in our verse under examination, it seems best to focus on the cessation of gifts (especially their misuse and abuse) as Paul's plan for their maturation process—when love would reign supreme and disunity be dispelled. He uses similar wording in Ephesians 4:11-16, when unity based on maturity was to rule out being tossed to and fro by every wind of teaching. Certainly, the completed revelation would be a part of that, as it would in 1 Corinthians 13:10, which would help eliminate immaturity based on pride. Just knowing that the gifts were partial, temporary and inferior to love would help the hearts and attitudes to change. This interpretation fits the context in showing that the partial, miraculous gifts were to cease, but keeps the real focus on maturing in love and respect for one another. The completed NT in writing was not incidental to Paul's purpose in writing, but neither was it his main focus.

Regulation. The *regulation* of the miraculous gifts is found in chapter 14. As long as these gifts did remain in effect, they needed to be exercised with God's restraints. Prophecy was a much greater gift than tongues, because it was understood much more easily (verses 1-19). Some find a supposed basis for ecstatic utterances in verses like verse 2: "For anyone who speaks in a tongue does not speak to men but to God. Indeed, no one understands him; he utters mysteries with his spirit." If one only read verse 2, such an interpretation would seem possible. However, verse 2 could also be explained as being a situation where a person was speaking a real language which neither he nor anyone in the audience understood. Thus, it would be a mystery to everyone present except God.

The above explanation is in perfect accord with the context of the discussion, as verses 22-23 show:

Tongues, then, are a sign, not for believers but for unbelievers; prophecy, however, is for believers, not for unbelievers. So if the whole church comes together and everyone speaks in tongues, and some who do not understand or some unbelievers come in, will they not say that you are out of your mind?

It is true that just knowing that God was speaking such a language through someone would provide some building up for them (verse 4). However, it would not do anyone else real good unless someone present had the gift of interpretation (see verses 5, 13, 27, 28, in this regard). This explanation takes into account all other considerations which we have studied, such as the meaning of "glossa"—*a language*—whereas the ecstatic utterance position does not.

In verses 26-40, the specific regulations for using the supernatural gifts in the first-century assemblies are outlined. Everything in the assembly was to be done for strengthening the hearers (verse 26). When tongues were being used, three people at the most could speak, one at a time, and only if an interpreter were present. If no interpreter was present, no tongues could be spoken (verses 27-28)! Two or three prophets would speak, one at a time, only until the next prophet received a revelation, and then the speaker had to stop and sit down (verses 29-33). Note that in verse 12, a warning is given against getting "carried away" and saying that you could not stop because you were "in the Spirit."

Women were to be silent in the assemblies, not being permitted to speak (verses 34-35). As we discuss in Appendix III, these women were most likely the wives of the inspired speakers in the service. The wives were interrupting their husbands, and in doing so, were disrupting a service which was to be conducted in an orderly manner. Paul then warns people against *over-reacting* and forbidding certain people with the gift to speak in tongues entirely. However, they were to be careful about keeping within these regulations as long as the gifts were operative (verses 39-40).

In view of the foregoing biblical consideration, the charismatic movement today is not based on the Holy Spirit's activity. Although its adherents are often well-intentioned and sincere, it is a movement based on emotionalism. Therefore, the purpose of this study is to promote truth in a spirit of gentleness and love. May God help us to help others who have been misled in this area of exercising so-called spiritual gifts!

Baptism with the Holy Spirit

Baptism with the Holy Spirit is another closely related subject to the miraculous gifts and must be carefully studied when examining the views of the Pentecostal churches. But other religious people have a misunderstanding of this subject as well. On the one hand, the Pentecostals believe that every Christian is to experience Holy Spirit baptism and the miraculous gifts which accompany it. On the other hand, there are those who spiritualize water baptism and claim that Holy Spirit baptism is the inner experience which brings salvation. In both cases, the biblical texts have been twisted considerably on this vital subject. Therefore, let us examine exactly what baptism with the Holy Spirit was in its original setting of Acts 2.

The promise of Spirit baptism was first seen in the preaching of John the Baptist in Luke 3:16-17:

> John answered them all, "I baptize you with water. But one more powerful than I will come, the thongs of whose sandals I am not worthy to untie. He will baptize you with the Holy Spirit and with fire. His winnowing fork is in his hand to clear his threshing floor and to gather the wheat into his barn, but he will burn up the chaff with unquenchable fire."

The baptism of fire is a reference to a *judgment* against the unbelieving Jews, which seems certain to be the destruction of Jerusalem in A.D. 70. No harm is done if this verse is applied to hell, but the other is the more probable judgment described. This impending destruction of their city was often mentioned in both OT and NT (see Luke 21:5-24; 23:27-31; Acts 2:14-21; Malachi 4:1-6 for examples).

The baptism of the Spirit is a reference to a *blessing* for the believing group. The purpose of baptism with the Spirit must be understood. Beginning with the negative, baptism with the Spirit was *not* connected with a number of things.

- It was not to enable people to do miracles, because they had already been doing that previous to Acts 2 (Luke 10:17-20).

- It was not to inspire people as prophets, for inspiration had been around for hundreds of years in the Old Testament prophets.

- It was not to "fill" people with the Spirit. John the Baptist was filled with the Spirit from birth, many years before Holy Spirit baptism occurred (Luke 1:15). Yet, he did *no* miracles (John 10:41). All Christians are commanded to be "filled" with the Spirit always (Ephesians 5:19—compare this passage with Colossians 3:16).

- It was not to *save* someone. The Holy Spirit indwells a Christian *at the point of conversion* (Galatians 4:6; Acts 2:38). Spirit baptism is never a *command* but is always a *promise*; Great Commission baptism in Matthew 28:19-20 is a command (see also Acts 2:38).

On the positive side of the coin, the purpose of Spirit baptism was to mark the beginning of the kingdom of Christ, the church. When the Spirit came, the apostles were promised to receive special power connected with their witnessing to the whole world (Acts 1:8). Acts 2 describes this "baptism" or "outpouring" of the Spirit. This occurrence marked the gathering of the Jews into Christ's kingdom. The only other mention of Spirit baptism in Acts was in 11:15-17, a reference to the Gentiles coming into the kingdom (and we will examine this passage more carefully below).

It is essential that we understand the exact definition of baptism with the Holy Spirit. In Acts 2:16-17, the "pouring out" of the Spirit is equated with the "baptism" of the Spirit. Pouring is from God's vantage point; baptism (a *covering,* or *overwhelming*) is from man's vantage point. For example, when water is poured over a coin in a glass, the coin is covered or overwhelmed. Thus, "pouring" and "baptism" are both accurate terms to describe Holy Spirit baptism in Acts 2. The reason that this outpouring was called a "baptism" is because of the overwhelming nature of his coming and subsequent availability. Before Spirit baptism occurred, the Holy Spirit was available only to a select few in the Old Testament (the prophets). Once this baptism occurred, he was then available for everyone who became a Christian (Acts 2:38-40).

However, he did not do the same thing with everyone who received him. The apostles could lay hands on people to give them the ability to perform a miraculous gift (Acts 6:6-7; 8:5-6, 14-19). Those with these gifts could not all do the same thing, because they normally had only one or two specific gifts (1 Corinthians 12:28-30). The need for the miraculous gifts ceased when the New Testament was complete in written form (2 Timothy 3:16-17; John 20:30-31).

Holy Spirit baptism, then, was the coming of the Spirit into the world in an *overwhelming* measure. He became *available* for everyone who would receive him. A similar parallel may be made between Jesus' work and the Spirit's work. Jesus' death was for *all* (Hebrews 2:9), but only those who *obey* him receive the benefit of salvation (Hebrews 5:9). Similarly, the coming of the Spirit was for *all,* but only those who *obey* receive the indwelling Spirit (Acts 2:38; Galatians 4:6).

The Case of Cornelius

In Acts 10 and 11, we find the account of Cornelius and his conversion. His is an unusual case, in that he had a miraculous gift from the Spirit *before* baptism, which is the only case like it in the Acts' record. If we are to understand why his conversion was an exception to the rule (Spirit before baptism), then we have to understand the setting and the reasons for the exception. At this time, only Jews had become a part of the kingdom. These Jews (including Peter), given their past history of extremely prejudicial attitudes toward the Gentiles, were not ready to accept Gentiles as fellow members of God's kingdom. But, when Cornelius and the others with him received the Spirit *directly*, accompanied by speaking in tongues, no one could deny them entrance (Acts 10:44-48; 11:15-18).

The result was that the Jews were satisfied, and Cornelius was baptized into Christ. However, this experience with the Spirit did not make him a Christian before baptism. According to Acts 11:15, the Holy Spirit came before they had even heard the message, and thus before they had developed the necessary faith in Christ: "As I began to speak, the Holy Spirit came on them as he had come on us at the beginning." No matter what one's theology on the Spirit or on baptism, the case of Cornelius must be viewed as an exception in these areas!

Another important consideration in this account is whether this falling of the Spirit on Cornelius constituted a second example of Holy Spirit baptism. A number of things in the text may support that understanding. Acts 11:15 is a key consideration: "...the Holy Spirit came on them as he had come on us at the beginning." Whatever else may be said, Holy Spirit baptism was not a regular occurrence, because this situation reminded Peter of the *beginning,* a reference to the Day of Pentecost back in Acts 2. This present account took place *years* later. The Pentecostal view that baptism with the Holy Spirit is an everyday occurrence does not agree at all with what Peter said.

Since Peter used the "keys" of the kingdom (means of entrance—Matthew 16:19; Acts 2:38) to usher in the Jews at the time of that first outpouring, he now used the same "keys" for the Gentiles at a similar outpouring (Acts 10:44-48). If this view is correct, baptism with the Holy Spirit was a *two-time-only* event in connection with ushering in the kingdom of God to both Jews and Gentiles. However, another view has more to commend it, as seen in the next explanation.

The account in Acts 10 and 11 is not necessarily a second example of Holy Spirit baptism. As we have seen, that view does make sense, but another similar view takes some other aspects into consideration. In Acts 2:17 (quoting Joel 2:28), Holy Spirit baptism was in the *future* tense, for it had not occurred before the Day of Pentecost. Then, in Acts 2:33, the pouring out of the Spirit was in *aorist* tense, which corresponds closely to our past tense, for it had just occurred. But in Acts 10:45, the Spirit poured out on the Gentiles was in *perfect* tense. Perfect tense denotes a past action with continuing results, like Jesus' statement "it is written," which means that the Scriptures are written and stand written, that they remain in force.

With this definition in mind, consider the wording of the passage: "The circumcised believers who had come with Peter were astonished that the gift of the Holy Spirit *had been poured out* even on the Gentiles." The perfect tense could well be pointing back all the way to Pentecost in Acts 2, as a past action with continuing results. Thus, the miraculous demonstration of the Spirit with Cornelius showed that Spirit baptism back at Pentecost was indeed for *all* men and not just for Jews. This similar *direct* falling of the Spirit on Cornelius, without human hands being laid on him, caused Peter to *remember* back to Christ's promise (Acts 11:16).

Another evidence of support for this *one time* outpouring on Pentecost is that "poured out" in Acts 2:33 means literally "to be drained." The word is often translated "spilled," meaning *emptied* instead of having something partially poured out, leaving some of the contents in the container for later pourings. In my view, the evidence strongly suggests that the outpouring of the Holy Spirit was a *one-time* event, making him forever available for those who become Christians. As Jesus died "once for all" for all men, so the Spirit was poured out "once for all" for all men. Of course, we must keep in mind that he does not do exactly the same things for us today as he did for those in the miraculous age of the church. But he does seal, strengthen, lead and love us. Praise God!

QUICK REFERENCE GUIDE: _____

1. **Pentecostal Claim:** Every Christian needs spiritual gifts, especially the gift of speaking in tongues. **Bible Truth:** The purpose of the miraculous gifts was to reveal and confirm the Word (Mark 16:15-20; Hebrews 2:1-4). Now that the Word has been confirmed and written, the written accounts of miracles can produce the same faith in us that the direct miracles did in the early church (John 20:30-31). Furthermore, the Scriptures completely equip us (2 Timothy 3:16-17).

2. **Pentecostal Claim:** These miraculous gifts are available to Christians today. **Bible Truth:** The gifts of the Spirit were passed on by the laying on of the apostle's hands (Acts 6:6; 8:14-19; 19:1-7; Romans 1:11). Therefore, when the apostles died, the gifts could no longer be passed on to others. Besides this necessary conclusion, 1 Corinthians 13:8-10 predicted such an ending.

3. **Pentecostal Claim:** Speaking in tongues is possible for all Christians, and it is a type of ecstatic utterance. **Bible Truth:** Even in the first century, not everyone spoke in tongues (1 Corinthians 12:29-30). Those who did speak in tongues spoke in a foreign language which could be understood by those from that country (Acts 2:6, 8, 11). That is the meaning of glossa, the Greek word translated "tongue" or "language."

4. **Pentecostal Claim:** We can be baptized with the Holy Spirit today, enabling us to speak in tongues. **Bible Truth:** Baptism of the Spirit was the outpouring of the Spirit, which took place on Pentecost. It was a "once for all" event. Peter was reminded of it by the experience with Cornelius (Acts 10:44 and 46; 11:15-17), but no one was ever commanded to be baptized with the Holy Spirit, and no individual in the NT is ever said to have received "the baptism of the Holy Spirit."

5. **Pentecostal Claim:** 1 Corinthians 14 proves that we should have spiritual gifts in the church today. **Bible Truth:** 1 Corinthians

14 regulated gifts for the time when they were available. A close examination of the passage shows that the Pentecostal practice totally contradicts that chapter. For example, no one could speak in tongues unless an interpreter was present, and even then, no more than three could speak in any service, one at a time (verses 26-28).

CHAPTER ELEVEN

EVANGELICALISM IN THE 21ST CENTURY

A Definition

The Evangelical Church in the 21st century has many faces and wears many hats. For that reason, its definition is no longer a simple matter. You can trace its roots back to Martin Luther and to the basic meaning of the word—meaning "to evangelize." Hence, the definition in simple terms would describe its adherents as those who share the gospel. At this point, their definition of gospel becomes quite important. Evangelicals have been characterized historically as Protestants who espouse a fairly specific set of basic doctrines. Claiming to be a "born again Christian" and an "evangelical Christian" are generally considered one and the same. According to George Barna, "'Born again Christians' are defined as people who said they have made a personal commitment to Jesus Christ that is still important in their life today and who also indicated they believe that when they die they will go to heaven because they had confessed their sins and had accepted Jesus Christ as their Savior." His definition of evangelicals is that they "meet the born again criteria plus seven other conditions: believing they have a personal responsibility to share their religious beliefs with non-Christians; believing that Satan exists; believing that eternal salvation is possible only through grace, not works; believing that Jesus Christ lived a sinless life on earth; asserting that the Bible is accurate in all that it teaches; and describing God as the all-knowing, all-powerful, perfect Deity who created the universe and still rules it today."[1]

The evangelical movement was known (until fairly modern times) primarily for its evangelistic outreach efforts and fundamental beliefs in the Bible—as compared to more liberal Protestant churches that were being infiltrated by those who were enamored with more modern views of evolution as it applied not only to the development of man from lower forms of life, but as they applied it to the supposed humanistic development of the Bible itself. Thus, in former times, the term "fundamentalism" was also basically equivalent to being an evangelical. In recent years, especially dating back to the Ronald Reagan presidential era, evangelicalism has been often identified as a right-wing political group that is interested in preserving traditional morality, at least partially through politics. Without doubt, the political clout of this side of evangelicalism has been felt by both Republicans and Democrat candidates alike in recent years. Even in the most recent presidential campaign, most evangelicals voted Republican. However, younger evangelicals appear to be distancing themselves from political interests, while maintaining traditional values such as their pro-life stance. Whether an aging political arm of evangelicalism can maintain its previous influence remains to be seen.

Other aspects of what has come to be identified with the evangelical movement seem to be losing their strong influence on the younger generation as well. The eschatology of premillennialism in its various forms, especially the dispensationalism made popular by Hal Lindsay and others like him, appears to be far less important to younger evangelicals than are current cultural challenges and needs. Their interest in the "now" far supersedes their interest in the "then." Even their contemporary spiritual music is fairly void of themes about heaven. What is certain is that most Protestants are evangelical, and what they think and do has a large influence on Christendom in America and other countries with large evangelical populations. The popularity of evangelical leaders is evidence of that continuing influence, and the popularity seems to be actually enhanced by those embracing and touting change in Christian circles. Leaders appear to be a ripe field for new ideologies and approaches. We are reminded of the words in Acts 17:21: "All the Athenians and the foreigners who lived there spent their time doing nothing but talking about and listening to the latest ideas."

In the remainder of this chapter, three "new things" will be examined, because all three are having, or are beginning to have, tremendous influence on the direction of Protestant Christianity in America. We will start our examination on the oldest of the three and proceed to the most recent.

The Mega-Church Movement

The Mega-Church Movement has, without question, had more influence on Evangelicalism than any other source—by far. We are not talking simply about growing churches with large memberships; we are mainly talking about a philosophy that has invaded and pervaded the thinking of the majority of church leaders in America. The Willow Creek Church in the Chicago area has led the way in selling other churches on the idea of becoming *selling* churches themselves, using consumer driven techniques. Bill Hybels, Senior Pastor at Willow Creek Church, has become a famous leader at whose feet many church leaders have sat, anxious to learn and anxious to imitate what has appeared to be hugely successful. Matt Branaugh, a writer on the *Christianity Today* website (christianitytoday.com) posted an article on May 15, 2008, describing the Willow Creek philosophy of church growth and ministry. One excerpt reads:

> Since 1975, Willow Creek has avoided conventional church approaches, using its Sunday services to reach the unchurched through polished music, multimedia, and sermons referencing popular culture and other familiar themes. The church's leadership believed the approach would attract people searching for answers, bring them into a relationship with Christ, and then capitalize on their contagious fervor to evangelize others.

Another article on the *Christianity Today* website (October 18, 2007), on a blog entitled, "Out of Ur," made it perfectly clear that calling this church a consumer-driven church is in no sense an exaggeration:

> Few would disagree that Willow Creek Community Church has been one of the most influential churches in America over the last thirty years. Willow, through its association, has promoted a vision of church that is big, programmatic, and comprehensive. This vision has been heavily influenced by the methods of secular business. James Twitchell, in his new book, Shopping for God, reports that outside Bill Hybels' office hangs a poster that says: "What is our business? Who is our customer? What does the customer consider value?" Directly or indirectly, this philosophy of ministry—church should be a big box with programs for people at every level of spiritual maturity to consume and engage—has impacted every evangelical church in the country.

Bob Burney, a pastor and radio show host, described the consumer-driven philosophy in slightly sarcastic terms that are nonetheless quite accurate and alarming:

> The size of the crowd rather than the depth of the heart determined success. If the crowd was large then surely God was blessing the ministry. Churches were built by demographic studies, professional strategists, marketing research, meeting "felt needs" and sermons consistent with these techniques. We were told that preaching was out, relevance was in. Doctrine didn't matter nearly as much as innovation. If it wasn't "cutting edge" and consumer friendly it was doomed. The mention of sin, salvation and sanctification were taboo and replaced by Starbucks,

strategy and sensitivity.

Thousands of pastors hung on every word that emanated from the lips of the church growth experts. Satellite seminars were packed with hungry church leaders learning the latest way to "do church." The promise was clear: thousands of people and millions of dollars couldn't be wrong. Forget what people need, give them what they want. How can you argue with the numbers? If you dared to challenge the "experts" you were immediately labeled as a "traditionalist," a throwback to the 50s, a stubborn dinosaur unwilling to change with the times.[2]

Perhaps the most shocking thing is not that the Mega-Church philosophy is so different from the message of Jesus Christ and the NT writers; it is that so many church leaders bought into the philosophy with such reckless abandon. In the Phoenix area where I live, it is the pervading foundation upon which most large churches are built. I often describe it as being like a health club whose dues are paid for by your company or health insurance (thus, its services are potentially free). When you walk into a health club, you are welcomed by some friendly, beautiful people and are free to choose what you want to do while there, and just as free to choose what you do not want to do. No questions are going to be asked about your life or your absence for the past six weeks (if that is the case). The staff is there to serve you in whatever ways you desire, and will be most careful not to offend you in any way. Health clubs are a consumer-driven business. You are the customer and they want to satisfy you. Mega-Churches have almost exactly the same philosophy. They want you to be entertained and happy, and to return regularly. You will not be asked if you are sleeping with your girlfriend or getting high on drugs or alcohol daily, or about anything else. Such probing would be offensive and could run you off as a potential paying customer.

Biblically, this whole approach to church is drastically different from anything you read in the NT, and the results are surely an abomination to God. In his book entitled, *Repentance*, Ed Anton addressed this whole consumer-driven approach in the first chapter. As a former marketing director for Coca-Cola, his words in this chapter alone are worth the price of the book (but the whole book is excellent). Hear well what Ed says:

> Sin no longer stands front and center as a heinous problem for biblical repentance to solve. Instead, I learn from consumer-driven pastors that I am a wayward victim of "sermons that are boring and don't relate to my daily living...And many churches seem more interested in my wallet than me...And members are unfriendly to visitors...And I wonder about

the quality of the nursery care for my children." So this is why I'm an uncommitted sinner? Eureka! Now let's enjoy some of that upbeat music with contemporary flavor. Meanwhile, barely audible amidst the upbeat din, Jesus continues to introduce us to the real source of our sin:

> "What comes out of a person defiles him. For from within, out of the human heart, come evil ideas, sexual immorality, theft, murder, adultery, greed, evil, deceit, debauchery, envy, slander, pride, and folly. All these evils come from within and defile a person." (Mark 7:20-23 NET)

Therefore sin requires an inside-out operation. Much more than a pat on the back, repentance reaches into the heart to eradicate sin's destructive force. This is worth accentuating. It's a good thing; in fact, it's a God thing.

Absolutely no minister wants to think of himself as "behaving with deceptiveness or distorting the word of God" (2 Corinthians 4:2 NET). In his mind, he is simply exploiting effective marketing techniques to attract a crowd who will then hear the gospel preached and the truth set forth plainly. He harbors the best of intentions. Someday soon he will work up to the unvarnished message of repentance and preach it with its requisite moral vigor.

But he never does, and he evades his guilt, because he is so busy working on the ever-increasing problems and demands of a growing congregation of unrepentant consumers—who inevitably consume the pastor himself! [3]

While anyone conversant with the real teachings of the Bible would have to be alarmed and dismayed at the Mega-Church message, it is at least somewhat satisfying that Bill Hybels and the staff of the Willow Creek Church finally figured out that what they had totally embraced didn't really work. In a fairly new book entitled, *Reveal: Where Are You?*,[4] co-authored by Cally Parkinson and Greg Hawkins (executive pastor of the Willow Creek Church), they admitted their false assumptions and subsequent failures. Hybels himself said, "Some of the stuff that we have put millions of dollars into thinking it would really help our people grow and develop spiritually, when the data actually came back, it wasn't helping people that much. Other things that we didn't put that much money into and didn't put much staff against is stuff our people are crying out for." He further quoted Greg Hawkins as saying, "We made a mistake. What we should have done at about this point, when people crossed the line of faith and became Christians, we should have started telling people and teaching people that they have to take responsibility to become 'self feeders.' We should have gotten people, taught them how to read their Bible between services, how to do the spiritual practices much more aggressively on their own."[5]

While we commend them for their honesty, we could only wish they had made their discovery from the Bible rather than having to evaluate three decades of going down the wrong road in the first place. Therein lies the danger for the future. Learning through experience alone about what does not work is not the same as going back to the Bible and digging out its truths. Burney, in the same article quoted earlier, provided us with a very relevant warning. "Unless there is a return to simple biblical (and relevant) principles, a new faulty scheme will replace the existing one and another generation will follow along as the latest piper plays."[6]

The Bible's message is simply not that hard to determine, and its warnings are not that difficult to understand. Sadly, not much has changed since Jeremiah's day, when he wrote: "From the least to the greatest, all are greedy for gain; prophets and priests alike, all practice deceit. They dress the wound of my people as though it were not serious. 'Peace, peace,' they say, when there is no peace" (Jeremiah 6:13-14). In some of the last words the apostle Paul penned, he reminded Timothy of what a true leader for Christ will always do. And with these words, we close this section of the chapter.

Preach the Word; be prepared in season and out of season; correct, rebuke and encourage--with great patience and careful instruction. 3 For the time will come when men will not put up with sound doctrine. Instead, to suit their own desires, they will gather around them a great number of teachers to say what their itching ears want to hear. 4 They will turn their ears away from the truth and turn aside to myths. 5 But you, keep your head in all situations, endure hardship, do the work of an evangelist, discharge all the duties of your ministry (**2 Timothy 4:2-5**).

Emerging Churches

One definite reaction against both the deadness of many Protestant churches and the Mega-Church Movement is a movement of sorts called "Emerging Churches." I call it a movement of sorts because it is primarily a philosophy finding its way into many religions settings. Its adherents agree on certain broad principles, but are very diverse in some of their specific beliefs. Most of them are simply sick and tired of religion as they have seen it practiced, although they still maintain many of its basic beliefs. The majority of those in emerging churches (or holding to its basic philosophy) come from Evangelical backgrounds.

Although describing emerging churches accurately is somewhat of an elusive task, it is safe to say that they are reacting to the weaknesses they see in Evangelicalism, which includes both the staid, traditional approach of some Protestant groups and the more recent Mega-Church approaches to Christianity. One reason that defining Emerging Churches is difficult is that they don't want to be defined in the normal sense. Rather than seeing themselves as a movement, they prefer to be called a "conversation." By that they mean that they value dialogue on any spiritual subject with all others who hold to any type of spiritual values. They want to be broad-minded about all religious topics and see what they are seeking as a progressing, emerging church of the future, without the shackles of traditional religion. Those who adopt this approach to religion are especially put off by dogmatism and drawing lines regarding absolute right and wrong, and making judgments about who is lost and who is saved. They are on a spiritual journey that indeed focuses more on the journey than the destination, in a variety of ways.

While some of the emphases of the Emerging Church philosophy are understandable and even commendable, some of their positions are quite unbiblical and dangerous. Understanding the terminology they use is very important to gaining an understanding of what this philosophy is all about, and as we describe strengths and weaknesses, it will be through the explanation of their choice conceptual words by which they seek to be known. Two terms that some would seem to use interchangeably probably should not be used in that way. Emerging Churches is the broader term that encompasses those (mainly) in traditional Protestant churches of one sort or another, and also those who have left those churches and are seeking to be very different churches. Many in the "House Church" movement are of the emerging philosophy, though not all. The term "Emergent Church" is most often descriptive of the "Emergent Village" group, a more organized group of churches developing in the late 1990s. The name most associated with this movement in America is Tony Jones, author of many books, including *The New Christians: Dispatches from the Emergent Frontier*[7] and *The Sacred Way: Spiritual Practices for Everyday Life*.[8] Jones is described as a leader in the emergent church movement and a renowned expert on postmodern theology and the American church landscape.[9]

Strengths

The very fact that those in the emerging church movement are reacting to Protestantism and Evangelicalism is a strength. Like most new religious movements, they are, in fact, reacting against some things that merit reaction. The emerging church adherents are looking for a simpler, more accepting approach to Christianity. They believe that one's life is the ultimate test of his religion, not his belief system. They see a world around them which has lost its moorings, in ways ranging from the destruction of families to the destruction of our environment. They desire to become more like Jesus in making a difference in the world around them by dealing with all of the issues of human suffering in the physical, emotional and spiritual realms. They are much more interested in a focus on the "here and now" rather than on the "hereafter." Comparisons to the Social Gospel Movement[10] are not unwarranted, but do not nearly provide the whole picture.

At least three terms are involved in describing the primary emphases of the Emerging Church: missional living, praxis and orthopraxy. Missional living is simply their focus lived out—not in isolation from society through a life that revolves around one's church, but through a life lived among the world to influence it toward change for the better. This change is brought about through sharing practical spiritual values and beliefs, but especially through simply serving the hurting and needy all around us. Passages from the Bible like Hosea 6:6 are emphasized: "For I desire mercy, not sacrifice, and acknowledgment of God rather than burnt offerings." The emerging church folks would be quick to point out that, in the New Testament Judgment scenes, like the one in Matthew 25:31-46, all focus is on the life one has lived in serving his fellow man, not on his doctrinal beliefs. It should be noted that they would not want to discuss what the same passage says about everyone either going to heaven or hell. They have difficulty with absolutes, especially in matters of eternal destination—which will be addressed later when discussing their weaknesses in doctrine from a biblical perspective.

The term "praxis" refers simply to how one's faith is to be lived out, and "orthopraxy" is right living. Thus, all three of these terms are interrelated, showing the focus on living a "Jesus life," as they see it. Of course, who of us hasn't wrestled with our own focuses in daily living regarding how much we are giving to others. Certainly, it is very important to live with our lives intertwined with our brothers and sisters in Christ as protection from Satan's influence, and for our maturation in Christ. However, there is still a badly hurting world surrounding us. As vital as sharing our faith is and believing that most people are on the broad road that leads to destruction (Matthew 7:13-14), the physical and emotional pain of those we are around daily is usually far more of a perceived need for them than would be a lesson on how to go to heaven. But Jesus found a way to wrap his arms around all of the world's hurts at the same time, as Matthew 9:35-36 well states: "Jesus went through all the towns and villages, teaching in their synagogues, preaching the good news of the kingdom and healing every disease and sickness. When he saw the crowds, he had compassion on them, because they were harassed and helpless, like sheep without a shepherd." The old saying is true: people don't care how much we know until they know how much we care.

This focus on what others are feeling and needing, combined with the determination to connect in both meaningful communication and service, is certainly commendable. Much of the focus for the people of God in the Old Testament was to keep separated from the world around them in order to avoid being tainted with the teachings and practices of pagan nations. That seems quite clear from reading the OT. God was intent upon keeping the Jewish nation righteous so that they could give birth to the Son who would then be able to reach the whole world with a message of redemption. This same focus of separation is not found in the NT, except for the distinction that, while we are to live in the world, we are not to be a part of it in heart and life (John 17:15-16). But we are to be the salt, the leaven and the light; and to exert that influence, we must be in the world in order to influence it.

It should be mentioned that because of their emphasis on social justice and concern for the needy, most Emerging Church adherents are considerably further left politically than are their spiritual ancestors of the 20th century. The fact that they value actions far more than a belief system makes them tend toward, as a whole, the stances of the Democrats rather than the Republicans, which is counter to the right-wing evangelicals of recent years. Most traditional evangelicals would argue that right practices come from right beliefs, whereas emerging church types would argue the opposite. That is an interesting topic to ponder, given the history of positions held on subjects like war and materialism by those holding supposedly orthodox biblical beliefs. The dogmatism of much of orthodoxy has not led to agreement doctrinally on a variety of subjects, and it is this failure to reach agreement that leads the emerging church to avoid doctrinal dogmatism, at least in their own minds. It is true that having right beliefs doesn't necessarily lead to living out those beliefs. No matter what the weaknesses of the emerging churches may be, reactions to traditional religion are not only understandable— they are called for by the teachings of the Bible itself! The question is whether the reactions of the Emerging Church are in fact biblical reactions producing biblical directions. Therein lay the deeper problems with this emerging movement.

Weaknesses

It is striking to me that the very claim of Emerging Churches to be built upon a foundation of "both/and" reasoning rather than "either/ or" reasoning is a foundation they reject time and time again. While rejecting dogmatism in some areas, they seemingly are almost blind to their own forms of dogmatism. This leads us to introduce one of the main tenets in their philosophy—the claim to be post-modernistic rather than modernistic in their thinking and reasoning. To them, modernism is the outmoded way of describing truth in propositional terms, saying that something is absolutely true and anything that varies from it is untruth. It is this dogmatism that drives the postmodernist up the wall, because he believes that history has not only shown that absolute truth in morals and religion is unreachable, but also that the insistence upon it has led to calamities of all sorts. The postmodernist would say that if definite truth and error are so obvious, why have leading proponents of it not agreed on so much of what they define as truth?

That is a challenge for all of us. The conclusion we usually reach is that the truths in the Bible that are salvation issues are clear enough to understand and agree upon, whereas other more peripheral issues are not. Deuteronomy 29:29 states the principle in these terms: "The secret things belong to the Lord our God, but the things revealed belong to us and to our children forever, that we may follow all the words of this law." In other words, the Bible gives us all that we need for life and godliness (2 Peter 1:3-4), but some subjects are not addressed at all, or too little is said about them to reach definite conclusions. The Bible uses the term *truth* more than 200 times and the term *understand* about 300 times. Obviously, God says that his Word is truth and that we are expected to understand and obey it. If we cannot understand the Bible enough to be saved, then it must be due to one of two reasons: either God did not want us to understand, or he was unable to have it written clearly enough for us to understand it. Either horn of that dilemma is untenable.

There are many reasons that religious men have not interpreted certain parts of the Bible correctly, but the fact remains that Jesus said that his words were truth. It could not be said in clearer terms than Paul said it in Ephesians 3:2-5: "Surely you have heard about the administration of God's grace that was given to me for you, that is, the mystery made known to me by revelation, as I have already written briefly. In reading this, then, you will be able to understand my insight into the mystery of Christ, which was not made known to men in other generations as it has now been revealed by the Spirit to God's holy apostles and prophets."

Postmodern thinking is very similar to the term *existentialism*, a term that was in vogue a generation ago. Existentialism was essentially the teaching that truth was relative and had to be determined by each individual for himself. Therefore, for me, truth might be one thing, and for you, it might be different. Sex before marriage with a "significant other" might be perfectly acceptable for one person, but not for another. Truth was relative generally, but could be arrived at more specifically on an individual basis. This approach reminds us of the statement in Judges 17:6 (also Judges 21:25): "In those days Israel had no king; everyone did as he saw fit." Postmodernism is somewhat different from existentialism in that it is more of a general philosophy, stating that propositional truth is unattainable. Thus, they argue that, while we all have our opinions about what is true, absolute certainty is ruled out, as history has proved with failures of sincere people to reach agreement in key areas.

Any philosophy claiming that truth is relative is restrictive in the areas in which the claims are made—most often in the areas of morals, philosophy and religion. A postmodernist might well say that one religion may be as good as another if it produces right living, but he will not apply that principle to certain other areas. He will not go to the pharmacist and say, "Give me any medicine you have, no matter what the doctor prescribed, because one prescription is as good as another." He believes in absolute truth when it comes to how airplanes and space shuttles are to be constructed. In those areas that could threaten his entire being, he wants scientific exactness with no variation!

Even in the area of religion, the postmodernist takes positions that should raise Shakespeare from the grave, crying out, "O Consistency, thou art a jewel." The embracing of "both/and" while rejecting "either/or" is used only as long as it is useful for the emerging church philosopher. Some common statements in postmodern religious thinking would be along these lines: "Christianity should be presented through loving attitudes rather than through doctrines." "It is not what we believe that matters; it is what we do in serving others." "The Bible is intended to teach us through narratives lessons about life, not through statements of propositional truth." These statements may sound good, and they do contain partial truths, but they are "either/or" fallacies nonetheless. In statements like these, along with their consistent and none-too-friendly reactions against status-quo religion, the "both/and" plea has been thrown out the window. The above quotes all happen to be "both/and" statements, by the way.

In reading the claims of the postmodernist, I'm reminded of an experience I had years ago with a young, single member of our congregation in Boston. After graduating from college, he found a good job and was a very serving member of our church. A few years later, he entered Harvard University as a graduate student (in a non-religious field). Soon, his exposure to postmodern reasoning (if it may be called that) became evident. The older leader of a small group in which our budding postmodernist was a member brought him to me, hoping to get some help for him. As we talked, the young man expressed his dismay that we leaders were fundamentalists. I asked for his definition of that term to which he replied, with something to the effect that we believed in absolute truth and were thus intolerant and out of touch. After patiently talking with him for a good while, I decided to go ahead and lead him into the trap that he had set for himself. The conversation continued something like this: "So, you don't believe that in the area of morals and religion that we can affirm absolute truth?" The answer: "No." Another question: "Are you sure about that?" The answer: "Yes." The final clincher: "Therefore, you are absolutely sure that we cannot be absolutely sure of anything." Silence!

Those who run from dogmatism often end up in dogmatism. Those arguing for their rights cry for tolerance, but are typically totally intolerant of anyone who won't tolerate their views. They are like the man who hated prejudice so much that he had only one prejudice left: his prejudice against prejudiced people! The philosophies of existentialism and postmodernism are biblically indefensible and an insult to the God who revealed truth to the writers of the Bible! It cannot be denied that postmodern thinking pervades our society, especially the youth. In an effort to avoid the mistakes of supposed logical reasoning processes, they have run to the extreme of illogic, and we are all reaping the harvest of substituting man's wisdom for God's teaching once again. The face of it all may look and sound different, but it's simply an old message dating back centuries, just dressed in different clothes.

Other weaknesses can be added to the list with regard to the Emerging Church, depending on which church or which emerging philosopher you are following. Church services, if they should even be called that in some cases, are conducted with a blend of religions, old and new, including some elements from Eastern religion. It is understandable that some distancing would be sought from the current "slick performance, smoke and mirrors, bells and whistles" services that find the audience giving standing ovations for performers while the more spiritually minded folks are left wondering where God is in all of it. But the question is: "How much distancing is biblically right?" Will all of the old, traditional ways of worship be discarded in favor of what will become new traditions in a fairly short time?

Besides the postmodern reasoning approach, the greatest danger of the Emerging Church Movement may be the rejection of leadership and authority in the church. It has been called a "bottoms up" movement, in which planning plays a very small role, and in which spontaneity reigns supreme. Concepts like organization, structure, expectations, accountability, leadership and authority are often looked upon as strongly suspect, if not with disdain. Have we really come so far since the days of the judges centuries ago, when "every man did that which was right in his own eyes"? This Emerging Church philosophy is having more effects at the grassroots level than most of us realize. It is seeping in at the seams in various ways, most of them unnoticed. Satan is smart and the master of deceit, knowing that we would reject the bottom-line conclusions of false teachings if we could see them clearly. It is vital for us to understand this developing movement, which is not easily understood because it is a varying philosophy or set of philosophies that present themselves by seemingly caring and aware people. They have things to offer that are good and right, and some other things to offer that are bad and damaging. Let's not become enamored with the latest and greatest, especially with regard to the emerging church wave that is breaking on the shores of Christendom rather strongly at this juncture of history.

The Breakout, Simple Church Movement

To call this a movement is admittedly premature, but the recent admissions of failure by the Mega-Church gurus are going to lead to some other philosophy to take its place. Mega-Churches will not simply disappear, but it seems likely that they are going to look for different ways to conduct business, so to speak. Gaining large audiences and offering a myriad of programs did not lead to the desired result of helping people increasingly take on the image of Jesus. Attendance and involvement on the larger level with hundreds and thousands of co-seekers did not equate with the spiritual growth of individuals. That analysis is theirs, not mine (though I would certainly agree). So, what's next?

The Emerging Church previously discussed is one item on the "what's next" list. It has a fairly broad appeal, but more to the younger generation than the older one. The older generation is never as reactionary or rebellious as the younger generation, so their changes will be more measured and less drastic; and they will take place within the confines of the current structure of the existing churches. Large churches and church buildings are already built. They are not likely to be discarded by those who built them and by those who became a part of them. In fact, it is often the leaders who see the failures more clearly than the members, who might in fact be quite satisfied with the status quo. In the case of the Mega-Church Movement, this has to be true of most members, because the church was built with the consumer in mind. They were consumer-driven churches by definition and design. But we have to give credit to many leaders who got caught up in the whirlwind—they did what they did with many good intentions. Now they are looking for something different and better because they want genuinely better results. The majority of them sincerely want to help people. Charitable attitudes must grant that most church leaders, regardless of the type and amount of errors they end up embracing, generally have good motives. With that in mind, we can expect some changes in 21st-century evangelicalism within the current structures of many of the larger churches, and also in the smaller ones who were trying to imitate them. So, we ask again, what's next?

Breakout Churches

Back in 2001, Jim Collins wrote a highly popular business book entitled, *Good to Great*.[11] In this book, Collins described the results of quite a broad survey of businesses in America that had moved from being mediocre or good to the level of being great. The criteria used to determine greatness were quite high, so high that only 11 companies qualified. When the dust settled and the good-to-great companies were identified, the author and his researchers found distinct patterns of behavior in those who led each company and the people who followed them—patterns that included disciplined people, thought and action. The criteria used to determine greatness were as follows:

1. The companies had to have experienced 15-year cumulative stock returns that were at or below the general stock market, punctuated by a transition point, then cumulative returns at least three times the market over the next fifteen years.

2. Each company had to demonstrate the good-to-great pattern independent of its industry.

3. Each company had to demonstrate a pattern of results.

4. Each company was compared to other similar companies that either never made the good-to-great leap (or made it but did not sustain it), in order to determine what distinguished the good-to-great company from all others.

This book not only made a hit in the corporate world, many religious leaders read the book with great interest, looking for insights that would apply to church leadership. For me, the most remarkable finding was the study they did regarding the type of leader at the helm of the company when it jumped to the category of great. Regardless of what we might have expected, without exception, those leaders were humble, self-effacing types who took the blame for failures and gave the credit for success to those under their leadership. They were ambitious leaders, but only ambitious for the success of the organization, not for themselves. In fact, the researchers had difficulty determining what label to use for these leaders, and were admittedly tempted to call them "Servant Leaders," but did not make that choice since they thought the business world would discount that terminology. That should make quite a statement to church leaders.[12]

Not surprisingly, a church leader then decided to do a broad survey of churches to see if he could identify churches that had experienced similar results—breaking out of the pack. So in 2005, Thom Rainer wrote a book entitled *Breakout Churches*.[13] The Breakout Churches studied are churches whose leaders hold a high view of Scripture, are intensely committed to implementing the Great Commission and exist to bring glory to God through their work. The underlying principle of striving to be great churches was this one: it is a sin to be good if God has called us to be great. The criteria he used to identify such churches and the process of their breaking out were described thus:

Stage 1—Define the Criteria
- The church has had at least 26 conversions annually since its breakout year. Any healthy church should be reaching at least one person with the gospel every two weeks.
- The church averaged a conversion ratio no higher than 20:1, at least one year since its breakout year, meaning it takes 20 members one year to reach one person.
- The church had been declining, plateaued or had stagnated for several years prior to breakout.
- The church broke out of its slump and sustained new growth for several years.
- There was no change in leader—only a change in leadership values.
- The church made clear and positive impact on the community.

Stage 2—Find the Churches
- The project was started with data on some 50,000 churches and they found 13 that clearly met the strict criteria.

Stage 3—Look for Comparison Churches
- "Good" churches became the source for direct comparison with the Breakout Churches.
- These have good pastors and laypeople, but haven't broken out of their mediocrity, are not making a significant impact on their communities and do not see significant numbers of changed lives.
- The differences between "good" churches and breakout churches became the focal point, or the "Chrysalis Factor."

Stage 4—Discover the Chrysalis Factor
- This refers to identifying as clearly as possible the events, patterns, plans, strategies, crises and other factors that took place when a church made the transition to greatness.

Stage 5—Apply What We Learned
- There are six major components of the Chrysalis Factor delineated in some detail by Rainer.

Of course, this book has made quite an impact on the evangelical community, and with its companion book mentioned next, may well be setting the stage for churches to get off the consumer-driven approach of the Mega-Church Movement and adopt the principles described by Rainer.

Simple Church

One year after *Breakout Churches* was written, Rainer and Eric Geiger wrote a sequel of sorts, entitled *Simple Church*.[14] In this book, also highly researched and supposedly based on much data, they discovered what they believed to be the reasons for some churches breaking out of the pack while others did not. Essentially, the authors contrasted two types of churches: one based on having a variety of programs designed to meet a variety of needs, and the other based on maintaining a focus on three key concepts. These three concepts were relationship with God, relationships within the church and outreach through serving the community. Statistically, the simple churches grew much more than the program-oriented churches. In the simple church approach, every activity of the church was viewed with the filter of the three goals in mind, and whatever fit into that filter was implemented, and whatever did not was discarded. The discarding of long held traditional activities was likely very painful in the beginning, but seemed to pay off in the long run. In reading the book, it seems that Sunday lessons are centered on helping people develop their relationship to God; the second focus of building relationships within the church is done through small groups; and the outreach focus is done by serving the community in various ways.

The description of a program-driven church seems very similar to what I would call an "event driven" church, and that is how the churches I have been in could often be described. My early days in our own movement of churches found our organizational approach to be centered on small groups which both met the needs of one another and reached out to non-Christians. Bible Talk groups were expected to minister to one another through discipling relationships and meeting the various needs of each other as they arose. Weekly Bible study sessions and Bible Talk activities were the means of introducing new members to the church. We were not focused on bringing visitors to church until they were already in personal studies and making progress spiritually. Sunday sermons were focused on the needs of the church, not on visitors. The small group evangelistic focus resulted in growth and new leaders being raised up. Every Bible Talk had an assistant who understood, at some point in the process, that the group would grow and split; at which time they would lead the new group, and both groups would designate new assistants to help repeat the process.

I think this approach is basically the right approach if we are to make our church "simple" and effective. As churches in our movement became more and more event driven (with the "push" to get visitors), we became less and less effective. We may have still had baptisms, but due to getting away from a real small-group focus, needs stopped being met and the number of people who left our churches increased—sometimes dramatically. I have personally never seen an event-driven church be as genuinely effective as the earlier approach was. That being said, I think we can do two things to improve our old approach. One, teach and emphasize the "gifts" each of us has in order to function in our small groups more effectively and to help each person feel really needed and useful. Two, in our day and age, use small-group activities of various sorts in which to include visitors—focusing on both relational building times and Bible study times. After all, Jesus said that people will know we are disciples by the love we show to one another. We just need to get non-Christians around us in natural, fun settings and then move things to spiritual activities (discussions and studies) with them, both in groups and on an individual basis.

Conclusion

Biblically, both the Mega-Church Movement and the Emerging Church Movement leave a lot to be desired. However, both have some things from which we can learn. Sunday services, Bible classes and all of our activities should be as excellent as we can make them—not in order to attract the "consumers," but to glorify God and to impact lives for him. The emerging churches can be commended for wanting to get back to a simpler relationship with God and a kinder approach to others who disagree with them, with a focus on promoting dialogue toward greater understanding of one another's values. But in the end, there has been so much about these approaches that was unbiblical that we can hardly be positive about the end results produced. Making the church into a "business" that is to be promoted and sold is a mockery to God. Under the umbrella of postmodernism, to reject the absolute truths of Scripture is to reject the God who inspired them.

On the other hand, the Simple Church Movement (and it seems destined to become a movement) has much more to commend it. Of the three strong strands of 21st-century evangelicalism, it is the one from which we likely can learn the most, although it will have to be filtered more closely through biblical principles and examples than is likely to be the case in the evangelical world. In reading the criteria that determine what simple churches are, certainly questions are raised. One of those questions is this: where does the idea come from that having visitors to church is the main evangelistic tool for conversions? Surely, it is not from the New Testament and the example of the early church. However, when we are so busy with church activities that we don't have time to effectively build relationships with non-Christians, something is wrong and needs to be changed. While we must be able to spit out the bones and eat the fish of any human description and plan, we must not miss the fish by worrying too much about swallowing a bone.

As a movement, we too are in a mode of looking for better ways to accomplish God's will and mission for us on planet Earth. May he help us to learn from those around us as we seek to put biblical principles into practice! We are not of the mind that we have arrived at the end of the rainbow with all of the answers. Even though we can be assured of many truths in the Bible, and be assured likewise that whatever varies from these truths is in fact error, self-righteousness and spiritual smugness are unholy responses to having learned much about real truth and error. As disciples, we are continual learners and constant followers of the Christ. Above all, let us keep our eyes on him and our feet set firmly in his paths—paths written in Scripture, but paths trodden by Jesus two centuries ago. He is our compass and our guide.

In the end, we must keep in mind that even the good that may be found in 21ˢᵗ-century evangelicalism doesn't change the fact that it is still the evangelical movement, with its erroneous doctrines regarding the salvation process. Praying Jesus into your heart, or praying the Sinner's Prayer, or accepting Jesus as your personal Savior are still common evangelical terminologies, and the underlying doctrines are still contrary to the teaching of the Bible. The biblical conversion process cannot be compromised simply because sincere believers in Christ and the Bible can be found in these evangelical churches. We are disciples of Jesus, which means we are both constant learners from him (through his Word) and followers of him. May we simply walk in his steps, with the help of our God and through the strength of the Holy Spirit who indwells us! While we can learn from the good that other religious folks have to share, Paul's command to Timothy must still be our chosen path:

"Watch your life and doctrine closely. Persevere in them, because if you do, you will save both yourself and your hearers" (**1 Timothy 4:16**).

QUICK REFERENCE GUIDE: _____

1. **Mega Church Claim:** The goal of the church is to attract members by offering programs and meeting their felt needs, while avoiding anything that would offend them. Church is all about the "consumer" and what he or she finds attractive. **Bible Truth:** The purpose of the church is to honor and exalt God, calling for people to meet his standards as described in the Bible, not define their own self-focused standards for Christianity. Paul's last letter makes it clear that the church leader's role, practically speaking, is to "comfort the afflicted and to afflict the comfortable" (2 Timothy 4:1-5)!

2. **Emerging Church Claim:** We are all on a journey toward God in which absolute truth is not attainable by sinful humanity. Engaging in meaningful dialogue with others and serving a hurting world in concrete ways are the real essence of religion. **Bible Truth:** We are indeed on a journey, but a journey mapped out by Scripture. The Bible provides the format for our discussions and the directions for serving others in Jesus' name. Life and doctrine are both essential to pleasing God (1 Timothy 4:16).

3. **Simple Church Claim:** Three main emphases are what build churches—relationship with God built through Sunday services; relationship with other Christians built through small group participation; and outreach to the world through community service, thus attracting those served to one's church. **Bible Truth:** Sunday services are to be both inspirational and corrective in nature, as we glorify God by seeking to please him in praise and in righteous living. But Sunday services are not the primary path through which the early church evangelized. Individual sharing and group sharing appeared to be that primary path, to which we need a return. Therein, many needs are met for Christians and potential Christians alike.

Notes _____

[1]The Barna Group (www.barna.org). Article on "Evangelical Christians."

[2]Bob Burney, A Shocking "Confession" from Willow Creek Community Church (Crosswalk.com, October 30, 2007).

[3]Edward J. Anton. *Repentance* (Waltham, Massachusetts: Discipleship Publications International, 2005), pp. 21-22.

[4]Cally Parkinson and Greg Hawkins, Reveal: Where Are You? (Willow Creek Association, August 2007).

[5]Bill Hybels, Leadership Summit 07 (oral presentation on the website http://revealnow.com).

[6]Bob Burney, A Shocking "Confession" from WIllow Creek Community Church (Crosswalk.com, October 30, 2007).

[7]Tony Jones, *The New Christians: Dispatches from the Emergent Frontier* (San Francisco: Jossey-Bass, 2008).

[8]Toney Jones, *The Sacred Way: Spritual Practices for Everyday Life* (Grand Rapids, Michigan: Zondervan, 2005).

[9]A number of articles on the Emerging Church can be found on the internet to provide an overview of the emerging church movement, Wikipedia, Theopedia, Christianity Today, and beliefnet.com being among them.

[10]The Social Gospel Movement is a Protestant Christian intellectual movement that was most prominent in the late 19ᵗʰ century and early 20ᵗʰ century. The movement applied Christian ethics to social problems, especially poverty, inequality, liquor, crime, racial tensions, slums, bad hygiene, child labor, weak labor unions, poor schools and the danger of war. Above all, they opposed rampant individualism and called for a socially aware religion. Theologically, the Social Gospel leaders were overwhelmingly post-millennialists—that is because they believed the Second Coming could not happen until humankind rid itself of social evils by human effort. Social Gospel leaders were predominantly associated with the liberal wing of the Progressive Movement and most were theologically liberal. Important leaders include Richard T. Ely, Washington Gladden and Walter Rauschenbusch. (wikipedia.org)

[11]Jim Collins, *Good to Great* (New York: HarperCollins Publishers, 2001).

[12]Although this book about business has some good spiritual applications to the church and its leadership, the most relevant business book to our movement I have ever read is one entitled, *Primal Leadership.* I recommend it highly. Daniel Goleman, Richard Boyatzis and Annie McKee, *Primal Leadership* (Boston, Massachusetts: Harvard Business School Press, 2002).

[13]Thom S. Rainer, *Breakout Churches* (Grand Rapids, Michigan: Zondervan, 2005).

[14]Thom S. Rainer and Eric Geiger, *Simple Church* (Nashville, Tennessee: B&H Publishing Group, 2006).

SECTION THREE

THREE MAJOR
SECTS

The word "sect" is normally applied to religious groups whose fundamental doctrines do not coincide with those of more traditional groups.
The three sects under consideration in this book have been chosen
because they are probably the most influential due to their evangelistic
outreach. Due to the nature of our study, which is more of a general
overview than an exhaustive research, we will discuss only the most
fundamental doctrines of each group. The history of each of these
groups is full of questionable, sensational and, in some cases, quite
unbelievable events. Further study of these histories would be both in-
structive and entertaining.

CHAPTER TWELVE

THE JEHOVAH'S WITNESSES

Founded by Charles Russell in the late 19th century, and still operating today from the Watchtower Bible and Tract Society in Brooklyn, New York, the Jehovah's Witnesses have experienced remarkable growth around the world through on-going door-to-door canvassing and the extensive distribution of literature. They are widely known for using only their translation of the Bible, for their interpretation of the Book of Revelation, for their opposition to blood transfusions, for their refusal to salute the flag or to serve in the military and for their willingness to engage in almost endless discussions concerning more difficult Biblical passages. However, their central heresy is in their message that Jesus was somehow the Savior, but that he was not fully God.

The Nature of the Triune God

The designation "Jehovah's Witnesses" comes from Isaiah 43:10, 12, and 44:8. In the first of these verses, we read:

"You are my witnesses," declares the LORD, "and my servant whom I have chosen, so that you may know and believe me and understand that I am he. Before me no god was formed, nor will there be one after me."

The word for "Jehovah" is translated "LORD" (all capitals) in most modern versions, but the older *American Standard Version* of 1901 uses the word "Jehovah." The passages in Isaiah declare that there is only one God, and that he is Jehovah. The Jehovah's Witnesses then declare what Isaiah does *not,* namely that there is no Trinity composed of God the Father, God the Son and God the Holy Spirit. They teach that the Spirit is not a person, but only God's active force, and that Jesus is a created being, a lesser "god," an archangel to be precise, but certainly not God.

The Jehovah's Witnesses have a *plethora* of strange and unbiblical doctrines in their system of theology. To deal with even a majority of these would take an entire book. Obviously, in one chapter, we will need to concentrate on the key issues which could help in dissuading a Witness or someone influenced by them. We will focus primarily on their teaching about the nature of God, including their false doctrines of the Holy Spirit and the nature of Jesus. Finally, we will look at what they teach about the nature of man and their misunderstanding of Biblical prophecy.

General knowledge regarding the nature and work of the Holy Spirit is definitely lacking in most religious groups, but the Jehovah's Witnesses' view of the Spirit is blatantly false. In light of the Witnesses' teaching about the Holy Spirit, a good question might be: "Is the Spirit an 'it' or a 'he'?" We can start out with the unequivocal declaration that the Spirit is definitely a person, a *he* and not an *it*! One rule of grammar does come into play here, and that is that the pronoun is determined by the gender of the noun. Therefore, the Spirit (neuter gender) may be designated by either an "it" or a "he," but the Biblical descriptions clearly show the Spirit to be a Person, a *he*.

In Matthew 12:31-32, we find that the Spirit can be *blasphemed against*. In John 14:26, we see that he is capable of *teaching*. Acts 5:3 tells us that he can be *lied to*, and Acts 7:51 says that he can be *resisted*. In Acts 13.2, he *spoke* directions for evangelism. Romans 8:14 promises that he *leads* the children of God, and in verses 26-27 of the same chapter, we are told that he helps us by *interceding* for us with the Father. We can enjoy *fellowship* with the Spirit (2 Corinthians 13:14), which necessarily means that he is a "fellow," a person! He can be *grieved* (Ephesians 4:30); he clearly says that an abandoning of the faith would come (1 Timothy 4:1); and he *testifies* (Hebrews 10:15). All of these attributes and activities provide *proof-positive* that the Spirit is a person. Therefore, the "active force" theory is a poor theory indeed.

Having shown that the Spirit is a personality, we need to demonstrate that he is Deity, and as such, a part of the Trinity. The Bible is absolute in its declaration that there is only one God. Yet, the Bible is equally clear in describing that one God with a three-fold personality—the Father, the Son and the Holy Spirit. Roy Lanier, Sr., in his book, *The Timeless Trinity*, stated it this way:

> We do not affirm that one God is three Gods; we affirm that there is but one infinite Spirit Being, but within that one Spirit essence there are three personal distinctions, each of which may be, and is, called God; each capable of loving and being loved by the others; each having a distinct, but not separate, part to

play in the creation of the universe, and in the creation and salvation of man.[1]

Several errors regarding the Trinity have been taught through the centuries. One is the view held by the Witnesses, which is a denial of the whole concept, in which case the Deity of Christ and of the Holy Spirit are both denied. Another view could be called the "manifestation" view, which affirms that one divine substance assumes different forms at different times. Thus, at some points, God *is* the Father; at other times, God *is* the Son; at other times, God *is* the Spirit. But this teaching does not allow God to manifest all three personalities at the same time. Some of the holiness groups espouse this basic view, with some variations. Their "Jesus only" doctrine is that the one person in the deity is Jesus—by any of the three designations. A third view could be called "tritheism," which teaches that the Trinity is composed of three separate spirit essences, three distinct minds and substances. They are one, *only* as a husband and wife are one—in unity. This teaching is a form of polytheism.

The two key concepts which must be held are that God is one (Deuteronomy 6:4), and that God has a plural personality. In Genesis 1:1, the Hebrew word for God is *Elohim,* which is a *plural* word. Then, in Genesis 1:26, we read: "Let us make man in our image." Again, the plural is obvious. The Hebrew *yachid* means an absolute one, while *achid* means a unified one. In the well-known Deuteronomy 6:4-5 passage, the word for God is *Elohim* (plural), and the word for *one* is "achid" (a unified one). In the NT, a number of passages show all three persons of Deity in the same Scripture, among which are Matthew 1:18-23; 3:16-17; 28:19; John 15:26; 2 Corinthians 13:14; and Ephesians 2:18, 21-22. The 2 Corinthians 13:14 passage puts it in a beautiful way: "May the grace of the Lord Jesus Christ, and the love of God, and the fellowship of the Holy Spirit be with you all."

When we accept the doctrine of the Triune God, we still may have misconceptions about his nature. Years ago, I remember seeing these two diagrams which helped to clarify the interrelationships within the Trinity:

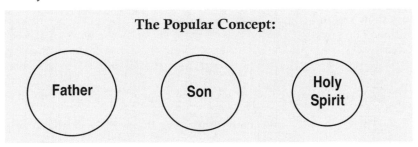

The Popular Concept:

The Biblical Concept:

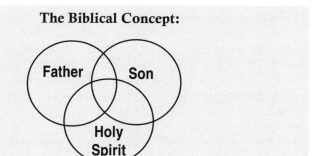

Frankly, the doctrine of the Trinity is difficult for humans to grasp, but that is to be expected. How could those created really understand the nature of their Creator? It is on this very point that the Witnesses go so far afield. They begin by saying that the concept of the Trinity is confusing, and then they quote 1 Corinthians 14:33, which states (KJV): "For God is not the author of confusion..." Therefore, they argue, if this doctrine is confusing and God is not the author of confusion, then the doctrine was not authored by God! This is shallow, humanistic reasoning! Referring to the divine nature and work of the Son and the Spirit, Paul plainly says: "Beyond all question, the mystery of godliness is great" (1 Timothy 3:16). The very idea that we humans are equipped to understand the nature of God is laughable. The Bible teaches a number of truths which are beyond human comprehension, such as the existence of eternity and the human spirit, but they are true because the Bible says that they are true. We walk by faith, not by sight; by the Scriptures, not by reliance on human reasoning.

Although temporal man is not able to comprehend eternal God, some simple illustrations may be helpful. Teachers of children often use two examples which demonstrate how one item can be a composite of three different elements. One example is that of an egg. A single egg is composed of the shell, the white and the yolk. Another example is that of three wooden matches held together and lit. Three stems are evident, but only one flame.

The beautiful unity and power of the Trinity working together may be shown with a Biblical consideration of two different types of creation. The physical creation was brought about by the work of the Father as designer (Revelation 4:11), Jesus as the agent of creation (John 1:1-3) and the Holy Spirit as the perfecter (Genesis 1:2ff). In a similar way, the spiritual creation (the church) was produced by the Father as designer (Ephesians 3:10-11), Jesus as the agent (his earthly ministry) and the Spirit as the perfecter (John 14:26; 16:7-15).

These passages, and many others like them, make it abundantly clear that the Spirit is a person and is Deity.

The Nature of Jesus

A key teaching of the Jehovah's Witness sect is that Christ is a created being and therefore not Deity. According to their doctrine, he is a lesser "god" or godlike creature, or more specifically, an archangel. This view has been considered heretical since the early centuries of Christianity, when a man named Arius said of Jesus that "there was a time when he was not." The Jehovah's Witness doctrine is simply the Arian heresy resurrected, and it must be rejected today as it was then.

First, consider the OT references to the eternal nature of Christ. Isaiah 9:6-7 alone should establish the point beyond any doubt.

> For to us a child is born, to us a son is given, and the government will be on his shoulders. And he will be called Wonderful Counselor, Mighty God, Everlasting Father, Prince of Peace. Of the increase of his government and peace there will be no end. He will reign on David's throne and over his kingdom, establishing and upholding it with justice and righteousness from that time on and forever.

This child who would be born and sit on David's throne can be no other than Jesus Christ. And yet this child who graced Bethlehem's barn was to be called "Mighty God" and "Everlasting Father." The Jehovah's Witnesses *dodge* on this passage is that Jesus is "mighty" God but not the "almighty." However, the same term is applied to Jehovah in Isaiah 10:20-21. Furthermore, Micah 5:2 indicates that the ruler who would come from Bethlehem was one whose "goings forth are from long ago, from the days of eternity" (NASV).

Isaiah 43:10 and 44:6 clearly state that there was no God but Jehovah ("LORD" in NIV). Either the term Jehovah (from the original "Yahweh") refers to the Godhead (Father, Son and Spirit), or Jesus is *not* Deity. The Jehovah's Witnesses' claim that Jesus is a lesser god is unscriptural polytheism. A number of passages demonstrate that Jesus is in fact Jehovah. Some people mistakenly assume that Jehovah is a name applied only to the Father. In Jeremiah 23:5-6, however, the righteous Branch from David's lineage is called specifically "the LORD (Jehovah) our righteousness." Let's look at that passage in its context:

> "The days are coming," declares the LORD, "when I will raise up to David a righteous Branch, a King who will reign wisely and do what is just and right in the land. In his days Judah will be saved and Israel will live in safety. This is the name by which he will be called: The LORD Our Righteousness."

Consider also the following parallels. Isaiah 45:18-23 states that unto Jehovah every knee would bow and every tongue swear because he was the *only* God. Paul states in Philippians 2:11 that this event refers to Judgment, when all will confess and bow to *Christ*. A comparison of Joel 2:32 and Romans 10:9-13 shows that calling on the name of Jehovah is equated with confessing Christ and calling on him. Since John the Baptist was to prepare the way of Jehovah (Isaiah 40:3-5), and he did prepare the way for Jesus (Mark 1:1-7), Jesus *must* be Jehovah. Again, Jehovah is said to have created all things (Isaiah 42:5; 44:24), and the same is recorded of Christ (John 1:1-3; Colossians 1:16). Thus, Jesus must be Jehovah. Many other such comparisons demonstrate, beyond a shadow of a doubt, that Jesus *is* Jehovah. Compare Isaiah 45:5 with Titus 2:13; Revelation 1:8 with Revelation 22:13-16; and Exodus 3:14 with John 8:58.

But also, there are the claims of the NT. The NT contains numerous passages which directly affirm the deity of Christ. Jesus is called "God" in John 1:1; 20:28; Titus 2:13; 2 Peter 1:1; and 1 John. 5:20. The Jews understood that Christ's claim to be the Son of God meant that he was equal to God in his nature (John 5:18). They had no doubt that his claims about himself were claims to be God (John 10:33). Men may be sons of God by *adoption*, but Jesus was the unique Son by *nature* (John 3:16; Philippians 2:6).

It is, of course, true that certain NT passages relegate Jesus to a lesser position than that of the Father (see John 14:28), but this was due to Christ's temporary fleshly existence. There was a voluntary departure from his pre-flesh glories (Philippians 2:5-8; John 17:5), but his ascension back to heaven changed this temporary humiliation (Ephesians 1:20-21). This lowered earthly role of Jesus concerned his *position*, not his *person* or *nature*. A person in a job setting may have a superior *position* over another person, but that says absolutely nothing about the one in submission being inferior in *nature*. The same situation exists in the case of Jesus and his heavenly Father.

A third and final observation about the Deity of Christ involves his reception of worship. Matthew 4:10 clearly teaches that *only* God is to be worshipped. Men could not be worshipped (Acts 10:25-26; 14:12-15), and neither could angels (Revelation 19:10; 22:8-9). However, Christ was worshipped by both men (Matthew 8:2; 9:18; 14:33; 15:25; etc.) and angels (Hebrews 1:6). Therefore, the only possible conclusion is that Jesus is *God*. The very foundation of the church is the Deity of Christ (Matthew 16:16-18), and any teaching that would reject this marvelous truth must be firmly and convincingly resisted by the Book of books. Christ is indeed *eternal*, "the Alpha and the Omega, the First and the Last, the Beginning and the End" (Revelation 22:13).

The Nature of Man

The Jehovah's Witnesses teach that a person has no conscious existence after death. This doctrine, with its related tenets, is often referred to as the "soul-sleep" doctrine. Those who teach this error deny that man has both an outer man (physical body) and an inner man (the spirit). Such false teachers boldly affirm that "man does not *have* a soul, he *is* a soul." Thus, when one dies, he is like the dog *Rover*—dead all over! If this concept were correct, "soul-sleep" would be a misnomer. It then should be called "soul-cessation," and "resurrection" should be called "recreation."

In the OT, the term "soul" (from *nephesh*) in the KJV was often used to designate the composite person. For example, in Genesis 2:7, we read that man became a living "soul" ("being" in the NIV). The NT equivalent (*psuche*) also is used in the same way (Acts 7:14). However, the OT also uses *soul* to refer to the inner man in contrast with the *body* (Genesis 35:18). That passage reads: "And it came about as her soul was departing (for she died), that she named him Ben-oni; but his father called him Benjamin." This verse is quoted from the *New American Standard Version*, which is the most accurate modern translation from the original languages, and is quite literal in this passage. The NT develops this usage of *soul* in much more detail. Matthew 10:28 and Revelation 6:9-10 are two key passages which show beyond any doubt that the soul lives after bodily life ceases.

The term "spirit" also is used to designate this inner being (Luke 23:45; Acts 7:59; Hebrews 12:22-23). This part of man is that which we share in common with our Maker. When God said, "Let us make man in our image" (Genesis 1:26), he had to mean his *spiritual* image, since he is *spirit* (John 4:24). Therefore, even though we receive our physical bodies from our parents, our *spirits* come from God. He is the "Father of our spirits" (Hebrews 12:9), the one who "forms the spirit of man within him" (Zechariah 12:1), and thus when we die, "the spirit returns to God who gave it" (Ecclesiastes 12:7).

The Sadducees of Jesus' day taught the same erroneous doctrine regarding the spirit of man (or lack of it) as the "soul-sleepers" teach. Jesus assured them that Abraham, Isaac and Jacob were yet alive, though their bodies had decayed (Matthew 22: 23-32). The fact that a person can live apart from his body is clearly taught in numerous passages. In 2 Corinthians 5:6-8, Paul teaches we can be *absent* from the body and *present* with the Lord. "Therefore we are always confident and know that as long as we are at home in the body we are away from the Lord. We live by faith, not by sight. We are confident, I say, and would prefer to be away from the body and at home with the Lord." Who is that *we*, if not the spirit or soul of man? The body of Dorcas was present, but *she* was no longer present (Acts 9:39). For similar passages, see Romans 14:8; Luke 23:43; Philippians 1:21-23; and Luke 16:19-31.

The soul-cessation teachers naturally deny the possibility of punishment after death or after Judgment Day. The teaching of the immediate *annihilation* of the lost rather than the *punishment* of the lost carries some strong implications. It does away completely with the Biblical concept of degrees of punishment. Consider the following passages in this light: Matthew 11:20-23; 26:24; Luke 12:47-48; Hebrews 10:28; and 2 Peter 2:20-21.

In Hebrews 10:28-29, we are told that the one who leaves Christ deserves to be punished *more severely* than those in the OT who were physically executed. Then, in the 2 Peter passage, those who leave Christ are worse off at the *end* than at the *beginning*. If there is no punishment after death at all, how could these Scriptures make sense? If physical death is tantamount to immediate annihilation, a man could burn another person to death and inflict punishment more severe than God can inflict after Judgment Day.

The Nature of Biblical Prophecy

From their earliest history, the Jehovah's Witnesses have focused much on their interpretation of Biblical prophecy. They have set many dates for the return of Christ, and once these dates had passed, they spiritualized the "return" in some way in order to save face. They have ignored the apocalyptic style of the Book of Revelation and twisted it into some bizarre doctrines—for example: the 144,000 of Revelation 7 and 14 are literally descriptive of an exact number of highly spiritual people who will go to heaven (which, by their own admission, does not include most of the Witnesses!). They have a "kingdom first" focus, to be sure, but the problem is that their concept of the kingdom is that it is not here yet!

The idea that Christ will reign on earth as a physical king is a widespread belief that crosses nearly all denominational lines. Not all groups believe exactly the same things about it, but the general outline they all accept. The explanation that I am giving in this section contains more of this general outline and does not exactly represent the Jehovah's Witnesses teaching. But it will be largely representative of what they believe and teach. This doctrine, usually called "premillennialism," was once rejected by many religious groups who have now come to accept it. The reasons for the current acceptance of the doctrine are not Biblical ones, as we shall show. Rather, people have become materialistic to the point that they cannot envision anything good apart from this earth, even heaven! Also, the teaching appeals to the emotions because of its "mysterious" elements, and many people are looking for mystical fancy rather than fact.

The doctrine of premillennialism, briefly stated, is the view that Christ will come back to earth at some future point and reign for a literal thousand years. A large segment who hold this view believe that, seven years before this return, the righteous will experience a *rapture* (catching up) from the earth while those left on earth will experience a great tribulation. The concept of such an earthly reign supposedly finds its foundation in Revelation 20:1-10. But in approaching this or other difficult passages, several fundamental rules of interpretation need to be kept in mind.

1. Truth does not contradict itself. If two verses seem to do so, there is either a misunderstanding of one of the verses, or possibly both of them.

2. Doctrine cannot be based on difficult passages without due consideration of less difficult passages on the same subject. To establish a theory on symbolic passages forces you to completely ignore literal passages which contradict it, and also forces you to apply figurative interpretation to obviously literal Scriptures.

3. One does not have to know exactly what a difficult passage means in order to know what it *does not* mean. For example, a person could be unsure of the exact interpretation of 1 Corinthians 15:29, but at the same time, be absolutely sure that it does not teach proxy baptism for the physically dead. Too many plain passages render that explanation impossible. In a similar way, one could be somewhat uncertain of the precise meaning of some of the symbolism in Revelation, while rejecting the doctrine of premillennialism itself.

Revelation 20

The actual examination of Revelation 20 reveals some important facts: first, the text does not mention a number of things that people assume are taught there. The second coming of Christ is not mentioned. Christ is not mentioned as being *on earth*. No mention is made of *anyone* reigning on earth. A bodily resurrection is not mentioned; and finally, no one living in modern times is mentioned in connection with this 1,000 year reign. The *persecuted* of the early church are the ones who sit on thrones and reign with Christ. How can a passage which mentions *none* of these things be said to teach *all* of them?

Second, this passage is full of figurative symbolic language. If we insist on making the 1,000 years literal, why are not the key to the abyss, the great chain, the beast, etc. also literal? Actually, the Book of Revelation employs apocalyptic language, as it portrays (by means of symbols) the victory of God's persecuted people over the Roman Empire. This type of writing was well understood in its day, although it may well be unfamiliar and strange to people today. The book dramatizes the victory of good over evil to bring hope to the persecuted saints of the first century. If the book really taught what many people advocate, it would have been of scarce comfort to those in the early church who were dying for their faith!

Now to a brief explanation of the passage: the binding of Satan (verse 2) was to stop him from deceiving the nations (verse 3). The text does not suggest that he would be tied in such a way as to be totally inactive (1 Peter 5:8). The nations as a whole had been deceived into *emperor* worship (see chapter 13:11-18), but the binding of Satan would limit this blasphemy for a thousand years (symbolic of a long period—see Deuteronomy 7:9; Job 9:3; Psalm 50:10, 90:4).

In verses 4-6, the persecuted Christians in the early church are promised a victory. Their cause looked as if it had been defeated, but here God assures them that Christianity would be vindicated. Their cause would be raised from the dust of defeat into a resurrection of victory. The souls under the altar (6:9) are now elevated to thrones as their cry has been heard and answered. See Ezekiel 37:1-14 and Isaiah 26:13-19 for the idea of a resurrection of a cause in victory. Revelation 20:5 calls this the "first resurrection" to avoid confusion with the general bodily resurrection at the end of time (1 Corinthians 15).

"The rest of the dead" in the first part of verse 5 (which is a parenthetical statement) are the non-Christians, the persecutors. Their cause lies in defeat for a long time-period (1,000 years symbolizes this period), but it will briefly arise at some future date (verses 7-10). Fortunately, this renewed deception of the nations is short lived, as Christ brings his judgment upon the wicked (verses 9-15).

Although this explanation seems logical to me, I claim no infallibility in my interpretation. The passage is a difficult one, and dogmatism is not urged in such cases. However, in spite of how Revelation 20 is to be explained in its various details, it assuredly does not teach the doctrine of premillennialism.

The premillennialists claim that Jesus will not begin his reign until the time of his return. He will then reign on a literal throne in a literal Jerusalem for a literal 1,000 years. When this concept is examined in light of OT prophecy about the Messiah, and in its NT fulfillment, the idea is shown to be false.

Zechariah 6:12-13 is one of the key passages. Once again, we will quote from the NASV.

"Then say to him, 'Thus says the LORD of hosts, Behold, a man whose name is Branch, for He will branch out from where He is; and He will build the temple of the LORD. Yes, it is He who will build the temple of the LORD, and He who will bear the honor and sit and rule on His throne. Thus, He will be a priest on His throne, and the counsel of peace will be between the two offices."'

The NT makes it clear that Jesus built his church, and that his church is God's temple (Matthew 16:18; 1 Corinthians 3:11, 16; 2 Corinthians 6:16; Ephesians 2:19-22). Now look at the Zechariah passage in light of the church being the temple of God.

Christ would sit on his throne (Zechariah 6:13), and Acts 2:32-35 says that he began occupying that throne on the Day of Pentecost when the church was established. He was to be a priest on his throne (Zechariah 6:13), and he is a priest now (Hebrews 4:14). This Branch was to rule on his throne while sitting (Zechariah 6:13), and he began sitting on this throne nearly 2,000 years ago (Acts 2:32-35). Therefore, he is ruling on his throne now. Since he was said to be a priest on his throne, and he is a priest in heaven (Hebrews 4:14), his throne must be in heaven. In fact, he *cannot* be priest on earth, for Hebrews 8:4 says, "If he were on earth, he would not be a priest..." Therefore, his throne *cannot* be on earth.

Psalm 110:1 and 110:4 also speaks of Christ ruling as a priest. In this case, his rule will last until his enemies are conquered. 1 Corinthians 15:25-26 says: "For he must reign until he has put all his enemies under his feet. The last enemy to be destroyed is death." Therefore, Jesus is reigning now and will continue to do so until the resurrection of the dead, at which point he will *cease* to reign over the Messianic kingdom as heaven begins. This truth is exactly opposite to what the premillennial doctrine teaches. They say he will *begin* reigning at his return, and Paul says he will *cease* reigning! It should be mentioned that, as a part of Deity, he reigns over heaven and all of its subjects, which includes all of the redeemed from all ages.

It should be obvious that Jesus is reigning in his spiritual kingdom now. In his earthly ministry, he claimed that the kingdom was *near* in fulfillment of prophecy (Daniel 2:44; Mark 1:15; Hebrews 12:28). This kingdom would come in the lifetime of some of the apostles, and it would come with power (Mark 9:1). Power came when the Spirit came on the day of Pentecost (Acts 1:8; 2:1-4). Therefore, the kingdom was established on the day of Pentecost. After this point, the kingdom is spoken of as a present reality (Colossians 1:13; 4:11; Revelation 1:6). The kingdom is equated with the church in Matthew 16:18-19. Any future view given concerning the kingdom is referring to the heavenly state after it has been delivered up to the Father by Christ (1 Corinthians 15:24).

Additional Considerations

In this discussion, several aspects pertaining to the end of time need to be considered. The first question to be answered regards physical Israel. Will there be a restoration of Israel in fulfillment of biblical prophecy? The answer is negative, for several reasons.

1. Christ is *already* on David's throne (Acts 2:30-33).

2. The tent of David has been rebuilt (Acts 15:14-17). The saving of the Gentiles is in fulfillment of Amos 9:11-12, according to James, the Lord's brother. The argument in Acts 15 is clearly that the tent was to be rebuilt before the Gentiles were to "seek the Lord." Therefore, either the tent here is *spiritual* in nature (the church), or Gentiles are yet in their sins and the Great Commission is nullified!

3. God's promises to Israel concerning the land inheritance have all been fulfilled (Joshua 23:14). Notice that the boundaries God specified to Abraham in Genesis 15:18 were reached by the time 1 Kings 4:21 and 2 Chronicles 9:26 were written.

4. God said, through Jeremiah, that Israel could not be made whole again (Jeremiah 19:11).

5. Jesus promised that the kingdom would be taken away from the Jews (Matthew 21:33-43).

6. The last state of the Jews would be worse than the first (Matthew 12:43-45).

7. God's special people are *spiritual* Jews (Christians) and not physical ones (Romans 2:28-29; 9:6; Galatians 3:26-29; Philippians 3:3). Philippians 3:2-3 could not state the point any more directly nor bluntly, as Paul contrasts the physical and spiritual "Jews": "Watch out for those dogs, those men who do evil, those mutilators of the flesh. For it is we who are the circumcision, we who worship by the Spirit of God, who glory in Christ Jesus, and who put no confidence in the flesh."

Our second consideration involves *the second coming of Christ*. When he comes, there will be only one bodily resurrection of the dead. The good and the bad are raised simultaneously, and then they will all be judged (John 5:28-29). All nations will be gathered for this great day (Matthew 25:31-34). Note that this is a judgment of every person within all nations, not a judgment of entire nations as nations, as some premillennialists claim. Compare the wording of 25:32 with Matthew 28:19.

Contrary to popular theory, there simply cannot be two separate bodily resurrections. The righteous are raised on the *last day* (John 6:40). The unrighteous are judged on the *last day* (John 12:48). Is not the last day really the last day? Furthermore, at the last trumpet, the dead are raised and the living are changed (1 Corinthians 15:51-52). If the wicked are raised 1,000 years later, they will not be awakened by the last trumpet, for it will have already sounded! When it does sound, the physical universe will be destroyed (2 Peter 3:10-12; Revelation 21:1). The OT passages which speak of the earth remaining "forever" mean only that it is "age-lasting." See in chapter 12 a related discussion under the heading, "The Sabbath, a Perpetual Covenant?"

A final consideration might be a look at *the real dangers of the premillennial view.*

1. This theory denies that Christ is reigning now and therefore pronounces failure upon God's eternal purpose in Christ (Ephesians 3:10-11).

2. It contradicts every passage which speaks of this present period as "the last days" (Acts 2:15-17; 1 Corinthians 10:11; Hebrews 1:1-2; 1 Peter 1:20).

3. It makes Jesus false to his promises when he said that the kingdom was near (Mark 1:15).

4. It alternates between Judaism and Christianity, by reviving the old law that Jesus nailed to the cross (Colossians 2:14; Ephesians 2:15).

5. It demotes Christ from the throne of his majesty to the earth, his footstool.

6. It denies that Amos 9:11-12 is fulfilled, and thus denies salvation to the Gentiles (Acts 15:14-17).

7. It is the same mistake that the first-century Jews made by expecting an earthly kingdom which was political in nature.

Paul said in Philippians 1:23 that he wanted to *go* be with the Lord, but the premillenialists say, "Lord, you come be with us; we like it here." Actually, the Jehovah's Witnesses' doctrine of the 144,000 is that only those individuals will go to heaven, while the rest of them will stay on the Earth. All of the ones I have questioned have said that they were a part of those who would stay on the earth for eternity, and they were happy that this was their lot. They did not even want to go to heaven. Jesus makes it plain in John 14:1-3 that eternal rewards have absolutely nothing to do with this earth.[2]

> "Do not let your hearts be troubled. Trust in God; trust also in me. In my Father's house are many rooms; if it were not so, I would have told you. I am going there to prepare a place for you. And if I go and prepare a place for you, I will come back and take you to be with me that you also may be where I am."

What about the 144,000?

Since the Witnesses place so much emphasis on this figure, we will provide a brief explanation of it. The symbolic number is found in Revelation 7 and 14. The Book of Revelation is a book of symbols, written near the end of the first century to Christians who were facing heavy persecution. The kind of writing used was called "apocalyptic," which means to "reveal" or to "uncover." The title *Revelation* is a translation of the Greek word *apokalupsis*. This revelation of God's victory message to his persecuted people was done through the use of symbols, which were familiar to the original readers. Many of the OT prophetic books employed this style of writing. The purpose of this style was to provide drama, to appeal to the imagination more than to the intellect. The people were facing dire circumstances and needed encouragement that stirred the emotions and inspired them to remain strong in the spiritual battle.

To the Jewish mind, numerology was very important. Many numbers had well-defined meanings, and they conveyed spiritual lessons. For example, the number "1" carried the idea of *unity*. Think of the series of "ones" in Ephesians 4:4-6. The number "2" carried the idea of *strengthening*. Jesus sent out his early preachers two by two. Revelation 11:3 mentions God's two witnesses. Then, the number "3" was the *divine* number (Father, Son and Spirit). Next, "4" was the cosmic or *world* number. In Revelation 7:1, you find four angels, four corners of the earth and the four winds of heaven.

Combine the divine number and the world number and you get "7," the number of *perfection*. Thus, in Revelation 4:5, the seven spirits most likely refer to the Holy Spirit in his perfection. The number "6" was an *evil*, sinister number because it fell short of the perfect number. In America, many of our hotels do not designate a 13th floor. In that Jewish setting, they would not have had a designated sixth floor. The "666" of Revelation 13:18 carries with it the idea of evil and failure. The next significant number was "10," which signified *completeness* (all fingers or all toes). You find this number often in the Revelation. A multiple of that number would be 1,000, denoting *ultimate* completeness. The 1,000 years in Revelation 20 show this kind of completeness, as a look at the references mentioned earlier will demonstrate.

The number of *organized religion* was "12," calling to mind the twelve tribes of Israel and the twelve apostles. In Revelation 7, the twelve tribes are connected to John's mention of the 144,000. If you take the organized religion number, multiply it by itself, and then multiply it by 1,000, the number of ultimate completeness, you come up with 144,000. Therefore, if you understood the way that numbers were used symbolically, you would expect this number to signify the *ultimate number of a religious group*. And we will see that this is precisely what is being done in Revelation 7. Finally, the other key number in Revelation is "3 1/2," found as three-and-a-half years, forty-two months, 1,260 days, and from Daniel, *a time, times and a half a time.* This number, in whatever form, symbolized the *period of persecution* itself, an unstable time, but one with an end to it.

With this explanation in mind, let's look at the passages in Revelation 7:4-8 and 14:1-5.

[4] Then I heard the number of those who were sealed: 144,000 from all the tribes of Israel.
[5] From the tribe of Judah 12,000 were sealed,
from the tribe of Reuben 12,000,
from the tribe of Gad 12,000,
[6] from the tribe of Asher 12,000,
from the tribe of Naphtali 12,000,
from the tribe of Manasseh 12,000,
[7] from the tribe of Simeon 12,000,
from the tribe of Levi12,000,
from the tribe of Issachar 12,000,
[8] from the tribe of Zebulun 12,000,
from the tribe of Joseph 12,000,
from the tribe of Benjamin 12,000 (**Revelation 7:4-8**).

[1] Then I looked, and there before me was the Lamb, standing on Mount Zion, and with him 144,000 who had his name and his Father's name written on their foreheads. [2] And I heard a sound from heaven like the roar of rushing waters and like a loud peal of thunder. The sound I heard was like that of harpists playing their harps. [3] And they sang a new song before the throne and before the four living creatures and the elders. No one could learn the song except the 144,000 who had been redeemed from the earth. [4] These are those who did not defile themselves with women, for they kept themselves pure. They follow the Lamb wherever he goes. They were purchased from among men and offered as firstfruits to God and the Lamb. [5] No lie was found in their mouths; they are blameless (**Revelation 14:1-5**).

In chapter 7, the 144,000 are used to represent the church during the time of persecution. Earlier in this chapter, all of them were "sealed," showing God's protection of them. See Ezekiel 9:4 for this usage. Since the persecutors were often Jews, or were aided by Jews, it should be obvious that the twelve tribes were not literally the twelve tribes of the Jews. The ones being sealed, or being guaranteed God's protection, were the Christians, those who were now a part of the *new* Israel of God

(Galatians 6:16). When you look closely at the listing of these tribes, it becomes even more obvious that the list has been "spiritualized." For example, the fourth tribe (Judah) is mentioned first, because that was the tribe out of which Jesus came (Genesis 49:10). Also, we find Levi in the list, although that tribe was not normally listed, because they did not inherit a land area in the OT. But, since all Christians are priests (1 Peter 2:5, 9), Levi here is to be identified with spiritual Israel, the church. Furthermore, Dan and Ephraim were excluded from the list, because Dan and Bethel (in Ephraim) were centers of calf worship under Jereboam. Therefore, they were excluded here. Finally, Joseph's name is added, even though, in the OT, his sons were the tribes listed and not Joseph himself. But to the Bible reader, this name has only good connotations.

After the 144,000 are thus described in chapter 7, the next section (verses 9-17) goes on to talk about a great multitude that no one could count. This great multitude was composed of those who "have come out of the great tribulation" and are now before the throne of God (verses 14-15). Therefore, the 144,000 showed the church on earth during the persecution, and the symbolism taught that God knew every one of them and would protect them spiritually, even if they had to die physically. Therefore, the great multitude did not need to be counted, because they had passed from time to eternity. The lesson of the chapter was that God would be with them and ultimately get them to heaven.

In Revelation 14, we simply find a description of Christians, the 144,000 (all of the redeemed). They were not defiled with women (literally, virgins), showing spiritual purity (2 Corinthians 11:2) as opposed to spiritual adultery through idol worship (Jeremiah 3:6; James 4:4). They followed the Lamb by keeping his words (John 10:4-5). They were purchased by the blood of Christ (Acts 20:28). As such, they were the firstfruits to God. Just as the first of all physical harvests was to be set apart for God (Deuteronomy 26:1-11), Christians are likewise set apart for the service of God (James 1:18). No lie was found in their mouths, but lying was one of the chief characteristics of pagan Rome and emperor worshippers (see Revelation 21:8).

Now, once we understand biblically who the 144,000 actually are, what should we say about the Jehovah's Witnesses interpretation? Simply this: if they insist on making the 144,000 a literal number, then you insist on making their description literal. When you do that, the 144,000 would have to all be Jewish (from the twelve tribes), and they would have to be male virgins (had not defiled themselves with women). No Witness would agree to those things, but if the passage is to be taken literally, these points would have to be accepted, because the wording itself is quite clear.

QUICK REFERENCE GUIDE: _____

1. **Jehovah's Witnesses Claim:** The Holy Spirit is simply God's active force, not a person. **Bible Truth:** The Spirit has the attributes and activities of a person. See Matthew 12:31-32; John 14:26; Acts 5:3; 7:51; 13:2; Romans 8:14, 26-27; 2 Corinthians 13:14; Ephesians 4:30; 1 Timothy 4:1.

2. **Jehovah's Witnesses Claim:** The concept of the Trinity is confusing and false. **Bible Truth:** God is one God, consisting of three distinct personalities (Matthew 1:18-23; 3:16-17; 28:19; 2 Corinthians 13:14; Ephesians 2:18, 21-22).

3. **Jehovah's Witnesses Claim:** Jesus is a created being, an archangel, and not Deity. **Bible Truth:** Jesus is eternal, a part of the triune God (Isaiah 9:6-7; Jeremiah 23:5-6; Micah 5:2; John 1:1; 20:28; Titus 2:13; 2 Peter 1:1; 1 John 5:20).

4. **Jehovah's Witnesses Claim:** Man does not have a soul, or spirit, that lives past the death of the body. **Bible Claim:** Man receives a spirit directly from God (Zechariah 12:1; Ecclesiastes 12:7; Hebrews 12:9). Our basic nature is that we are a spirit who lives in a body, not a body which happens to have a spirit. See Matthew 22:23-32; Luke 16:19-31; 23:43; Acts 9:39; Romans 14:8; 2 Corinthians 5:6-8; Philippians 1:21-23.

5. **Jehovah's Witnesses Claim:** Christ is coming back to earth to establish a literal 1,000-year kingdom. **Bible Truth:** The kingdom was set up on the Day of Pentecost as described in Acts 2. Revelation 20 is a symbolic passage showing the persecuted disciples of the first century that their cause would soon triumph over the persecutors. The symbols of this book cannot be forced into a literal interpretation. Compare Zechariah 6:12-13 with Acts 2 in order to see that Jesus is now reigning in his kingdom. The kingdom on earth is the church (Matthew 16:18-19), and after Acts 2, it is described as a present reality (Colossians 1:13:4:11; Hebrews 12:28; Revelation 1:6). Actually, when Jesus comes, it will be to take us home with him (John 14:1-3; 1 Thessalonians 4:16-17) and to destroy the physical universe (2 Peter 3:10-12; Revelation 21:1).

6. **Jehovah's Witnesses Claim:** The 144,000 depicts a literal number of spiritual Jehovah's Witnesses who will go to heaven, leaving the rest of the Witnesses on the earth for eternity. **Bible Truth:** This number, in the contexts of Revelation 7 and 14, depicts all of the

redeemed on earth who were undergoing that persecution, and who were going to be protected spiritually by God. If the Jehovah's Witnesses are going to take the number literally, then they need to make the rest of those passages literal as well. In this case, the 144,000 are all Jewish male virgins! As to the rest remaining on earth, there will be no earth on which to remain (2 Peter 3:10-12).

Notes _____

[1]Lanier, Roy H., Sr. *The Timeless Trinity*. Denver, Colorado: Roy H. Lanier, Sr. Publisher, 1974, p. 46.

[2]I received valuable help on both the doctrines of premillennialism and Seventh Day Adventism from the rather exhaustive work, *God's Prophetic Word*, by Foy E. Wallace, Jr. (Oklahoma City: Foy E. Wallace, Jr. Publications, 1960).

CHAPTER THIRTEEN

THE SABBATH-KEEPERS

A number of different groups, mostly small, are characterized by their keeping of the Sabbath day as the day of worship. All such groups claim that the Sabbath day, or the seventh day of the week (our Saturday), was the day of worship for the early church. They normally blame the supposed "change of the Sabbath" from Saturday to Sunday on the Pope of the Catholic Church. They say that since the OT Sabbath was a seventh-day observance, neither the Pope nor anyone else can change that. However, the problem for the Sabbath-keepers is that this day was never bound on Christians. Once the church was established in Acts 2, the first day of the week became its special day of worship.

Probably the two best known Sabbath-keeping groups are the **Seventh Day Adventists** and the **Worldwide Church of God.** The former is much larger, but the latter has exerted a good deal of influence through a widely circulated publication, *The Plain Truth*. They differ in some respects, but both of them are adamant about observing the Sabbath and are opposed to those who do not. In theory, they do not condemn other groups who worship on Sunday, but in practice, they go a long way in this direction. Since the OT is the basis for much of their Sabbath doctrine, it is not surprising that they would tend strongly toward legalism, and such is the case.

The Adventist group has quite the colorful history. Their origins trace back to the influence of a "date-setting" Baptist preacher named William Miller. Through intense study of prophecy, he came to the conclusion that Jesus would return in 1843. Once the year came and went, he recalculated (with the help of one of his leaders) and found the date to be 1844. When this date failed, Miller got out of the date-setting business. Several of those influenced by him kept working with the following he had acquired. The one who later united the group and became its leader was Ellen G. White.

White added the seventh-day emphasis, and served as the prophetess of the group. Subsequent Adventist writers have downplayed her prophetic role, but her earliest followers accepted her own testimony as inspired. She had a supposed vision from God in which he showed her that the fourth commandment was to be exalted above the rest. The apostle Paul may not have been allowed by God to talk about the contents of his heavenly vision (2 Corinthians 12:1-10), but White was able to speak freely! This "vision" occurred in 1847, and by 1860, the name "Seventh Day Adventist" had been officially adopted, although the first General Conference of the group did not meet until 1863. Therefore, the date normally given for the beginning of this denomination is 1863.

The second "sabbath-keeping" group, The Worldwide Church of God, under the leadership of Herbert W. Armstrong, separated from the Church of God. Armstong's influence spread rather quickly due to his use of the media. In 1934, he began broadcasting a radio program known as the "Radio Church of God," later changing the name to *The World Tomorrow*. Also, the publication known as *The Plain Truth* was begun and distributed without charge to promote Armstrong's views. Like the Adventist Church, his group has two very strong emphases: the Sabbath day and the study of prophecy. As far as prophecy is concerned, much of what was covered previously in this book in connection with the Jehovah's Witnesses applies. All three of these groups are premillennial, and continuing along with that materialistic focus, they also agree that man's nature is material, with no spirit which survives the body.

The Sabbath issue is our major concern here, but we will take a brief look at the food laws that most sects seem to accept. The way that the Sabbath-keepers influence other religious people is to convince them that they have been totally misled about worshipping on Sunday. Then, once they have their foot in the door on that issue, they work on other issues such as the food laws. Given the Biblical ignorance of the general religious population in America, it is no wonder that these groups are able to unsettle others. However, the Sabbath-day questions are not difficult to answer from a Biblical standpoint; nor are the related questions about the food laws of the Old Testament.

The Old and New Covenants

The most basic issue with these seventh-day-worshipping sects is how they view the Mosaic Law. Since the Sabbath law was one of the Ten Commandments, a part of that Mosaic covenant, the question of how to bind that specific command without also accepting the rest of the covenant naturally arises. This is not easily answered, as we will see. The Adventist way of solving it is to make a separation between the ceremonial laws and the moral laws (or the Ten Commandments). Sup-posedly, the former legislation was called the "Law of Moses," and the latter was called the "Law of God." But the whole argument falls apart in the light of Scripture.

There is a difference between ceremonial laws and moral laws, but this difference does not mean that the Sabbath law is binding today. Moral laws come out of the nature of God himself, and are, to a major extent, self-evident. In the absence of a written law, Cain still knew that the world's first murder was wrong (Genesis 4:9). Other laws come from the voice of God in revelation and are not self-evident. To state it an-other way, some things are in the Bible because they are *true* (the moral laws), while other things are true simply *because they are in the Bible*. The moral laws were true from the beginning, whether or not they were writ-ten down by God in a revelation. However, when God did inspire men to write, these types of laws were always included in that written revela-tion.

The Sabbath law, unlike the other nine commandments in the Dec-alogue, was not one of these *true-for-all-time principles*. There may be a principle *behind* the Sabbath law, which demands that we not be worka-holics and that we set time aside each week to pay special honor to God. But such a principle would certainly not have an obvious, logical day of observance in connection with it. The specific *day* would have to be a matter of revelation from God, which it was. The day of the OT was the seventh day of the week, and the day of the NT is the first day of the week.

Even in the case of the other nine commandments in the Ten, we do not observe them because they are in the Ten Commandments. We are not under the Mosaic legislation as a binding covenant. The principles contained in these moral commandments are all restated in some form in the NT. In fact, Jesus *strengthened* the application of these principles. He taught that it is not enough to say "don't murder" or "don't commit adultery." We have to deal with the *heart* by avoiding lust and anger (Matthew 5:21, 27-28). Certainly we learn tremendous lessons from the OT; and it is a part of the Bible for Christians from which to study and learn. It contains many applicable principles of spirituality that can bless our lives. But, we are not bound by the specifics of that legislation. This lesson is paramount if we are to understand the Sabbath-day issue.

Several NT passages shed much light on the relationship between the two covenants, between the Law and the Gospel. Galatians 4:21-31 contains a very interesting allegory, which compares the old covenant to Hagar, who was thrown out, and the new covenant to Sarah, who was the free woman. The lesson here is that we are *not* under the Law of Moses, and that includes the Ten Commandments, as we will see. In

Galatians 5:4, Paul shows the seriousness of holding on to that covenant: "You who are trying to be justified by law have been alienated from Christ; you have fallen away from grace." The whole Book of Hebrews contrasts the two covenants, proving that we are not under the Mosaic covenant. But, how can we be sure that the Ten Commandments are included in the Law from which we have now been released?

Furthermore, Romans 7:4-6 informs Christians that they have died to the law, and then in verse 7, the identity of the law in view is given: "What shall we say, then? Is the law sin? Certainly not! Indeed I would not have known what sin was except through the law. For I would not have known what coveting really was if the law had not said, 'Do not covet.'" The law against coveting was one of the Ten Commandments. Similarly, 2 Corinthians 3 is a lengthy treatment contrasting the two covenants, and the one engraved on stone can be none other than the Ten Commandments. The Sabbath-day worshippers try to identify this stone as something other than the Decalogue, but the tablets of stone were connected to the time when Moses' face shone. A reading of Exodus 34:29-35 shows that this event was definitely at the time when the Ten Commandments were given. Nothing else in Israelite history will fit the description found in 2 Corinthians 3.

Additionally, Hebrews 8:7-12 mentions the new covenant God promised to make, thereby releasing us from the old one. The writer quotes from Jeremiah 31:31-34, and states that the new covenant will not be like the one that he made when he took the Israelites by the hand to lead them out of Egypt. What was this old covenant to which he referred? 1 Kings 8:9, 21 make it perfectly clear that the Ten Commandments are included in that covenant:

> There was nothing in the ark except the two stone tablets that Moses had placed in it at Horeb, where the LORD made a covenant with the Israelites after they came out of Egypt. I have provided a place there for the ark, in which is the covenant of the LORD that he made with our fathers when he brought them out of Egypt.

The commonly advanced idea by the seventh-day people is that the "Law of Moses" (ceremonial law) was the law done away with by Christ, while the "Law of God" (Ten Commandments) was for all time. This distinction does not hold up under the light of the entirety of Scripture. For example, in Ezra 7:6, it says that God had given the "Law of Moses," while in 2 Chronicles 34:14, it says that the "Law of God" was given by Moses. In 2 Chronicles 31:3, the burnt offerings and holy days are said to be a part of the "Law of the Lord." Then in the NT, we see that Mark 7:10 says that the command to honor father and mother (one of the Ten) was given by Moses. Luke 2:22-23 uses the terms "Law of Moses" and "Law of the Lord" interchangeably:

When the time of their purification according to the Law of Moses had been completed, Joseph and Mary took him to Jerusalem to present him to the Lord (as it is written in the Law of the Lord, 'Every firstborn male is to be consecrated to the Lord').

The Sabbath law, as a part of the Ten Commandments, was done away with when Christ died. Colossians 2:14-17 could not be clearer:

...having canceled the written code, with its regulations, that was against us and that stood opposed to us; he took it away, nailing it to the cross. And having disarmed the powers and authorities, he made a public spectacle of them, triumphing over them by the cross. Therefore do not let anyone judge you by what you eat or drink, or with regard to a religious festival, a New Moon celebration or a Sabbath day. These are a shadow of the things that were to come; the reality, however, is found in Christ.

In her vision, Ellen G. White may have thought that the Fourth Commandment was the glorious one to be exalted, but the two greatest commands, to love God with all your being and to love your neighbor as yourself, were not even from the Ten Commandments (Matthew 22:35-40).

The Sabbath: A Perpetual Covenant?
The Sabbath-keepers claim that the Sabbath was not simply a facet of the Mosaic Law, but that it predated the law and was to last forever. A key text for them is Exodus 31:14-17, quoted here in the NASV:

"'Therefore you are to observe the sabbath, for it is holy to you. Everyone who profanes it shall surely be put to death; for whoever does any work on it, that person shall be cut off from among his people. For six days work may be done, but on the seventh day there is a sabbath of complete rest, holy to the LORD; whoever does any work on the sabbath day shall surely be put to death. So the sons of Israel shall observe the sabbath, to celebrate the sabbath throughout their generations as a perpetual covenant. It is a sign between Me and the sons of Israel forever; for in six days the LORD made heaven and earth, but on the seventh day He ceased from labor, and was refreshed."

At first glance, this passage seems to say exactly what the Sabbatarians claim. After all, it does say "perpetual" and "forever." You can see just why the Sabbath-keeping doctrine makes an impact on those who do not know the Bible well. But, a closer examination of the passage is needed.

Notice that this Sabbath covenant was to be a sign between God and the sons of Israel. It was not made with anyone but the Jews. If it had really been in effect since the creation of the world, how could it have been a sign with this new nation? In verse 17, the fact that God mentions the time he ceased from his work of creation does not mean that the covenant itself goes back to that time. That statement was preceded by the one about the sign being between him and his new nation. In Deuteronomy 5:15, God ties in the observance of the Sabbath with the fact that the Israelites had been slaves in Egypt. In slavery, they may have had no opportunity to observe the Sabbath, but now God wanted them to have this special day for him. Nehemiah 9:13-14 and Ezekiel 20:12, 20 say that the Sabbath law was not given until Mount Sinai. All of these statements show definitively that the Sabbath was given to the Jews alone, and was not demanded of other nations before the Mosaic Law.

But what about the word *perpetual?* In verse 16, the covenant's duration is given as being "throughout your generations." This phrase is used to denote the generations of the Jews as God's chosen people. They were his chosen people during the time of their covenant with him, which lasted from Mt. Sinai until the cross of Christ. The term "perpetual" is defined and limited by that phrase, which is very easy to prove. Many aspects of the Mosaic covenant are said to be "perpetual." To mention a few, the Aaronic priesthood was according to a perpetual statute (Exodus 29:9); incense burning was perpetual (Exodus 30:8); the washing of feet and hands by the priests was a perpetual statute (Exodus 30:21), as was the observance of the Feast of Tabernacles (Leviticus 23:41); and the blowing of trumpets by the priests (Numbers 10:8).

The word "everlasting" was used simply to mean *age-lasting,* which for the Jews was until the cross. For example, in Genesis 17:13, circumcision is called an "everlasting covenant." However, in the new covenant, Paul made this radical statement: "Mark my words! I, Paul, tell you that if you let yourselves be circumcised, Christ will be of no value to you at all" (Galatians 5:2). Therefore, the length of "everlasting" depends on the context in which it is used. And don't worry—heaven will be *age-lasting,* meaning, in this case, *forever and ever* (1 Corinthians 15:50-54; 1 Thessalonians 4:17).

The Adventists also try to tie together Mark 2:28 and Revelation 1:10 in order to make the "Lord's Day" equivalent to the Sabbath. The Mark 2:28 passage says that Jesus is "Lord of the Sabbath," and Revelation 1:10 uses the term "the Lord's Day." In Mark, it is obvious (in context) that Jesus is not trying to exalt the Sabbath Day. On the contrary, he is saying that he can do just what he wants to do on any day, *even* on the Sabbath! In regard to Revelation 1:10, the Adventists are assuming the very point to be proved. As we will see, "the Lord's Day" is the first day of the week.

The First Day of the Week Is the Lord's Day

The first day of the week is the day of emphasis in the new covenant. Jesus arose from the dead on the first day of the week (Mark 16:1-9). Jesus first appeared to his group of disciples on the first day of the week (John 20:19), and his next appearance to them was one week later, also on the first day of the week (John 20:26). Since Jesus was "declared with power to be the Son of God by his resurrection from the dead" (Romans 1:4), this marvelous declaration is inseparably connected to the first day of the week. The church was established on the Day of Pentecost, which was always the first day of the week. Therefore, it is not surprising that the long-awaited outpouring of the Spirit occurred on the first day of the week (Joel 2:28-32; Acts 2:1-4, 16-21); the first gospel sermon was preached on this day; and the first converts were baptized into Christ on this first day of the week. How could the events of a Judaistic Sabbath compare with these highly significant events on this new day of emphasis in the new covenant?

Another important passage is Acts 20:7, which reads: "On the first day of the week we came together to break bread. Paul spoke to the people and, because he intended to leave the next day, kept on talking until midnight." The previous verse tells us that Paul had arrived a week before in Troas and stayed seven days. The implication from the text is that Paul waited for all those days in order to meet with the church in Troas before continuing on his journey. Since their day of meeting was on the first day of the week, he waited until then, met with them and departed the next day. This one passage provides rather conclusive proof that the church met regularly on the first day of the week, rather than on the Sabbath.

Several other passages also cast light on this first day of the week emphasis. Jesus commanded the observance of the Lord's Supper (Matthew 26:26-29; 1 Corinthians 11:17-34). The church was also commanded to assemble (Hebrews 10:25). They observed the Lord's Supper when they assembled; and in fact, assembled for the very purpose of celebrating this memorial (Acts 20:7; 1 Corinthians 11:33). And the day of this assembling was on the first day of the week, as 1 Corinthians 16:2 clearly says: "On the first day of every week, each one of you should set aside a sum of money in keeping with his income, saving it up, so that when I come no collections will have to be made." Therefore, the first-century church assembled on the first day of the week and not on the Sabbath.

This being true, the Lord's Day designation in Revelation 1:10 is, without a doubt, the first day of the week. If all of the earth-shaking events of the new covenant had already occurred on this day of the week, it is only fitting that the apostle John should be in the Spirit on that day as he received the final revelation of God's will from the Lord Jesus Christ!

Jesus Made All Foods Clean

Most of the sects, being legalistic in mindset, make the keeping of OT food laws a high priority. This priority is seen plainly in both the Seventh Day worshippers and Mormons. Although they tell outsiders that their emphasis is only for health reasons, they absolutely bind these laws on people who become members of their group. But what does the Bible say about these matters? In Mark 7:17-19, Jesus could not have stated it any clearer:

> After he had left the crowd and entered the house, his disciples asked him about this parable. "Are you so dull?" he asked. "Don't you see that nothing that enters a man from the outside can make him 'unclean'? For it doesn't go into his heart but into his stomach, and then out of his body." (In saying this, Jesus declared all foods "clean.")

Several other passages may also be mentioned, although Jesus' word cannot be misunderstood in Mark. In 1 Timothy 4:1-5, Paul strongly denounced those false teachers who ordered others to abstain from certain foods, concluding with these remarks in verses 3-5: "...which God created to be received with thanksgiving by those who believe and who know the truth. For everything God created is good, and nothing is to be rejected if it is received with thanksgiving, because it is consecrated by the word of God and prayer." When Jesus or Paul commented on the issues of eating foods, they were not ambiguous.

In Romans 14, Paul was discussing what he called "disputable matters," which were matters of opinion. Among those matters was the issue of clean or unclean foods. Verse 3 of that chapter says quite specifically: "The man who eats everything must not look down on him who does not, and the man who does not eat everything must not condemn the man who does, for God has accepted him." In other words, the possibility exists in the will of God for a Christian to eat *everything*! That would mean that a nice, hot breakfast of eggs, bacon and coffee would be fine with the Lord. Amen. In the later context, Paul states what sectarians have not yet learned about the real focus of the spiritual life: "For the kingdom of God is not a matter of eating and drinking, but of righteousness, peace and joy in the Holy Spirit, because anyone who serves Christ in this way is pleasing to God and approved by men" (Romans 14:17-18).

Finally, the last passage to consider is Colossians 2, beginning in verse 16:

> Therefore do not let anyone judge you by what you eat or drink, or with regard to a religious festival, a New Moon celebration or a Sabbath day. These are a shadow of the things that were to come; the reality, however, is found in Christ...Since you died with Christ to the basic principles of this world, why, as though you still belonged to it, do you submit to its rules: "Do not handle! Do not taste! Do not touch!"? These are all destined to perish with use, because they are based on human commands and teachings. Such regulations indeed have an appearance of wisdom, with their self-imposed worship, their false humility and their harsh treatment of the body, but they lack any value in restraining sensual indulgence.

If a person will allow the Bible to settle any question of doctrine, these passages will totally settle the issue of binding food laws in the Christian covenant. Whatever we may personally decide about eating healthily, food requirements have absolutely no place in the church of Jesus. Even on the health issue, just think of what Jesus could have taught about that one, and yet he did not! Since he did not, we must not! The kingdom of God is about much more important things. Let's get busy with those things and help all other people to do the same.

QUICK REFERENCE GUIDE: _____

1. **Sabbatarian Claim:** The Ten Commandments are moral commands for all times and for all covenants of God with men. **Bible Truth:** Nine of the Ten Commandments are restated in the NT, as is the principle behind the Sabbath (man is not to be a workaholic and should set aside a special day for honoring God). However, we are not under the Ten Commandments. Romans 7:4-7 identifies the law to which we have died as the law which contained the law on coveting (Ten Commandments). Hebrews 8:7-12 say that we are under the new covenant rather than the old, and 1 Kings 8:9, 21 shows that the old covenant being discussed includes the Ten Commandments. 2 Corinthians 3 calls the covenant engraved on stones—the one which was done away in Christ; and this one can be none other than the Ten Commandments.

2. **Sabbatarian Claim:** The ceremonial law, called the Law of Moses, was ended at the cross, but the Ten Commandment moral law,

called the Law of God, remains today. **Bible Truth:** No such distinction can be made biblically. God gave the Law of Moses (Ezra 7:6) and Moses gave the Law of God (2 Chronicles 34:14). The ceremonial parts of the law were said to be a part of the Law of the Lord in 2 Chronicles 31:3, and the moral parts were called the Law of Moses (Mark 7:10). Luke 2:22-23 uses the two designations interchangeably.

3. **Sabbatarian Claim:** The Sabbath observance was to be a perpetual, everlasting covenant based on Exodus 31:14-17. **Bible Truth:** This passage shows that the Sabbath was given only to that new nation as a sign between them and God. It also shows that words like "perpetual" and "everlasting" are to be qualified by the phrase "throughout your generations," a reference to the generations of the Jewish covenant (which ended at the cross). Nehemiah 9:13-14 and Ezekiel 20:12, 20 make it clear that the Sabbath law was not given until Mount Sinai. Furthermore, if the Sabbath-keepers want to make their argument on the word "perpetual," then they will also have to accept the other "perpetual" requirements of Judaism (Exodus 29:9; 30:8, 21; Leviticus 23:41; Numbers 10:8).

4. **Sabbatarian Claim:** The seventh day of the week is the day of emphasis for the church. **Bible Truth:** Even though Jesus observed the Sabbath, since he was born and died under the Law of Moses (Galatians 4:4), and even though the early preachers went into Jewish synagogues on the Sabbath in order to preach to the Jews, the first day of the week was clearly established as the day of emphasis in the early church. Jesus arose on the first day of the week (Mark 16:1-9), he appeared to his disciples on two different first days (John 20:19, 26), and the church was established on the first day of the week (Acts 2). The early disciples observed the first day as their day of assembly (Acts 20:7; 1 Corinthians 16:2).

5. **Sabbatarian Claim:** OT food laws are designed to promote good health, and they should be kept in the new covenant. **Bible Truth:** Jesus made all foods clean (Mark 7:17-19), nothing is to be rejected (1 Timothy 4:1-5), God can accept the man who chooses to eat everything, and so must other disciples (Romans 14:3); and finally, we should refuse to let anyone judge us by what we eat or drink, because these things have absolutely nothing to do with spirituality (Colossians 2:16-23).

CHAPTER FOURTEEN

THE MORMONS

Early Beginnings

Joseph Smith, Jr. was born in 1805 in Vermont, and moved with his family to the state of New York when he was a small boy. As a teen, supposedly looking for the correct church to join, he claimed to have received a vision of God and Jesus, followed by several visions in which an angel named "Maroni" appeared to him. This angel is said to have told him about the existence of some buried golden plates containing a divine history of the former inhabitants of the American continents. These plates, so goes the story, contained the "fullness of the everlasting gospel." Several years later, Maroni told Joseph to dig up the plates and to translate them with the help of the Urim and Thummim stones which were found with them. (Of course, the Bible reader is familiar with two stones by those names attached to the breastplate of the Jewish High Priest. In the Biblical account, the stones were used to determine God's will for specific decisions, not for translation purposes.)

Within weeks, Joseph claimed to have translated these plates, resulting in *The Book of Mormon*. The Mormon Church officially began on April 6, 1830, in Fayette, New York. Smith and his followers eventually migrated to Ohio, and then to Illinois. As the practices of this strange new group started to become evident, the local townspeople rose up against Smith and put him and his brother, Hyrum, in jail. When the jail was mobbed, the two Smith brothers were killed, as Joseph fought back with a smuggled six-shooter in his hand.

Had he not died in this manner at this time, the history of the religion which he started may well have turned out very differently. But, six-gun or not, he had now become a martyr, who in death inspired his followers to continue in their quest for this new faith. A short time later, Brigham Young moved the group to Utah, and the rest is fairly well-known history, even to non-Mormons. This sect has grown to large proportions, in both numbers and influence.

At first consideration, the entire story sounds quite unbelievable to the average person. A knowledge of Joseph Smith's early years helps explain something of the nature of the supposed "miracles" which accompanied the origins of Mormonism. (His family history is well documented in many books written to expose the Mormon religion.[1]) As a teen, Smith was known to be a treasure-hunter who claimed to have discovered buried treasure by looking into "peep stones." Similarly, his father had similar inclinations, being preoccupied with digging for Captain Kidd's buried treasure![2] Neither of the Smith men had a positive reputation in their community, to put it kindly, which may help explain why the new religion grew much faster once it left the location where its founder was personally known.

Strange Doctrines

In beginning an examination of the Mormon religion, it is helpful to realize just how bizarre many of the Mormon doctrines actually are. This sect is not just another group in Christendom with a few untraditional views based on an erroneous interpretation of the Bible. Certainly, many of their teachings contradict the Bible, as will be dealt with later in the chapter, but it is important to be aware of just how far afield some tenets of this religion go. Mormonism has grown, not *because* of its beliefs, but in spite of them, demonstrating that that there are always gullible people who will accept certain ideas, especially when they are presented by those with a serious commitment to them.

Although some Mormon writings attest to the one God, the idea of multiple Gods is unmistakably presented in others. In the *Pearl of Great Price*, Joseph Smith wrote: "And then the Lord said: Let us go down. And they went down at the beginning, and they, that is the Gods, organized and formed the heavens and the earth" (Abraham 4:1). Not to be outdone by the Catholic exaltation of Mary, Mormon apostle Bruce McConkie stated: "Implicit in the Christian verity that all men are the spirit children of an Eternal Father is the usually unspoken truth that they are also the offspring of an Eternal Mother."[3]

Furthermore, Mormons teach that God has a physical body. *Doctrines and Covenants* 130:22 reads: "The Father has a body of flesh and bones as tangible as man's; the Son also; but the Holy Ghost has not a body of flesh and bones, but is a personage of Spirit." They also teach that God is a changing and growing Being. Another Mormon apostle, Orson Hyde, wrote: "Remember that God, our heavenly Father, was perhaps once a child, and mortal like we ourselves, and rose step by step in the scale of progress, in the school of advancement; has moved forward and overcome, until He has arrived at the point where He now is."[4] Brigham Young taught that Jesus was *not* begotten by the Holy Ghost, but was begotten by the Father through literal sexual intercourse! "The birth of the Savior was as natural as are the births of our children; it was the result of natural action. He partook of flesh and blood—was begotten of his Father, as we are of our fathers."[5]

The next (illogical) step of this physical doctrine of God is that Jesus himself fostered children. Orson Hyde wrote: "Jesus was the bridegroom at the marriage of Cana of Galilee."[6] He went on to say that Jesus was married to Mary, Martha and others, and that, through them, he begot children.[7] Mormon doctrine has demoted God to the point of being a glorified man, but this approach provides man the opportunity to climb up the ladder and become God also. A well-known saying in Mormonism puts it this way: "As man is, God once was; as God is, man may become."

Many other strange and unusual doctrines pervade Mormonism, but the above serve to illustrate what can happen when men's imaginations are allowed to run unchecked by Biblical authority.

Mormon Writings

In addition to the *Book of Mormon*, two other books were written by Joseph Smith, and the three together, along with the Bible (according to them), form the Mormon "Word of God." Both of these books are doctrinally more significant to Mormonism than the *Book of Mormon* itself. *Doctrines and Covenants* was published in 1876, and it contains 136 sections which are divided into verses. The final section is attributed to Brigham Young. The subject matter of this book includes Smith's theology on God, the church, the priesthood, salvation and other related subjects. In Section 132, verses 52-54, Smith addresses a "revelation" to his wife Emma, telling her that she must accept her husband's additional wives or suffer eternal damnation!

The *Pearl of Great Price* is a shorter book, containing the Book of Moses, the Book of Abraham, Smith's translation of Matthew, excerpts from his autobiography describing the discovery and translation of the golden plates and the Articles of Faith. The Book of Abraham was said to be a translation of some Egyptian papyri which Smith had purchased in 1835. Along with the supposed translation, Smith included some actual drawings from the papyri. This decision has proved to be an unwise one on Smith's part because a number of Egyptologists have declared that his translation was no translation at all. Modern archeology and related fields have consistently shown that Joseph's works and his "revelations" about the inhabitants of the Americas have no basis in fact.

Mormon Writings Are Contradictory

These basic books of Mormonism's trilogy, along with the other alleged writings of modern prophets, are frequently contradictory. As we have seen, Mormon prophets (including Joseph Smith) teach a plurality of Gods. Yet, The *Book of Mormon* also states quite clearly that there is only one God (Ether 2:8). The *Book of Mormon* teaches that baptism is necessary for the forgiveness of sins (3 Nephi 12:2), while *Doctrines and Covenants* asserts that baptism follows forgiveness (20:37). Furthermore, The *Book of Mormon* teaches that death seals the fate of man (Alma 34:31-35), but *Doctrines and Covenants* teaches the doctrine of a second chance (88:99).

Even more serious is the fact that the writings of the Mormon Church contradict Biblical facts. Consider these examples:

- In Helaman 14:20, the time of darkness at the crucifixion was stated to be three days, rather than three hours (Matthew 27:45).
- In Alma 7:10, we find that Jesus was born in Jerusalem rather than Bethlehem (Matthew 2:1).
- Mosiah 18:17 speaks of the establishment of the Church of Christ, but the date of this writing was in 147 B.C. Therefore, about a century and a half later, Jesus was evidently uninformed enough to think that he still had to establish his church (Matthew 16:18).
- Alma 46:15, describing the events of 73 B.C., says that people were called "Christians" because of their belief in Christ who was yet to come! Dr. Luke, in writing about the work of Barnabas and Saul in Antioch, was evidently about 100 years late in describing when this term came to be used (Acts 11:26).

Mormon Writings Fail the Practical Test

Joseph Smith unequivocally declared to the world that "The Book of Mormon" is the most correct of any book on Earth, contending that every word was dictated to him by God."[8] Yet, the grammar is incorrect and the historical contents of these books are not accurate. The book has undergone thousands of grammatical revisions, including corrections of basic issues like subject/verb agreement. The Mormons rationalize the poor grammar by appealing to the lack of formal education of their founder. (Amazingly, the corrected editions are still grammatically poor, even after a century of revisions.)

In Helaman 9:6, a judge was said to have been stabbed "by a garb of secrecy." One wouldn't think that a piece of clothing could have done enough damage to kill him! In Helaman 1:7, someone was trying to persuade people to rise up against their brothers, and Smith said that "he was about to *flatter* away those people" (italics mine). Then, Alma 27:4 speaks of people who were "so dearly beloved" by Ammon. Hopefully, they were dearly loved, but "beloved" is a noun. The book is no more than a weak effort at adopting King James English for an imagined story. In fact, it would have to be considered more than a little strange that God chose to translate Egyptian into outdated English. But to Smith, the English found in the King James Bible was the only religious language that he knew. Thus, we have an ancient document written in Reformed Egyptian, and translated word by word by God himself into an outdated language, replete with significant grammatical problems! Believe it if you can!

Besides the grammatical problems, the historical/archeological problems are even more damaging to the case of Mormonism. The main premise of the Book of Mormon is that God revealed how the Americas were originally settled by two different groups who migrated from the Holy Lands. However, no reputable archeologist attaches any significance to this alleged history. In fact, a 1987 statement from the Smithsonian Institute rejected numerous elements of Smith's whole thesis about this history. These archeologists did not merely question an issue or two—they questioned the entire theory![9] Contrast how completely modern archeology has shown the Bible to be accurate. As additional discoveries are made which relate to the Bible, the more reliable its details are considered to be; as more discoveries are made which relate to the Book of Mormon, the less believable it is considered to be.

Mormon Writings Fail the Biblical Test

The practical considerations demonstrate the falsity of Mormon writings, but the Biblical considerations are far more compelling. Basic Biblical doctrines are flatly rejected by Mormonism. The Bible teaches that only God is eternal and that he created our spirits. Mormons believe that our spirits are also eternal, and that God simply places them into human bodies. 1 Timothy 6:15-16 says that only God is immortal, and Hebrew 12:9 says that he is the Father of our spirits.

Yet another false doctrine is the practice of proxy baptism. Their practice is based on their interpretation of 1 Corinthians 15:29, which says, "Now if there is no resurrection, what will those do who are baptized for the dead? If the dead are not raised at all, why are people baptized for them?" Admittedly, this passage is a difficult one and has evoked a number of different interpretations. As with all difficult texts, it cannot be used in a manner which contradicts the teaching of clear passages. Everything in the NT points to a judgment which takes place when a person dies and is irreversible. See Luke 16:19-31, 2 Corinthians 5:10 and Hebrews 9:27. Also, keep in mind that Biblical baptism is always predicated on the personal faith and repentance of the one being baptized (see earlier discussion in chapter 8).

But what *does* 1 Corinthians 15:29 mean? In context, Paul is refuting those who were saying that the resurrection of the dead was already past. Therefore, whatever he was saying in verse 29, it was to demonstrate the fallacy of that claim and the truth of the resurrection. Actually, the NT shows that our baptism is not just for immediate forgiveness of sins. It definitely looks forward to our resurrection from the dead. Consider the following passages, and their relationship to this subject.

We were therefore buried with him through baptism into death in order that, just as Christ was raised from the dead through the glory of the Father, we too may live a new life. If we have been united with him like this in his death, we will certainly also be united with him in his resurrection (**Romans 6:4-5**).

Praise be to the God and Father of our Lord Jesus Christ! In his great mercy he has given us new birth into a living hope through the resurrection of Jesus Christ from the dead, and into an inheritance that can never perish, spoil or fade—kept in heaven for you, who through faith are shielded by God's power until the coming of the salvation that is ready to be revealed in the last time (**1 Peter 1:3-5**).

Therefore, the passage in 1 Corinthians 15 may well be saying that those disciples were originally baptized with a view toward the dead state, in that they were looking forward to their ultimate resurrection from this dead condition. Why now, Paul argues, are they allowing false teachers to take away their original conviction? This interpretation, or one similar to it, must be correct, for it takes the context into consideration and does not violate other plain teaching of Scripture. Regardless of the *specific* interpretation intended by Paul, we can know for sure what he did *not* intend!

One of the major *biblical* challenges to Mormonism is their teaching about the priesthood. Biblically, only the Levites, through the family of Aaron, could serve as priests during the OT period. The priest named "Melchizedek" was a priest during the days of Abraham, and the Book of Hebrews tells us that Jesus became a High Priest "after the order of Melchizedek." Additionally, this same book tells us that the Aaronic priesthood was done away with.

If perfection could have been attained through the Levitical priesthood (for on the basis of it the law was given to the people), why was there still need for another priest to come—one in the order of Melchizedek, not in the order of Aaron? For when there is a change of the priesthood, there must also be a change of the law (**Hebrews 7:11-12**).

The NT teaches that Jesus is the only High Priest, the one mediator between God and man (1 Timothy 2:5), and that all Christians are now priests (1 Peter 2:9). Yet, Mormons claim that God gave them both the Aaronic and Melchizedek priesthoods. The Book of Mormon is also in violation of the laws which limited the priesthood to the family of Levi during the OT period. In 1 Nephi 5:15, Nephi traces his lineage back to the family of Joseph. Then, in 1 Nephi 7:22, he declares that they offered sacrifices and burnt offerings. According to what we can read in Numbers 18:6-7, an offering such as this by non-Levites constituted a violation of God's law—which was punishable by death. A related problem in the Book of Mormon is the statement in 2 Nephi 25:24-2—that these people believed in Christ and yet kept the Law of Moses. Galatians 5:4 shows clearly that the two covenants could not both be observed.

One of the most *emotionally* objectionable teachings of Mormonism has been its blatant racism. Brigham Young claimed that the curse God placed on Cain was to make him black. His disdain for blacks was unmistakable in his writings, with the ultimate pronouncement that interracial marriage demanded the death penalty.

"Shall I tell you the law of God in regard to the African race? If the white man who belongs to the chosen seed mixes his blood with the seed of Cain, the penalty, under the law of God, is death on the spot. This will always be so."[10]

In 1978, bowing to the pressure of public opinion, Mormon President Spencer Kimball received a "revelation" which authorized the ordaining of black priests, which had been verboten before that time. But the statement by Young that "It will always be so" is an example of many such pronouncements of absolute finality which have later been rejected or proved false.

When God was establishing the line of prophets who were to follow after Moses, he gave this test of a true prophet in Deuteronomy 18:18-22:

I will raise up for them a prophet like you from among their brothers; I will put my words in his mouth, and he will tell them everything I command him. If anyone does not listen to my words that the prophet speaks in my name, I myself will call him to account. But a prophet who presumes to speak in my name anything I have not commanded him to say, or a prophet who speaks in the name of other gods, must be put to death. You may say to yourselves, "How can we know when a message has not been spoken by the LORD?" If what a prophet proclaims in the name of the LORD does not take place or come true, that is a message the

LORD has not spoken. That prophet has spoken presumptuously. Do not be afraid of him.

On this basis, we are justified in saying that the writings of Mormonism are decidedly not from God. Mistake after mistake has been noted in these writings involving historical facts, Biblical facts and Biblical doctrines. Joseph and all those supposed prophets who followed him were, and are, false prophets. The facts make any other conclusion untenable.

Mormon writings cannot be inspired because of their very nature, as already explained, but more than that, the NT teaching about the ending of the prophetic office rules out modern-day prophecy entirely. In chapter 10, we discussed at length the age of miraculous gifts in the church. We showed that these gifts were needed to bring the new revelation of the new covenant, and that only the apostles could confer these gifts on those early disciples. Therefore, by the time the apostles died, two realities became evident. One, the gifts had to cease because there were no apostles who could pass them on. Two, by then, the NT had been completely revealed and additional revelation was neither needed nor possible.

The biggest battleground with Mormons is certainly the issue of the all-sufficiency of the Bible against their claims for latter-day revelation. Hebrews 1:1-2 states:

In the past God spoke to our forefathers through the prophets at many times and in various ways, but in these last days he has spoken to us by his Son, whom he appointed heir of all things, and through whom he made the universe.

Jesus is the last revealer of the will of God, and we need to see how he accomplished this revelation. In John 14:25-26, Jesus promised the first-century apostles that the Holy Spirit would be sent to them, and he would teach them *all things* and remind them of *everything* that he had taught them. Similarly, in John 16:13, Jesus told the apostles that the Holy Spirit would come and guide them into *all truth*. From these two passages, it is clear that the first-century apostles would receive all truth when the Holy Spirit came to them. Since the Spirit came in Acts 2, they received the inspiration necessary to deliver this complete truth. Paul's last letter showed that he believed the Scriptures (which included his writing—2 Peter 3:16) "thoroughly equipped" the man of God for "every good work." Even though several letters of the NT were written after Paul's last letter, the truths were available through inspiration before they were written down. The point is that nothing else was needed then, and certainly not 1,800 years later!

2 Peter 1:3 states that God's divine power *had given* (past tense) our brothers and sisters *everything needed* for spiritual life through their *knowledge* of Jesus. Jude 3 says that no other revelation is needed nor expected: "Dear friends, although I was very eager to write to you about the salvation we share, I felt I had to write and urge you to contend for the faith that was once for *all* entrusted to the saints." The word translated "once for all" here is *hapax*, meaning *one time for all time*. In Hebrews 9:26-28, the same word is used in reference to Christ coming to earth to do away with our sins; to man's dying which leads then to judgment; and to the actual death of Jesus. Obviously, all of these events are *one-time* events. Entrusted (past tense) means that the faith had already been fully delivered. No more revelation is expected, nor needed!

It is important to note that this totally adequate message was delivered progressively over a period of years in the first century to the apostles (John 16:12-13). In the earliest stages of the church, the message was found in *only* the inspired man, then in *both* the inspired man and the inspired Book (2 Thessalonians 2:1-2), and finally, in the inspired Book *alone*. Since the Word was totally given by the end of the first century, nothing more is needed and nothing more is *allowed*. Paul leaves no doubt about there never being a need for any other gospel in Galatians 1:8: "But even if we or an angel from heaven should preach a gospel other than the one we preached to you, let him be eternally condemned!" The Book of Mormon, along with other supposedly inspired Mormon writings, clearly contradicts the NT message in *multitudes* of places. Therefore, these writings are inspired *only* by Satan and his demons! And that is not an unexpected thing, for 2 Corinthians 11:13-15 reads thus:

> For such men are false apostles, deceitful workmen, masquerading as apostles of Christ. And no wonder, for Satan himself masquerades as an angel of light. It is not surprising, then, if his servants masquerade as servants of righteousness. Their end will be what their actions deserve.

Mormonism presents itself attractively. From its university with great athletes to its famous politicians and entertainers, from wealthy businessmen to its slickly produced advertisements advocating strong families, it appears to be a stronghold of wisdom, values and spirituality. But the test of anything is how it appears in light of the Word of God. Here, Mormonism is weighed in the balances and found wanting.

QUICK REFERENCE GUIDE: _____

1. **Mormonism Claim:** A number of Gods exist, and they have flesh and bones. **Bible Truth:** There is only one God, and he is spirit (Mark 12:29; Ephesians 4:6; John 4:24; Luke 24:39).

2. **Mormonism Claim:** Jesus was begotten by the Father through literal intercourse. **Bible Truth:** Jesus was begotten by the Holy Spirit through a virgin mother (Matthew 1:18-23).

3. **Mormonism Claim:** In spite of some writings which are accurate, other Mormon writings talk about God being progressive in his knowledge and power. **Bible Truth:** God is perfect and cannot change in his nature, nor can Jesus (Malachi 3:6; Hebrews 13:8).

4. **Mormonism Claim:** Jesus was married to several women and had children by them. **Bible Truth:** The only wife that Jesus has ever had is the church (2 Corinthians 11:2; Ephesians 5:25-32).

5. **Mormonism Claim:** The *Book of Mormon* teaches that three days of darkness occurred at Christ's crucifixion (Helaman 14:20). Alma 7:10 has Jesus being born in Jerusalem. Mosiah 18:17 speaks of the establishment of the Church of Christ in 147 B.C., and Alma 46:15 says that people were called Christians (in at least 73 B.C.). **Bible Truth:** Three hours of darkness (Matthew 27:45); Bethlehem (Matthew 2:1); Jesus, the establishment of his church, and when the name "Christian" started to be used (Matthew 16:18; Acts 11:26).

6. **Mormonism Claim:** The spirits of humans are eternal. **Bible Truth:** Man was created totally in the beginning (Genesis 1:26-27), and our spirits are now created and placed in our physical bodies (Zechariah 12:1; Ecclesiastes 12:7). Only God is immortal (1 Timothy 6:15-16).

7. **Mormonism Claim:** Living humans can be baptized for the benefit of dead humans. **Bible Truth:** After death, no second chance (Luke 16:19-31; 2 Corinthians 5:10; Hebrews 9:27). Also, Biblical baptism is always based on the personal faith and repentance of the one being baptized.

8. **Mormonism Claim:** Both Aaronic and Melchizedek priesthoods were given to them by God. **Bible Truth:** The Melchizedek priesthood is occupied by Jesus alone, and the Aaronic priesthood was a part of the old covenant which has been done away in Christ (Hebrews 7:11-12). Now, all Christians are priests (1 Peter 2:9).

9. **Mormonism Claim:** The Mormon Church has a continuing line of prophets who reveal and interpret the will of God. **Bible Truth:** Prophecy ended with the death of the first-century apostles (Acts 8:9-18; 1 Corinthians 13:8-10). The apostles received all truth in the first century, and through inspiration, delivered it to us (John 14:25-26; 16:13; Ephesians 3:2-5). Finally, the NT was complete and gives man all that he needs to please God (2 Timothy 3:16-17; 2 Peter 1:3; Jude 3).

Notes _____

[1] A brief, but helpful, recent book written for this purpose is *The Truth about Mormonism* by Weldon, Langfield/Bakersfield, California: Weldon Langfield Publications, 1991.

[2] Langfield, p. 19.

[3] Bruce R. McConkie, *Mormon Doctrine,* Salt Lake City: Bookcraft, 1979, .516.

[4] F. D. Richards, *Journal of Discourses.* Liverpool: Latter-day Saints' Book Depot, 1854-1886, Vol. 1, 123.

[5] *Journal of Discourses,* Vol. 8, 115.

[6] *Journal of Discourses,* Vol. 2, 81-82.

[7] *Journal of Discourses,* Vol. 4, 210.

[8] *The History of the Church of Jesus Christ of Latter-day Saints.* Six vol. Salt Lake City: Deseret News, 1902-1912; quote found in Vol. IV, 461.

[9] Department of Anthropology, The Smithsonian Institution, *Statement Regarding the Book of Mormon,* Washington: National Museum of Natural History, Spring 1987.

[10] *Journal of Discourses,* Vol. 10, 110.

FINAL CONSIDERATIONS AND CAUTIONS

As I conclude the writing of this book, I feel numerous mixed emotions. I feel saddened over the need to even write such a book. False doctrines carry heavy consequences for humanity. It must be heart-breaking for God to have poured out his heart to men, in what could be called a *love letter*, and have them reject it and him; to watch as they have perverted its teaching almost beyond recognition. I feel saddened as I consider how multitudes, most with good intentions, have been led astray by these false teachings. The contemplation of their eternal destiny is heart-wrenching.

I also feel a good deal of righteous indignation at what religious leaders have presumed to do with God's Word. Their pride and presumption have wreaked havoc with the souls of men over many centuries. They have been god-players and, therefore, God-rejecters. Many leaders may have been victims of their particular religious system, but the originators of these systems have been rebels against God and truth. As disciples of Jesus, we need to develop his kind of heart, rise up against religious corruption and "turn over the tables" of the false prophets of our day.

Another feeling that the writing of this book produced in me is that of confidence. Regardless of what men have said, the Bible stands true. "Let God be true and all men liars." Once, in a series of discussions with a denominational preacher, he finally reached the exasperation point with me. He then said something like this: "Gordon, you don't seem to even care what great religious leaders like Martin Luther and Billy Graham have said." His point was that all of the famous leaders surely could not be wrong. My reply went something like this: "And you seem to care more about what they have said than what the Bible says." Whatever any man may have said that was true and helpful—Amen; but my ultimate allegiance is to God, not to any man. The Bible gives me the convictions to face any person holding any doctrine with the utmost confidence.

Along these lines, I also feel very thankful—thankful to have been born to parents who believed that the Bible was the Word of God; thankful to have been born in a country where Bibles were readily available; thankful to have been motivated to read it for myself; and thankful to have developed the convictions to follow it at all costs. Mostly, I am just thankful to the God who inspired and delivered it to us. His Word is truth, and that truth does make us free.

Finally, I feel cautious. We are but men. We can be mistaken, even with zeal and noble intentions. Therefore, we must remain rooted in the authority of God's message, and bathed in the humility which only a close relationship with him provides. I want to share my feeling of cautiousness with you, in the form of the following cautions.

1. In spite of our opposition, we can never be tentative about our key biblical stands. Although our convictions place us in a minority position among religious groups, so what? Only a remnant of religious people has ever been on the narrow road, and we should not feel insecure about how others view us. Never allow any man or group of men to make you feel ashamed of the Word of God.

2. However, as you stand firm for the truth, avoid the spirit of dogmatism and self-righteousness. If someone rejects the truths that you are sharing, make sure that their rejection is not based on your pride. As Peter said, give your answers with "gentleness and respect."

3. We cannot be naive enough to think that we have such a commitment to the Bible that it would be impossible for our leaders to move us away from truth and into error. Remember that many departures throughout history came through people who thought the same thing. The need is for us to keep a humble posture, asking God to show us clearly if we start to drift from the path.

4. Similarly, we cannot afford to become totally comfortable with what we believe. We are in trouble when we see no need to do fresh thinking and fresh study. Mental laziness is a plague, but a continual search for more truth is a reward. God's Word contains all of the truth, and none of us will ever have it all down pat.

5. We must understand that some doctrines are more central than others. Jesus talked about the "weightier" (KJV) "more important" matters. Some things are absolutely central and crucial. Others are important, but still "lesser" matters. We make a serious error and begin to distort the Bible when we make the minor things into major things.

6. We can never make traditions sacred. After we have done something for a long time, we can fall into thinking it should not be done any other way when, in reality, there may be a way that is more biblical, or at least more effective. Even if a practice is not anti-scriptural, we must remember that traditions are traditions and should not be put on par with the Word of God.

7. Finally, none of us should ever be unwilling to admit we have been wrong. Pride is what causes many people to hold on to their unbiblical views. This is a special challenge for leaders who may have taught a certain thing over and over and then do not want to admit that they may have misled or incorrectly taught others. When we openly admit mistakes and sins, others respect us more, not less. No one can see our humility without first seeing our humanity.

WHAT ABOUT THE APOCRYPHA?

The word "apocrypha" means "hidden" and is applied to a collection of 15 books, most of which were written during the intertestamental period. The Catholic Church accepts 12 of the 15 books of the Apocrypha, although some of them were interwoven with other books so that only seven additional books are found in the table of contents of a Catholic Bible. But what is *hidden* about these books? The Catholics would claim that they were hidden in a good sense, in order to be preserved, or the deeper truths were hidden to the unspiritual. The truth is that they were hidden in a bad sense, in that their genuineness was considered doubtful, and they were never accepted as Scripture until the Catholic Church adopted them as such fairly recently.

The study of which books belong in the Bible is often called a study of *canonization*. The word *kanon* was originally used by the ancient Greeks as a rod, ruler, staff or measuring rod. The Hebrew *kaneh* (reed) was an Old Testament term meaning measuring rod (see Ezekiel 40:3; 42:16). Later, the word came to be used as a standard for something, and early Christian usage applied the term to authoritative Scripture. The key point to keep firmly in mind is that canonicity is *determined* by God and simply *discovered* by man. The determination of which books really belong in the Bible is complex from the humanistic point of view, but quite simple from the godly point of view. The study of canonization has often focused on man's part of the process, since this is the part that people tend to question. However, God's part in the process is by far the most important. He uses men when they are willing to be used, and he works to accomplish his will in spite of them if they are not willing. If God has preserved the Bible during times when men were trying to destroy it (either literally or through higher criticism), then we have no reason to doubt that he was able to use men who had basically good intentions to collect and preserve it. We have exactly the books in the Bible that God wanted to be in it. But what does all of this mean in connection with the Apocrypha?

There are very good reasons the books do not belong in the Bible.

1. The Jewish people did not accept them as canonical, even though they were Jewish writings. The Jews did appreciate them from historical and literary viewpoints, but they did not believe them to be a part of the Bible. At least part of the reason was that these books did not fit into the divine chain from Moses to Malachi, having been written mostly during the intertestamental period. The Jewish Talmud stated: "After the latter prophets Haggai, Zechariah and Malachi, the Holy Spirit departed from Israel." (Michael L. Rodkinson, Tractate "Sanhedrin," *Babylonian Talmud*, VII-VIII, 24) Jesus expressed this same idea in Matthew 23:35 when he used the expression "from...Abel to...Zechariah." In the Hebrew arrangement of the OT, Abel was found in the first book of the Scriptures, and Zechariah in the last.

2. None of these books were quoted by Jesus or the New Testament writers.

3. The Council of Trent (1,500 years after Jesus!) was the first official Catholic proclamation on the Apocrypha, and this was an obvious move to fight against the Protestant Reformation.

4. Some teachings are clearly out of line with the teachings of the Old Testament and New Testament books, such as "prayers for the dead" (2 Maccabees 12:44-45).

5. Other accounts are more fairy tale than anything else (Bel and the Dragon).

6. Historical errors clearly exist. Tobit 1:3-5; 14:11 show Tobit being alive when the Assyrians conquered Israel in 722 B.C., and also when Jeroboam revolted against Judah in 931 B.C. However, his total life span was said to be only 158 years. Judith 1:1 has Nebuchadnezzar reigning in Nineveh instead of Babylon.

7. There is no claim of inspiration within the Apocrypha itself.

THE DOCTRINE OF ORIGINAL SIN

Much of the supposed Biblical basis for this doctrine comes from one passage—Romans 5:12-21. Although the passage is fairly lengthy, we will include it at this point because of its importance in relation to this doctrine.

[12] Therefore, just as sin entered the world through one man, and death through sin, and in this way death came to all men, because all sinned—[13] for before the law was given, sin was in the world. But sin is not taken into account when there is no law. [14] Nevertheless, death reigned from the time of Adam to the time of Moses, even over those who did not sin by breaking a command, as did Adam, who was a pattern of the one to come. [15] But the gift is not like the trespass. For if the many died by the trespass of the one man, how much more did God's grace and the gift that came by the grace of the one man, Jesus Christ, overflow to the many! [16] Again, the gift of God is not like the result of the one man's sin: The judgment followed one sin and brought condemnation, but the gift followed many trespasses and brought justification. [17] For if, by the trespass of the one man, death reigned through that one man, how much more will those who receive God's abundant provision of grace and of the gift of righteousness reign in life through the one man, Jesus Christ. [18] Consequently, just as the result of one trespass was condemnation for all men, so also the result of one act of righteousness was justification that brings life for all men. [19] For just as through the disobedience of the one man the many were made sinners, so also through the obedience of the one man the many will be made righteous. [20] The law was added so that the trespass might increase. But where sin increased, grace increased all the more, [21] so that, just as sin reigned in death, so also grace might reign through righteousness to bring eternal life through Jesus Christ our Lord.

By anyone's admission, this passage is one of the most difficult in the entire NT. In the case of difficult or obscure texts, the basic rule of interpretation is that you do not base a highly consequential doctrine on them, but rather look to other clearer passages. Under no circumstances should a doctrine based on a difficult passage be allowed to *contradict* plain passages. We may not be absolutely sure of the exact meaning of a text, but when compared to other less difficult texts, we can usually be sure of what it does not mean. In the case of Romans 5, these basic principles must be kept firmly in mind as we offer an interpretation.

Three primary interpretations of Romans 5 can be found in the writings and teachings of different religious groups. The first would be the concept of "original sin," as taught by the Catholic Church and a number of other churches as well. The doctrine claims that everyone is born guilty of the sin of Adam, and therefore everyone enters the world in a state of spiritual death. Infant baptism is then seen as a remedy to this problem. The second concept might be called the "original choice" concept. This explanation would argue that Adam introduced sin and Jesus introduced righteousness, and now we can choose which path we want to follow. In a sense, this is obviously true, but it does not fit well with the actual wording of Romans 5.

The view that I believe squares with both this passage and with others all through the Bible is one that we might call the "original consequence" view. The idea here would be that Adam introduced sin, which resulted in physical death for him, because he was shut out of the Garden of Eden where the Tree of Life was located (Genesis 3:22-24). He had been told, back in Genesis 2:16-17, that if he ate of that tree, he would surely die. This death penalty would have had to indicate or include physical death, because of the result that his sin brought. However, sin also separates man from God spiritually, and at the point of his sin, Adam experienced spiritual death as well. Romans 8:2 (the "law of sin and death"), and passages like Isaiah 59:1-2, refer to that principle.

What Adam did resulted in both types of death for him, and it certainly resulted in physical death for all of his descendants, since they were also barred from the Tree of Life. Therefore, his sin did affect us physically, as far as the *consequences* are concerned. But did his sin affect us spiritually in a way that makes us *guilty* of his sin? This is the real issue. Two passages in the OT are quite helpful on this point. In Exodus 20:5, God forbids idol worship with these words: "You shall not bow down to them or worship them; for I, the LORD your God, am a jealous God, punishing the children for the sin of the fathers to the third and fourth generation of those who hate me." Clearly, the consequences of a father's sins, be they idolatry or drunkenness, do hurt their families. But we are considering consequences, not actual guilt for another's actions.

Ezekiel 18:20 dispels the whole theory of inherited guilt. "The soul who sins is the one who will die. The son will not share the guilt of the father, nor will the father share the guilt of the son. The righteousness of the righteous man will be credited to him, and the wickedness of the wicked will be charged against him."

In 1 John 3:4, John says, "Everyone who sins breaks the law." Sin is a personal action for which only the sinner is responsible. Guilt cannot be passed on, but consequences can. If the President of the United States made decisions which brought the country into a war, we would likely not be responsible for his decision. We would, however, suffer the consequences. Therefore, we die physically because of Adam's first sin, but we die spiritually because of our own sins. But now, let's go back to Romans 5 and see if this explanation harmonizes with the teaching of this passage.

The early part of the chapter showed the efficacious effects of Christ's death for mankind. Paul's Jewish opponents were apparently arguing that Christ's death could not possibly affect every person in the entire world, as Paul was preaching. They felt that his emphasis on the work of Christ was far overstated and would discourage the personal responsibility of individuals. He countered by showing that even Adam had affected everyone, by sinning and being shut out of the Garden. Thus, we sinned in Adam in the sense that we share in the consequence of his actions.

The same basic analogy is found in 1 Corinthians 15:21-22 regarding the effects of Adam and Christ on all mankind: "For since death came through a man, the resurrection of the dead comes also through a man. For as in Adam all die, so in Christ all will be made alive." Compare this concept to a similar one in Hebrews 7:9-10 where the Levitical priests are said to have paid tithes in a representative manner through their ancestor Abraham when he paid tithes to Melchizedek: "One might even say that Levi, who collects the tenth, paid the tenth through Abraham, because when Melchizedek met Abraham, Levi was still in the body of his ancestor." It should be clear that the NT traces consequences back to our ancestors, but that is quite a different thing than tracing *our* guilt or responsibility back to *their* actions.

Much of Romans 5:12-21 discusses this type of *involuntary participation* on our part, in which we had absolutely no choice in the matter. Paul begins by showing that we die physically because of Adam's sin (verses 12-14). In verses 13-14, an interpretative paraphrase would go something like this: "Before the Mosaic Law was given, sin was in the world, but sin did not demand the death penalty where there was no such law stating it (as was the case before the Law, especially prior to the Flood). However, physical death still reigned between Adam and

Moses, even over those who did not have the command "sin and die" as did Adam. Therefore, the people in this period *must* have died because of Adam's sin rather than their own sins."

Then, verses 15-17 form a parenthetical explanation of how Jesus' impact on humanity is far *greater* than that of Adam. In verses 20-21, Paul concludes in a similar manner, showing the possibility of *voluntary participation* in the benefits of Christ's death. The "much more," the "gift," and "God's abundant provision of grace" refer to spiritual salvation which must be personally accepted. The "increased" sin in verses 20-21 refers to our own sins which bring spiritual death (but can be forgiven). Therefore, Adam affected everyone and Christ affected everyone. What we lost in Adam (life in a body), we gain back in Christ at the resurrection. However, Christ affected everyone much more (potentially) by also offering spiritual life.

The basic flow of Paul's earlier argument picks back up in verses 18-19. We are raised from the dead because of the death and resurrection of Christ. The "life" and being "made righteous" refer to being raised bodily, good and evil alike. The term "righteous" is used here in the sense of having the scales balanced out and earlier consequences offset. (The term does not always mean *spiritually* righteous, as Romans 5:7 demonstrates.) John 5:28-29 states: "Do not be amazed at this, for a time is coming when all who are in their graves will hear his voice and come out—those who have done good will rise to live, and those who have done evil will rise to be condemned."

The end result of Paul's line of reasoning is that he was not overstating the impact of Christ's work in man's behalf, and in the next chapter, he continues in a similar mode by dealing with the false charge that grace leads to a light view of sin (Romans 6:1-4). If the Jews could accept the universal impact brought about by Adam's sin, then they should have been able to apply the principle to Jesus and his work. This was especially a feasible idea when the factor of Christ's *Deity* was added to the formula!

Romans 5:12-21 is admittedly a very difficult chapter, but it cannot be interpreted in a way which causes it to contradict other clear passages. The interpretation which we have provided does seem to take these other passages into consideration, while attempting to deal honestly with the Romans text as well. To sum up this explanation, an interpretative paraphrase of the passage is now included.

[12] **Therefore, just as sin entered the world through one man** (Adam) and (physical) **death through sin, and in this way** (physical) **death came to all men, because all sinned** (representatively in Adam, as far as the *consequences* were concerned). [13] **For before the law** (of Moses) **was given, sin was in the world. But sin is not taken**

220

PREPARED TO ANSWERPREPARED TO ANSWER

into account (counted for the death penalty) **when there is no law** (demanding such a penalty). **[14] Nevertheless, (physical) death reigned from the time of Adam to the time of Moses, even over those who did not sin by breaking a command** (which carried the death penalty), **as did Adam, who was a pattern of the one** (Christ) **who was to come.**

[15] **But** (before we go on discussing the impact of Adam on the world, and how Christ offset that impact, let us understand that) **the gift** (of Christ's impact on the world) **is not like the trespass** (it is far greater!). **For if the many** (everyone) **died** (physically) **by the trespass of the one man** (Adam), **how much more did God's grace and the gift that came by the grace of the one man, Jesus Christ, overflow to the many** (everyone)! [16] **Again, the gift of God is not like** (not limited to) **the result of the one man's sin: The judgment** (consequences) **followed one sin and brought** (physical) **condemnation, but the gift followed many** (Adam's and our own) **trespasses and brought** (the possibility of spiritual) **justification.** [17] **For if, by the trespass of the one man,** (physical) **death reigned through that one man, how much more will those who receive** (by personal response) **God's abundant provision of grace and of the gift of righteousness reign in life through the one man, Jesus Christ.**

[18] (But let's return to our discussion of the impact of Adam's sin and how Christ's resurrection offset that impact.) **Consequently, just as the result of one trespass was** (physical) **condemnation for all men, so also the result of one act of righteousness** (Jesus' resurrection after a sinless life) **was justification** (from the death sentence) **that brings life** (in a body at the resurrection at the Last Day) **for all men.** [19] **For just as through the disobedience of the one man the many** (everyone) were made sinners (as far as the *consequences* are concerned), **so also through the obedience of the one man the many** (everyone) **will be made righteous** (from the death penalty, because they will be raised from the dead).

[20] (Now let's end this comparison by going back to the earlier idea of how Christ's impact did *far more* than offset the impact of Adam's sin—it ushered in the *opportunity* for spiritual life to all who accept it.) **The law** (of Moses) **was added so that the trespass** (each man's personal sins) **might increase. But where sin increased, grace increased all the more,** [21] **so that, just as sin reigned in death** (*physically* because of Adam's sin and *spiritually* because of our own sins), **so also grace might reign through righteousness to bring** (to those who choose it) **eternal life through Jesus Christ our Lord.**

Even when this Scripture is shown not to teach the doctrine of original sin, other passages are incorrectly used to support it, especially

Psalm 51:5. "Surely I was sinful at birth, sinful from the time my mother conceived me." This Psalm was written by David when he had faced his sin with Bathsheba, and was quite broken and repentant. The last thing that he was trying to do was shift the blame to his mother or anyone else. Contextually, original sin does not fit here. He was totally accepting responsibility by admitting that he had been born into a sinful world (verse 4) and had participated in its evil as long as he could remember. To make that point as strongly as possible, he used a figure of speech called *hyperbole*, in which a case is overstated for emphasis. The figure is used in other Psalms, such as Psalm 22:9; 58:3; 71:6. The passage in 58:3 is an excellent parallel, as it states: "Even from birth the wicked go astray; from the womb they are wayward and speak lies."

Another passage often used in an attempt to substantiate this doctrine is Ephesians 2:1-3. In verse 3, it says that "we were by nature objects of wrath." The word "nature" may refer to inborn nature or it may refer to acquired nature. In this context, the latter seems obvious, because the emphasis is on what we have done—our personal sins and sinful lifestyles—certainly not what *Adam* had done. The very idea that we could somehow inherit personal guilt for an act on the part of Adam raises numerous questions. One, why was there never a provision for granting forgiveness for this specific sin in any covenant of God with man? Not even the sacrificial laws of the Mosaic covenant, which covered all kinds of sins, ever mention this sin. Two, if our "fallen natures," which supposedly came from Adam's sin, now cause us to sin, why did Adam sin? Actually, he had much less temptations to deal with than we do at the time of his first sin. For example, he did not have a temptation to commit adultery or steal. He was tempted and sinned, just like us—no better or no worse. Three, why did we inherit only his *first* sin?

Perhaps the biggest fallacy in the whole idea of inherited sin ties in with our basic nature and how we became human beings in the first place. We receive our physical bodies from our earthly parents through the act of procreation. Thus, all that we can inherit from them are physical things. On the other hand, our spirits come directly from God, and only from him can we inherit spiritual things. In Zechariah 12:1, we read: "...The LORD, who stretches out the heavens, who lays the foundation of the earth, and who forms the spirit of man within him..." Ecclesiastes 12:7 speaks of both our bodies and spirits in this manner: "And the dust returns to the ground it came from, and the spirit returns to God who gave it." Hebrews 12:9 similarly reads: "Moreover, we have all had human fathers who disciplined us and we respected them for it. How much more should we submit to the Father of our spirits and live!" Therefore, we cannot inherit sin from our earthly fathers, for spiritual things (including our souls) come from our heavenly Father!

NEW TESTAMENT TEACHING ON WOMEN'S ROLE

1 Timothy 2:5-8

I want men everywhere to lift up holy hands in prayer, without anger or disputing. I also want women to dress modestly, with decency and propriety, not with braided hair or gold or pearls or expensive clothes, but with good deeds, appropriate for women who profess to worship God. A woman should learn in quietness and full submission. I do not permit a woman to teach or to have authority over a man; she must be silent. For Adam was formed first, then Eve. And Adam was not the one deceived; it was the woman who was deceived and became a sinner. But women will be saved through childbearing—if they continue in faith, love and holiness with propriety.

As we examine this passage, the first thing that stands out is a focus on *spirituality*. Men were to be holy, without hot tempers and disagreeable attitudes (verse 8). Women were to be modest in dress, adorned by good deeds (verse 8—see also 1 Peter 3:1-6 for similar admonitions). Were these commands intended to be *mutually exclusive*? That is, were *only* men allowed to pray in any type of assembly? The word for "men" here is not the one denoting *mankind*, from *anthropos*, but a reference to *males*, from *aner*. If we take the affirmative, then were *only* women to dress modestly and to practice good deeds? How could you bind one as law and not the other?

Women did apparently pray in mixed groups, according to Acts 1:14 and 1 Corinthians 11:3-16. We will look at the latter passage in detail later in this chapter. Clearly, men were to be the leaders in public services, but that would not *necessarily* rule out women praying in some type of format (such as a group prayer). Keep in mind that the focus of these directives was on the spirituality of the men and women in the Corinth church and their characteristic areas of need. The men needed to be harmonious in their relationships with one another, and the women needed to be modest in their dress and demeanor.

Next, we see a focus on *leadership*. The teaching here is not based simply on the culture of that day, for Paul goes back to the creation story to make his point (verses 13-15). The women are to show "full submission" (verse 11), which is a leadership issue that does not in any way demean women. It has nothing to do with value, intelligence or spiritual capacity. Submission is a necessary ingredient of life in many areas, but it demonstrates strength and not weakness! She is to learn in "quietness" (verse 11). The Greek word is not the one for "silence," as translated in some versions, and even in verse 12 in the NIV. The word for "silence" is found in 1 Corinthians 14:34, as we will see later. Actually, quietness is the correct translation of *hesukia*, and it refers to *demeanor* rather than *sound*! In 1 Thessalonians 4:11, the same Greek word is translated as "quiet life" in this phrase—"Make it your ambition to lead a quiet life, to mind your own business..." In 2 Thessalonians 3:12, it is rendered "settle down" in this sentence: "Such people we command and urge in the Lord Jesus Christ to settle down and earn the bread they eat." Then, in 1 Timothy 2:2, it reads: "...that we may live peaceful and quiet lives in all godliness and holiness." It should be clear that being quiet is a matter of character and behavior, not of audibility.

In verse 12, the women are forbidden to teach a man in a public setting in a manner which gives her *authority* over him. She can do some teaching in more private settings (with a submissive spirit, of course), for Priscilla had a part in teaching the eloquent Apollos (Acts 18:24-26). The real issue is having authority over a man, and in my judgment, she has the freedom to do *many* things without assuming authority. A wife has the freedom to do many things without assuming the authority of her husband. Why is the role of women in the church different in principle from the husband/wife relationship?

1 Corinthians 14:34-35

Women should remain silent in the churches. They are not allowed to speak, but must be in submission, as the Law says. If they want to inquire about something, they should ask their own husbands at home; for it is disgraceful for a woman to speak in the church.

To those with the more restrictive view of the woman's role, this passage seems to be proof-positive of their position. Of course, the charismatics think that this chapter is also proof-positive of their position on the use of miraculous spiritual gifts. But looking at passages without a consideration of their context produces all sorts of erroneous conclusions. Therefore, let's look at this text in its *context*.

Note that women were to be "in submission as the Law says." The Law here is likely a reference to the last part of Genesis 3:16, which reads: "Your desire will be for your husband, and he will rule over you." This desire for her husband is a negative in the context, perhaps a reference to her desire for his *position*. Compare the use of the word "desire" in Genesis 4:7. At any rate, the submission enjoined in 1 Corinthians 14:34 is enforced with a reference to the Law—the OT.

But just what did the Law allow generally in the case of women? Actually, it allowed a good deal more than the casual observer might think. It allowed Deborah to be a judge and to lead in battle (Judges 4:4-10). On the latter point, was her leadership allowed only because no man was willing to lead? Probably, but she exercised this leadership in a team situation with Barak, and I am confident it was done with a submissive demeanor! The Law also allowed Huldah to be a prophetess whose advice was sought by male leaders in 2 Kings 22:11-20. It allowed Anna to be a prophetess also, as seen in Luke 2:36-38. Whatever else may be said, the Law did not rule out women leadership, even very *prominent* leadership. Therefore, it would be *risky* to make too broad of an application from this passage!

In verse 34, *absolute silence* with *no speaking at all* was being demanded. Both the context and the meaning of the Greek word make this idea clear. The word is *sigao*, and its other usage will demonstrate the point. In Acts 12:17, the same word is translated "quiet," but the context shows what it means: "Peter motioned with his hand for them to be quiet and described how the Lord had brought him out of prison…" Then, in Acts 15:12, it says "silent": "The whole assembly became silent as they listened to Barnabas and Paul telling about the miraculous signs and wonders God had done among the Gentiles through them."

This command is found in an overall context of orderly worship (verses 26-40). Our word for "silence" is found three times in this section, and in each case, it means absolute silence without any speaking at all. In verses 26-28, those speaking in tongues were told that no more than three could speak at any assembly, one at a time, if an interpreter were present to interpret. If no interpreter was present, the tongue speaker was told to "keep quiet" in the church (from the word *sigao*, absolute silence). In verses 29-33, the prophets were told that no more than three prophets could speak at any one assembly, one at a time, and when the next to speak was given a revelation, the one speaking "should stop." (Again, this is the root word *sigao*—no speaking at this point.) Finally, in verses 34-35, the women were to "remain silent" in the churches (also from the root word *sigao*).

If this command were taken literally, with *no* attempt to determine the context, women would be forbidden to make any *sounds* at a public assembly. Of course, no one would interpret it in such an extreme way, but the reasoning is normally something like this: "Well, it cannot mean that the women are forbidden even to sing." Why *not*, if we insist on taking the passage at face value, with no real attempt to determine the meaning *in its context*! The word *sigao* means exactly that. It should be obvious that I do not take the traditional restrictive view, but what is the meaning of this directive in its context? Some questions raised and answered will be helpful in discovering the meaning.

First, *who* were the women being discussed in this passage? They were women who were disrupting orderly worship, acting disgracefully and not in submission. (Surely all the women present were not guilty of such behavior!) They were *married* women who could ask questions of their own husbands at home. From looking at 1 Corinthians 7, we know that there was quite a contingent of singles in the church at Corinth. However, only the married women are given the directive in chapter 14. At this point, many people will say "other women are included too." Of course, they have the liberty to *say* it, but we should keep in mind that it is their *opinion* and nothing more. God certainly appears to be addressing women *with husbands*! The word translated "women" is the Greek term *gune*, which can be translated either women or wives, depending on the context. This context seems clearly to be directed at *wives* and not women generally. Furthermore, these women appear to be a specific *group* of wives, the wives of the *prophets* and perhaps of the *tongue speakers* as well.

Second, what was their *wrongful speaking*? They were asking questions of their husbands (who were speaking), and thereby interrupting the assembly. In this contextual situation, it was disgraceful to speak in the church. However, to apply the passage more generally would be *assumptive*, and it would demand *absolute silence* on the part of women in assemblies if we stuck with the meaning of *sigao*. Unless the context is taken into consideration, you would have to forbid women even to sing! Therefore, 1 Corinthians 14 is dealing with a specialized situation which has little to do with the role of women generally (except to teach them not to disrupt services by asking questions).

It is tempting for those who want to reach their foregone conclusions without dealing with the context to take a very simplistic view, such as, "See, it plainly says that women must remain silent in the churches, and we need to simply accept that statement for what it says!" Those who take that approach often claim that an explanation like the one used in this present chapter is explaining away the clear and obvious truth. However, they themselves are accused of the same thing by the Pentecostals even within this same chapter! The Pentecostals quote verse 39: "Therefore, my brothers, be eager to prophesy, and *do not forbid speaking in tongues.*" Then they say that all of the explanation about why people do not speak in tongues today is simply a *dodge* of the *obvious* truth! The point is simply this: *just because a doctrine must be explained contextually and in some detail does not make it wrong!* Simplistic explanations of involved issues may sound *good*, but the conclusions thus reached may also be quite *erroneous!* Many examples of simplistic explanations which are quite wrong can be cited, including such false teachings as salvation by faith only, the literal thousand-year reign of Christ on earth and many others.

1 Corinthians 11:3-16

[3] Now I want you to realize that the head of every man is Christ, and the head of the woman is man, and the head of Christ is God. [4] Every man who prays or prophesies with his head covered dishonors his head. [5] And every woman who prays or prophesies with her head uncovered dishonors her head—it is just as though her head were shaved. [6] If a woman does not cover her head, she should have her hair cut off; and if it is a disgrace for a woman to have her hair cut or shaved off, she should cover her head. [7] A man ought not to cover his head, since he is the image and glory of God; but the woman is the glory of man. [8] For man did not come from woman, but woman from man; [9] neither was man created for woman, but woman for man. [10] For this reason, and because of the angels, the woman ought to have a sign of authority on her head. [11] In the Lord, however, woman is not independent of man, nor is man independent of woman. [12] For as woman came from man, so also man is born of woman. But everything comes from God. [13] Judge for yourselves: Is it proper for a woman to pray to God with her head uncovered? [14] Does not the very nature of things teach you that if a man has long hair, it is a disgrace to him, [15] but that if a woman has long hair, it is her glory? For long hair is given to her as a covering. [16] If anyone wants to be contentious about this, we have no other practice—nor do the churches of God.

In contrast to 1 Timothy 2, *this* passage has much to do with the issue of *customs* in the first century in the city of Corinth. At this time in Corinth, the wearing of a veil signified that the woman was an upright person, but the absence of a veil demonstrated the very opposite. Immoral women went without veils. Evidently, some Christian women were appealing to their elevation in Christ (Galatians 3:28) as an excuse for dismissing this customary dress for women. This connotation of the veil, or the lack of a veil, was a matter of custom at that *time* in that *place*, because back in Genesis 38:14-15, Tamar wore a veil, which apparently was the custom of *prostitutes*, since she was posing as one. Obviously, customs change with time.

What is the *veil* under discussion? The word for "cover" is from the Greek *katakalupto*, designating a woman's artificial covering. The word for "covering" in verse 15 is another Greek word, *peribolaion*, which refers to the hair as a natural covering. If you tried, as some have, to make the *covering* of the earlier verses the same as this one, then only *bald-headed* men could have prayed or prophesied, according to verse 4! Paul's point in verse 4 is that it is no more appropriate for a woman to refuse to wear her customary attire than for a man to wear a woman's garment (not that the men were really doing that). He states that if the women were going to discard the veil, then they might as well cut their hair (like the prostitutes) or even shave their heads (like the women accused of adultery).

What about the *angels* of verse 10? Although the question has little relevance to our discussion, it is a matter of curiosity. One good possibility is that the angels are *good* ones, who serve Christians (Hebrews 1:14). They would be offended, as would God himself, by the sisters' rejection of their veils, which were a "sign of authority." Another possibility is that these angels are *bad* ones, who lost their lofty positions with God because they did not stay in their submissive roles (Jude 6). If that interpretation is the one intended by Paul, the sisters had better learn from the angels' example of disobedience!

Thus far, what are the lessons for us in our setting? One, men and women are different by design, and this difference is not to be denied, either by dress or appearance. In verses 14-15, the issue seems not really to be the length of the hair, but the blurring of the sexes. That is always wrong, no matter what the specific customs may be. Two, custom is not to be discarded if the discarding hurts the influence of Christians with those whom they are trying to evangelize. If all prostitutes wore red dresses today, then Christian women should not wear them.

The most relevant issue in this text for our study involves the *praying* and *prophesying* of the women. In what context were they doing these things? If you were to take 1 Corinthians 14 out of its context, as many do, you would be forced to assign 1 Corinthians 11 to a setting where only women were present. Difficulties are readily apparent with such an assumption. For one thing, 1 Corinthians normally places the use of these particular spiritual gifts in a context of corporate worship (see 1 Corinthians 12:7-11, 28; 14:3-4). For another thing, the passage speaks of both men and women praying and prophesying. By what principle of interpretation can you limit one and not the other—the principle of *assumption*? Finally, why would women praying and prophesying need a "sign of authority" on their heads if the authorities to whom they were to show submission were not even present? Surely women did not have to wear veils with other women in a *private* setting.

I have no problem in assuming that their practice was based on the presence of supernatural gifts in the church and that women are no longer divinely directed to *preach* to a mixed audience (especially in view of 1 Timothy 2). But this passage strongly militates against the highly restrictive interpretation of 1 Corinthians 14 which would prohibit the sharing of a personal testimony. She cannot teach men the Bible in a public setting, thus taking an authoritative role, but *sharing* with a submissive demeanor is another matter, and I think a permissible one.

Several other areas of judgment about how to apply the principles of the woman's role need to be briefly addressed before closing this appendix. Can women serve as ushers and distribute communion to the assembly? It seem clear that such actions are issues of serving, not of exercising authority, unless a woman were the appointed leader in one of these functions and had to assume leadership over men. Our practice is mainly to use non-leader brothers for serving communion, as a way to encourage them as good disciples of Jesus. To use women for the same reason is an excellent practice. The *lead* usher should be a man, but women can surely serve as ushers.

Is it permissible for women to participate with men in chain prayers in devotional settings? As long as a man is in charge of the overall session, giving the instructions regarding procedure, then the women would not be in a leadership position. If they can comment in a Bible class setting with men and women present, then they can direct their comments to God in the presence of brothers and sisters. If men never hear women comment or pray, they are missing some very special spiritual encouragement.

How about women baptizing other women? Is that permissible? For some reason, this question stirs up a lot of emotions for some people when they first hear of this practice. But the reaction rises from an emotional concern more than from a Biblical concern. Matthew 28:19-20 commands disciples to make other disciples, baptize them and to train them after baptism. In the past, women have been able to do only two of the three things mentioned here. Why? *Tradition!* We have always said that any disciple can baptize, in contrast to the denominational practice of allowing only the clergy to baptize. But what we evidently *meant* is that any *male* disciple can baptize! It is time we followed our own statements. The Bible is totally silent on the subject, which allows us some freedom to choose. The practice does not necessarily give a woman authority, but even if it did, the authority would be over another woman. Can a woman baptize a man? Since the act can bond us in a special way, as seen in 1 Corinthians 1:14ff, it would not be an expedient practice. If men are present when women are baptizing women, a brother should be in charge of the overall activity. This will eliminate misunderstandings. But the practice of women baptizing those with whom they have studied is a very good one indeed!

APPENDIX IV

THE NEW AGE MOVEMENT

BY TOM JONES

In 1992, *The Celestine Prophecy* was released by a small publisher and sold for the most part in small, independent bookstores. Now, six years later, it is marketed by one of the world's most famous media conglomerates and has sold millions of copies, after running for weeks on the *New York Times* best-seller list. What is in this book that accounts for its phenomenal success?

A fictional work that could hardly be described as great literature, *The Celestine Prophecy* describes a man in search of an ancient manuscript that is supposedly to be found somewhere in the back country of Peru. In the process of searching for the manuscript, he learns "the nine great insights" needed for making life meaningful. While it is billed in its subtitle as an adventure, author James Redfield uses the novel as a device to communicate his own New Age theology. It is obvious from the sales of his book, and those of a massive number of other New Age titles, that people in our culture are very attracted to this message. It is meeting a felt need. A search of the Worldwide Web reveals hundreds of sites set up to disseminate New Age ideas. One can easily conclude that New Age religion is growing far faster than any traditional religious approach. This movement is on the cutting edge—thus, this new addition to *Prepared to Answer*.

But what does the New Age Movement teach? A Web page set up for supporters of Redfield's book summarizes "The Nine Insights" this way:

1) The awareness begins with a feeling of restlessness—an inner urging to find more meaning in life. As we respond to this inner prompting, we begin to notice the "chance coincidences"—strange synchronistic events in our life. We begin to realize that some underlying process is operating our life.

2) We take a look at the evolution of consciousness (thought) of humankind, and we begin to see everything in a larger prospective. We become conscious of our preoccupation with the material world and begin to seek a deeper meaning and purpose to our lives.

3) We begin to see our connectedness. We become aware of the subtle energy that infuses all things and the relationship we have with that energy. By consciously becoming co-creatures and choosing what we think, we can have a positive effect on our world.

4) We unconsciously compete for energy from other people and this competition underlies all conflicts. As we begin to become aware of these power struggles, we learn that there is, in Reality, no lack of energy—there is another Greater Source of endless energy.

5) The key to overcoming conflict is tapping into the Greater Source through the mystical experience. In this experience, we sense our connectedness and oneness with everything. This experience is available to everyone, as we allow ourselves to be filled with a sense of love.

6) Childhood traumas block our ability to fully experience the mystical. All of us carry wounding and false messages from our past. As we get in touch with our own personal control issues, we can begin healing the blocks of our past and transcending them.

7) Once cleared of our past traumas, we can build energy through contemplation and meditation. As we focus on our basic life question, we receive the guidance we need through intuition, dreams, and synchronistic connections that guide us in the direction of our own evolution and transformation.

8) Evolution can't be done alone, so practice uplifting those who cross your path. We are here to support and teach each other. Release addictive relationships, and integrate and embrace all parts of yourself, so that you become a whole person.

9) Our purpose here is to evolve consciously. As our planet evolves through greater technology, we are freed up to spend more time to evolve spiritually. As we spend more time connecting with our Higher Source, we experience a higher vibratory energy which nurtures ourselves, each other, and our planet. We eventually connect with God's energy in such a way that we become beings of light and the kingdom of heaven is manifested here on earth.

Redfield's work epitomizes New Age thinking, and is perhaps the most visible and popular of the New Age works. However, there are dozens of others, from the writings of actress Shirley MacLaine (*Out on a Limb*) to those of Thomas Moore (author of the best-selling *Care of the Soul*) and the prolific Depak Chopra.

The New Age Movement is not easy to describe. It is a broad, social, spiritual and intellectual movement, based in great part on the concepts found in Eastern religions—particularly Buddhism with some additions from Western evolutionary theory. It is believed to have taken its name from the optimistic belief that evolution has led us to the verge of a new age—the Age of Aquarius. While there is no one creed for New Agers, there are certain things that are generally true of its different manifestations:

1. Recognizing the Need for Spirituality

New Agers recognize that the emphasis on science, technology and material things has left modern man impoverished. Modern man extinguished Biblical faith and turned to secular humanism. But eventually, he found nothing there to meet the needs of his soul. New Agers recognize that there is another element in human beings that must be fed. As Redfield's second insight teaches, "We become conscious of our preoccupation with the material world and begin to seek a deeper meaning and purpose to our lives." Thomas Moore begins his book by saying: "The great malady of the twentieth century, implicated in all of our troubles and affecting us individually and socially, is 'the loss of soul.'"

Much as the mystery religions (including various Gnostic sects) attempted to the fill the spiritual vacuum of the first and second centuries, New Age theology attempts to do the same in our day. The New Agers' problem is not found in their description of man's need, but in the solution that they pose. One especially dangerous aspect of the New Age Movement is the way it sometimes gives new meanings to traditional Christian terminology. A Christian talking to a New Ager may think they are talking about the same things, when what you mean and they mean by the same word may be something quite different. (For example, they will sometimes speak of Christ, but when they use that terminology, they do not at all mean the incarnate Son of God. Instead, they have in mind the Christ we can all become—quite apart from faith in him, repentance and a new birth by the power of the Holy Spirit.)

2. Pantheistic View of God

New Age philosophies (like the Eastern religions from which they spring) are essentially monistic (meaning that everything is essentially one) and pantheistic (meaning God is all and all is God). Note Redfield's idea that the mature person senses "connectedness and oneness with everything." Shirley MacLaine describes an experience in an Andean mineral bath that demonstrates this idea:

> Slowly, slowly, I became the water...I was the air, the water, the darkness, the walls, the bubbles, the candle, the wet rocks under the water, and even the sound of the rushing river outside.

She goes on to write, "I am God, because all energy is plugged into the same source. We are all individualized reflections of the God source. God is in us and we are God."

In pantheism and in New Age theology, God is not the Creator, and he is not transcendent. God (or the eternal force) and the universe have both always existed. God is not the high and holy God of the Bible who is "wholly other" than those he has created. There is no great difference between God and man. As a result, adherents can define God in almost any manner they choose, something that is very attractive in our culture of independent and autonomous lifestyles. In New Age religion, you hear frequent admonitions to trust in "the god within you." How different this is from the words spoken by Isaiah:

> For this is what the Lord says—he who created the heavens, he is God, he who fashioned and made the earth, he founded it; he did not create it to be empty, but formed it to be inhabited—he says: "I am the Lord,and there is no other" (**Isaiah 45:18**).

> For this is what the high and lofty One says—he who lives forever, whose name is holy: "I live in a high and holy place, but also with him who is contrite and lowly in spirit, to revive the spirit of the lowly and to revive the heart of the contrite" (**Isaiah 57:15**).

The God of the Bible is the Lord and Creator, and there is no other. He is "high"; he is "holy"; he is "above" man. He loves man. He is committed to man. He revives and renews those who are humble and contrite, but the ultimate sin is found in confusing who man is with who God is. New Age theology may speak of man's spiritual needs. It may recognize that material possessions will never be enough. But as we hear their view of God, we must remember Paul's words to the Colossians:

I tell you this so that no one may deceive you by fine-sounding arguments (**Colossians 2:4**).

See to it that no one takes you captive through hollow and deceptive philosophy, which depends on human tradition and the basic principles of this world rather than on Christ (**Colossians 2:8**).

The god described by the New Age Movement is a god of man's own making. It is a god who is the product of man's speculations and philosophy. The god of the New Age Movement is not the true God who we see in the face of Christ. It is not the Father in heaven whom you need to love and obey. It is not the personal God who sends us his Son to bring us back to him.

3. Truth Found through Mysticism

Because there are no external standards or guidelines, truth is found through personal mystical experiences, and New Agers are open to almost any variety of these, including altered states of consciousness, astral travel, contact with spirit beings, channeling, use of crystals, meditation, mental telepathy, psychic healing, levitation and automatic writing, just to name a few. (Incidentally, most converts to the New Age movement do not come in through any kind of study or logical examination of a body of material. They are usually invited to an event where they are introduced to experiences like one of these.)

In New Age thinking, no one can define truth for you. No one can really correct your understanding. Both revelation and reason are rejected. In Redfield's insight, "We receive the guidance we need through intuition and dreams." New Agers have no concept of sin, and there is no conviction that the heart of man can profoundly mislead him. In Jeremiah 17:9, the Biblical prophet wrote: "The heart is deceitful above all things and beyond cure. Who can understand it?" New Agers will have none of that. Like the philosophers from the East, they believe that the greatest truths lie inside us. We are not in need of redemption or new birth. We just need to get in touch with the god within us. We are already one with him, and he is one with us. There is no need for outside revelation or a written standard.

Some New Age thinkers do not even like the word "truth." They see it as too rigid and too lacking in the fluidity needed to live a full life.

Listen to Thomas Moore:

> Truth is not really a soul word; soul is after insight more than truth. Truth is a stopping point asking for commitment and defense. Insight is a fragment of awareness that invites further exploration (Care of the Soul, p. 246).

Moore, a former Catholic monk who is still fond of quoting certain sayings of Jesus, has no use for this central idea in Jesus' teaching: "If you hold to my teaching, you are really my disciples. Then you will know the truth, and the truth will set you free" (John 8:31-32). New Age theology and Jesus could not be more at odds. New Agers see truth as harmful to the soul (or certainly not to be found in the standards of Jesus); Jesus sees it as the ultimate liberation.

4. No Need for Redemption or the Forgiveness of Sin

Because all is God and God is all, there is no separation between God and man. There is no gap to close. There is no sin for which to atone. For the New Ager, Isaiah was wrong when he wrote:

> But your iniquities have separated you from your God; your sins have hidden his face from you, so that he will not hear (Isaiah 59:2).

Being separated from God is an impossibility for New Age believers. Salvation (if the word is used at all) is not deliverance from one's sins. It is simply enlightenment or the gaining of insight. It is coming to understand that you are one with the universe and that you are already deity. As Redfield teaches: "We eventually connect with God's energy in such a way that we become beings of light and the kingdom of heaven is manifested here on earth." That connection with God's energy comes about through spiritual evolution, not through the death of a Savior, who gave his life on our behalf. Popular New Ager Neal Walsh (*Conversations with God, Book 1*) has everyone going to heaven, including Adolph Hitler. Newsweek magazine quotes one observer of various New Age philosophies as saying they advocate "religion without the hard parts."

5. No Moral Standard

For advocates of New Age philosophy, morality is the ultimate moving target. Any objective rule (like "adultery is wrong" or "lying is sin") is something rigid and ugly that interferes with the development of soul. Thomas Moore describes a woman he was counseling who was in a bad marriage. With his encouragement, she separated from her husband, moved into a new apartment and began dating other men. This whole experience led her to many discoveries about herself, which eventually led her back to her husband. The only rule seems to be that you need to do what is best for the development of your soul (however you understand that). Moore says that this woman's story shows us that caring for the soul will often take you to unexpected places (p. 89) (and quite possibly into bed with unexpected people!). Moore closes his book by saying that care of the soul "is not at all concerned with living properly." He writes,

> We care for the soul solely by honoring its expressions, by giving it time and opportunity to reveal itself, and by living life in a way that fosters the depth, interiority and quality in which it flourishes. *Soul is its own purpose and end* (p. 304, emphasis added).

"Soul is its own purpose and end." That is just another fine-sounding way of saying that the soul is its own god. And as its own god, it decides what is right and what is wrong for it.

All of this is totally at odds with Biblical revelation, where we find a definite standard of morality laid down. God clearly revealed what is right, what is loving and what is righteous. He has just as clearly revealed what is wrong, what is unloving and what is sinful. Paul's words in Romans 6 are a reminder of the consequences of ignoring God's truths or the rewards in embracing them:

> What then? Shall we sin because we are not under law but under grace? By no means! Don't you know that when you offer yourselves to someone to obey him as slaves, you are slaves to the one whom you obey— whether you are slaves to sin, which leads to death, or to obedience, which leads to righteousness (**Romans 6:15-16**)?

The Christian Response

As disciples considering the New Age Movement, we need to remember three things:

1. There is much about the New Age Movement that is not new at all. "Spiritual" teachers with an esoteric message who claimed to be enlightened and have a superior message to the apostles were found in the New Testament times. These "false teachers" are in the background of books like the Gospel of John, Colossians and 1 John. Gnostic teachers (from the Greek word *gnosis* which means "knowledge") attempted to infiltrate the church and hijack the gospel for their own purposes. The Biblical writers responded forcefully to this teaching, reminding their readers of the supremacy of Jesus, the efficacy of the cross and the need to face and deal honestly with sin. The first-century leaders were not intimidated by these men or their message. They saw in their teaching "human wisdom" (1 Corinthians 1-3), "fine-sounding arguments" and "hollow and deceptive philosophy" that was not at all rooted in Christ (Colossians 2:4, 8).

The false teachers were saying, "We have found something that you are missing." The Biblical response was: "We have Christ, and because he is the Cosmic Christ, we are missing nothing! Jesus is all-sufficient (see Colossians 1)!" The first-century equivalent of the New Agers might report some fantastic experience. "Such a person," Paul said, "goes into great detail about what he has seen, and his unspiritual mind puffs him up with idle notions" (Colossians 2:18), but his experience is no substitute for a real connection to the Head, who is Christ (v. 19).

2. Correct doctrine and correct life are still a powerful combination (1 Timothy 4:16). Even though the typical New Ager has rejected revelation, logic and reason, we should not doubt that the word of God is still living and active and can produce faith in anyone with an open mind to hearing the truth. Challenge the New Ager to read these "ancient spiritual documents" with an open mind. However, since New Agers are so oriented toward experience, we should prepare the way for the Scriptures by showing them a radical life in Christ, a robust confidence that God is at work within us and a fellowship of love and caring that far surpasses anything they have ever seen.

Many people have involved themselves in the New Age Movement because of a real desire to fill up a spiritual vacuum. They are looking for hope, for personal fulfillment and for spiritual experiences that have meaning. This search may lead them into a variety of strange practices, but because of their belief that everything is essentially "one," New Agers are often concerned for the environment, for animal rights, for an end to war and for the needs of the poor. Our compassion for and commitment to the poor, our all-pervasive spirituality and the racial diversity of God's kingdom will all speak powerfully to the New Ager with a good heart. Peter's advice to Christian wives of non-Christian husbands applies very well to our efforts to reach New Agers. We must in many ways win them over "without words." We must show them a genuine "experience" of real faith and heart.

Obviously, no New Ager will become a disciple until he opens his mind, accepts the Bible as the word of God, studies it and humbles himself before the God who is his Creator. But all evidence would indicate that we will not get him to that point without showing him something that is at the same time very different, very patient and very powerful.

Never will Paul's words to Timothy be more relevant than in our efforts to win the New Ager:

> And the Lord's servant must not quarrel; instead, he must be kind to everyone, able to teach, not resentful. Those who oppose him he must gently instruct, in the hope that God will grant them repentance leading them to a knowledge of the truth, and that they will come to their senses and escape from the trap of the devil, who has taken them captive to do his will (**2 Timothy 2:24-26**).

3. New Agers will become disciples! There is no one so far out, so into mystical experiences, so convinced that they are already one with God that they cannot be convicted by the Holy Spirit and brought to repentance. Many New Age writers ridicule Scripture, question all authority and express full confidence in their own opinions, but many followers of these writers can be shown the uniqueness of Jesus, the clarity of his message and the results that come when that message is believed and embraced. "I am not ashamed of the gospel, because it is the power of God for the salvation of everyone who believes" (Romans 1:16). Throughout the centuries, religious movements and philosophies have come and gone, but the message of the cross is still the power of God, and it still changes hearts of people from all kinds of backgrounds and experiences.

APPENDIX V

WATCHMAN NEE'S TEACHING ON SOUL AND SPIRIT: A FORM OF NEO-GNOSTICISM

A REVIEW BY GORDON FERGUSON

My Introduction to Watchman Nee and Witness Lee

In my first ministry job, I was one of several ministers on the staff of a local church. The main pulpit preacher was using terminology and concepts that were strange to my ears, which was significant, since I had just graduated from a very intense, two-year ministry training school in which we went through the whole Bible verse by verse and memorized hundreds and hundreds of Bible verses. What I was hearing sounded definitely different from biblical concepts and wording. Further inquiry led to discovering that the minister was reading books by Nee and Lee, and appeared to be rather drawn to what amounted to a "new teaching" in the churches of which I was a part.

I then purchased some of these books and read them, being struck quickly with the obviously allegorical approach to interpreting Scriptures. The allegorical approach to studying written documents certainly predated the Christian era, but it found its way into the Christian church fairly early. Philo, an Alexandrian Jew (20 B.C. to 42 A.D.), is credited with introducing this method of biblical interpretation to the Old Testament Scriptures. Origen (182-251 A.D.) was quite influential in spreading this method of interpreting the New Testament, as one of the early "Church Fathers." Augustine adopted a modified form of the system, and Jerome is said to be the main figure responsible for introducing it into the Roman church. But my most recent study, described in the following material, convinces me that Nee's system is also a form of neo-Gnosticism. Actually, the allegorical system of interpretation is quite closely related in a specific way to the Gnostic approach of interpreting the Scriptures, as we shall see.

Introductory Thoughts about Interpreting Nee

In Watchman Nee's classic book, *The Spiritual Man*, he combines three volumes into one comprehensive work, which well represents the school of theology that he has developed. The total number of pages in this compendium of his work is 694—hence a substantial work. The first chapter, *Spirit, Soul and Body*, forms much of the basis of what he writes later, and gives the reader the keys to interpreting and understanding the terminology used and the concepts they represent. It should be said that the terminology and concepts are unfamiliar to the average Bible reader, which suggests from the outset that we are being introduced to a system of interpretation developed by a man, rather than to the Bible itself. Instead of being taught biblical things in biblical terms, we are forced to learn a system before we can understand what is being taught about the Bible, and thus, this teaching must be run through the filter of the system of interpretation being employed.

A failure to learn the system makes a reading of Nee's work confusing and not really understandable to the uninitiated. For example, terms like "soulish" and "soulical" (neither of which are in the Bible or the English Dictionary) are used repeatedly. Soulish essentially represents worldly or non-spiritual attitudes and behavior, while soulical represents spiritual attitudes and behavior. Had Nee simply used the biblical terms themselves rather than inventing other terms, the book would be far more helpful to the average reader, and its errors more obvious. The insistence of using non-biblical terminology to represent fundamental teachings in Nee's system of theology is not only confusing and demands that the reader develop a familiarity with the system, it also introduces elements of Gnosticism—which will be explained later.

Spirit, Soul and Body: The Biblical Passages

This first chapter of the book lays the foundation for the rest of the book, and thus all quotes used from Nee come from Volume One, mostly Chapter One. A failure to understand the terminology and basic assumptions upon which it is based insures the reader's failure to grasp the rest of the book. With that in mind, I want to give a basic introduction to the theological system used by Nee. The two main passages which form the basis of the theology are the following:

1 Thessalonians 5:23: "May God himself, the God of peace, sanctify you through and through. May your whole spirit, soul and body be kept blameless at the coming of our Lord Jesus Christ."

Hebrews 4:12: "For the word of God is living and active. Sharper than any double-edged sword, it penetrates even to dividing soul and spirit, joints and marrow; it judges the thoughts and attitudes of the heart."

A few observations about these passages are in order: one, the mention of "soul" and "spirit" contained within one verse is only found in these two passages, and neither of them defines what is meant by the distinction. Hence, basing an entire system on one's interpretation of only two passages which are left divinely unexplained should raise eyebrows at the outset. Most biblical scholars do not elaborate upon this distinction, since it doesn't seem to be the focus of the passage, but they rather state what the overall emphasis of the passage appears to be (i.e., God saving us completely in 1 Thessalonians 5:23). The following comment by the College Press Commentary is typical of the type of explanations given:

That idea is further underlined with the combination "spirit, soul and body." Much discussion of this phrase has concerned whether it indicates that human beings are trichotomous, consisting of three distinct aspects described by these terms, or dichotomous, really consisting of two aspects, body and spirit. In favor of the former interpretation is the fact that all three terms are used here; in favor of the latter is the difficulty in distinguishing clearly between the meaning of "spirit" (*pneuma*) and "soul" (*psyché*). However, it must be conceded that Paul is not discussing the precise nature of humanity but is offering assurance of God's protection. The combination of three terms here is probably only intended as a means of underlining the comprehensive nature of that protection; it is no more a systematic presentation of human nature than is the combination "heart, soul, mind and strength" in Matthew 22:37; Mark 12:30; Luke 10:27. Paul, like the other New Testament writers, repeatedly indicates that God's purpose is to save the whole person, not just some part.

A representative example of what biblical scholars say about Hebrews 4:12 is as follows (from Expositor's Bible Commentary):

The Word of God is unique. No sword can penetrate as it can. We should not take the reference to "soul" and "spirit" as indicating a "dichotomist" over against a "trichotomist" view of man, nor the reference to "dividing" to indicate that the writer envisaged a sword as slipping between them. Nor should we think of the sword as splitting off "joints" and "marrow." What the author is saying is that God's Word can reach to the innermost recesses of our being. We must not think that we can bluff our way out of anything, for there are no secrets hidden from God. We cannot keep our thoughts to ourselves. There may also be the thought that the whole of man's nature, however we divide it, physical as well as nonmaterial, is open to God. With "judges" we move to legal terminology. The Word of God passes judgment on men's feelings (*enthymeseon*) and on their thoughts (*ennoion*). Nothing evades the scope of this Word. What man holds as most secret he finds subject to its scrutiny and judgment.

In other words, the main focus of these two passages is not to emphasize a distinction of soul and spirit, but to make a main point of practical application—namely, that God can save us entirely and that the Word of God exposes our inmost thoughts and motivations. Building a theological system on passages intended to provide practical motivations is highly suspect, to say the least. However, Nee has not only chosen a suspect approach, he has deemed it absolutely essential to our understanding of the Bible. A couple of quotes will illustrate that point:

> It is an issue of supreme importance for it affects tremendously the spiritual life of a believer (page 22).

> To fail to distinguish between spirit and soul is fatal to spiritual maturity (page 22).

It is obvious that Nee has not only developed a system of theology and interpretation, but it is equally obvious that he believes we cannot be spiritually healthy (or maybe spiritually saved) without seeing the Bible through the filter of his system. One brother, who came out of this background himself, said that it is not uncommon to hear the adherents to Nee's doctrine say that this issue is a salvation issue. Certainly, such strong assertions by Nee are both assumptive and arrogant, and insulting to the large body of believers who are either unaware of Nee's system or who have studied and rejected it upon biblical grounds. And as stated before, one of these grounds is the inclusion of certain Gnostic elements.

Spirit, Soul and Body: The System Introduced and Defined

It is important that we introduce the basics of Nee's theological approach and explanation of his terminology. Nee begins his explanation with the creation of man in Genesis 2:7, quoting from the American Standard Version: "And Jehovah God formed man of the dust of the ground, and breathed into his nostrils the breath of life; and man became a living soul." The term *soul* is from the Hebrew *nephesh*, which will prove to be very important in this study. Nee says that God breathing into Adam the breath of life meant that the breath of life became man's spirit, and when it came into contact with man's body, the soul was produced. Hence, the soul is the combination of man's body and spirit (and assumedly would not have been formed without the spirit). He states: "In other words, soul and body were combined with the spirit, and spirit and body were merged in the soul" (page 24). Another quote: "Soul is the organ of man's free will, the organ in which spirit and body are completely merged" (page 25). Thus, according to Nee, the soul chooses whether to go toward the flesh or the Spirit. We are told that the body gives us "world consciousness;" the soul gives us "self consciousness;" and the spirit gives us "God-consciousness." This interesting observation was made on page 27: "Before man committed sin, the power of the soul was completely under the dominion of the spirit...The spirit cannot itself act upon the body; it can only do so through the medium of the soul."

However, this observation was followed up by quoting Luke 1:46-47, which reads: "And Mary said: 'My soul glorifies the Lord and my spirit rejoices in God my Savior.'" This passage is typical of scores of passages which use soul and spirit interchangeably (which Nee denies strongly). In this case, we have a simple case of Hebrew parallelism, as any commentator will note. Hence, Nee uses a passage that makes a different case than the one he is trying to make. Nee's three-fold delineation of the supposed nature of both soul and spirit is this: Soul—the site of personality, consisting of will, intellect and emotions; Spirit—the site of conscience, intuition and communion (worship).

Biblical and Practical Inconsistencies

The word "soul" is used in a variety of ways biblically. Prior to Genesis 2:7, where man is said to be a "soul," animals, fish, birds and creeping things were all said to be "souls" (from *nephesh*). (Yet, they had no spirits to unite with their bodies to form their souls!) See Genesis 1:20-26 on the point of other animate life besides humans being souls. The word "creature" is most often the term used to translate *nephesh*. Thus, living "being" is a good translation for all of created animate life, including man. Furthermore, God himself is a soul (and has a soul):

Leviticus 26:11: "Moreover, I will make My dwelling among you, and My soul will not reject you."
Leviticus 26:30: "I then will destroy your high places, and cut down your incense altars, and heap your remains on the remains of your idols; for My soul shall abhor you."

Leviticus 26:43: "For the land shall be abandoned by them, and shall make up for its sabbaths while it is made desolate without them. They, meanwhile, shall be making amends for their iniquity, because they rejected My ordinances and their soul abhorred My statutes."

Psalm 11:5: "The Lord tests the righteous and the wicked, And the one who loves violence His soul hates."

Isaiah 42:1: "Behold, My Servant, whom I uphold; My chosen one in whom My soul delights."

Isaiah 53:11: "As a result of the anguish of His soul, He will see it and be satisfied; By His knowledge the Righteous One, My Servant, will justify the many, As He will bear their iniquities."

Zechariah 11:8: "Then I annihilated the three shepherds in one month, for my soul was impatient with them, and their soul also was weary of me."

In the Old Testament, as well as the New Testament, soul is often used to describe the inner part, or the spirit of man. *Nephesh* can describe only the man as a created being (like the animal, bird and fish world), or it can describe the part that is unique to man—the spirit.

Psalm 19:7: "The law of the Lord is perfect, restoring the soul; the testimony of the Lord is sure, making wise the simple."

Psalm 23:3: "He restores my soul; He guides me in the paths of righteousness for His name's sake."

Psalm 25:1: "To Thee, O Lord, I lift up my soul."

Psalm 30:12: "That my soul may sing praise to Thee, and not be silent."

Psalm 33:20: "Our soul waits for the Lord; He is our help and our shield."

Psalm 34:2: "My soul shall make its boast in the Lord; the humble shall hear it and rejoice."

Psalm 35:9: "And my soul shall rejoice in the Lord; it shall exult in His salvation."

Psalm 42:1-2: As the deer pants for the water brooks, so my soul pants for Thee, O God. My soul thirsts for God, for the living God; when shall I come and appear before God?"

Psalm 71:23: "My lips will shout for joy when I sing praises to Thee; and my soul, which Thou hast redeemed."

Psalm 94:19: "When my anxious thoughts multiply within me, Thy consolations delight my soul."

Psalm 103:2: "Bless the Lord, O my soul, and forget none of His benefits."

Psalm 108:1: "My heart is steadfast, O God; I will sing, I will sing praises, even with my soul."

Psalm 119:81: "My soul languishes for Thy salvation; I wait for Thy word."

Many other similar verses could be quoted, but why is this point important? The following quotes from Nee answer that question.

The spirit lies beyond man's self-consciousness and above his sensibility. Here man communicates with God (page 29).

The revelations of God and all the movements of the Holy Spirit are known to the believer through his intuition (page 32).

God is not apprehended by our thoughts, feelings or intentions, for He can only be known directly in our spirits (page 32).

Implications from the above quotes:

1. If the spirit lies beyond man's "self-consciousness" (his soul), and is the only place where man can communicate with God, the Psalmist was poorly informed of such.

2. If the revelations of God and all the movements of the Holy Spirit are only known through the intuition (which is a part of the spirit, not the soul—by Nee's definition), then the Psalms are mistaken.

3. If God cannot be known directly through our souls, the Psalmist is again mistaken.

These kinds of contradictions will always occur when the Bible is forced into an artificial system of interpretation. Other contradictions:

1. Before conversion, one cannot distinguish between soul and spirit (page 34).

2. Yet, on the same page, we are told: "The New Testament does not consider those with a sensitive conscience, keen intellect or a spiritual tendency to be saved individuals." (If conscience is a function of the spirit and is based on the intuition, which cannot be distinguished prior to conversion, how can the conscience become "sensitive"?)

3. If the revelations of God and the work of the Holy Spirit can only be known through his intuition, one's personal insight is exalted above the statements of Scripture. (Dictionary definition of intuition: "knowledge or conviction gained by intuition. The power or faculty of attaining to direct knowledge or cognition without evident rational thought and inference.") Such a conclusion is both unbiblical and dangerous.

The Soul and Spirit of Man in Normal Biblical Usage

Spirit refers to man's inner being, made in the image of God. Soul may refer to the animate life itself, or to man's inner being—depending on the context. Some Old Testament verses use Hebrew parallelism to show the interchangeable nature of soul and spirit, when soul is used to refer to man's inner being.

> **1 Samuel 1:15:** But Hannah answered and said, "No, my lord, I am a woman oppressed in spirit; I have drunk neither wine nor strong drink, but I have poured out my soul before the Lord."
> **Job 7:11:** "Therefore, I will not restrain my mouth; I will speak in the anguish of my spirit, I will complain in the bitterness of my soul."
> **Isaiah 26:9:** "At night my soul longs for Thee, indeed, my spirit within me seeks Thee diligently; for when the earth experiences Thy judgments the inhabitants of the world learn righteousness."

The New Testament is even clearer in its interchangeable usage of the terms soul and spirit:

> **Matthew 10:28:** "And do not fear those who kill the body, but are unable to kill the soul; but rather fear Him who is able to destroy both soul and body in hell." (According to this passage, man cannot kill the soul.)
> **Matthew 22:37:** "And He said to him, 'You shall love the Lord your God with all your heart, and with all your soul, and with all your mind.'"
> **Matthew 26:38:** "Then He said to them, 'My soul is deeply grieved, to the point of death; remain here and keep watch with Me.'"
> **Luke 1:46:** "And Mary said: 'My soul exalts the Lord.'"
> **Acts 2:27:** "Because Thou wilt not abandon my soul to Hades, nor allow Thy Holy One to undergo decay."
> **2 Corinthians 1:23:** "But I call God as witness to my soul, that to spare you I came no more to Corinth."
> **Hebrews 6:19:** "This hope we have as an anchor of the soul, a hope both sure and steadfast and one which enters within the veil."
> **Hebrews 10:39:** "But we are not of those who shrink back to destruction, but of those who have faith to the preserving of the soul."
> **James 5:20:** "...let him know that he who turns a sinner from the error of his way will save his soul from death, and will cover a multitude of sins."
> **1 Peter 2:11:** "Beloved, I urge you as aliens and strangers to abstain from fleshly lusts, which wage war against the soul."
> **2 Peter 2:8:** "...for by what he saw and heard that righteous man, while living among them, felt his righteous soul tormented day after day with their lawless deeds."
> **3 John 1:2:** "Beloved, I pray that in all respects you may prosper and be in good health, just as your soul prospers."

Many observations could be made on the preceding passages, but a mere reading of them pretty much makes the point. Trying to force biblical terminology to fit a system imposed upon it always leads to confusion and false teaching.

Dangers of Watchman Nee's Teaching (and those patterned after him)

His teaching is a system which is based on his theology and terminology, and cannot be understood without first being trained in that terminology. Thus, instead of just studying the Scriptures, time must be taken to study the philosophy of a man. Many of his teachings are merely assumptions and opinions, and yet are emphatically declared by him to be Scriptural. The essential ingredients of Gnosticism are present in both subtle and blatant forms.

Gnosticism (which was present in incipient forms in many places in the New Testament) has the following characteristics: the name comes from the Greek word, *gnosis,* for knowledge. It is built upon the premise that anything material was bad. In the realm of personal practices, the NT contains two manifestations of it: asceticism (see 1 Timothy 4:1-3 and Colossians 2:20-23) and libertinism (see 2 Peter 2:13-22 and Jude). The reasoning was that since the flesh was inherently bad, either deny it or indulge it. In the latter viewpoint, as long as you had the right knowledge (gnosis), what you did with the body didn't matter. In defining the nature of Christ, those with Gnostic tendencies denied that he could have come in the flesh. He just "seemed" to be in the flesh. We call this the Docetic doctrine. The Apostle John attacks this heresy in no uncertain terms in 2 John 1:7: "Many deceivers, who do not acknowledge Jesus Christ as coming in the flesh, have gone out into the world. Any such person is the deceiver and the antichrist."

Furthermore, and this is where Nee's and Lee's teachings especially converge with Gnosticism, those who succumbed to Gnosticism believed that they had a special insight to spiritual knowledge, and saw their insight (intuition) as more important than the Bible's specific teaching. They were very prideful and looked down on those who just simply clung to the specifics of the Bible. They had the idea that, in spite of what the Bible seemed to say on certain points, they had been given the illumination of the true will of God. (They could read between the lines to get the *real* meaning God intended.) This tendency is seen in some of the Christians in Thyatira, according to Revelation 2:24: "Now I say to the rest of you in Thyatira, to you who do not hold to her teaching and have not learned Satan's so-called deep secrets (I will not impose any other burden on you)." In other words, these people claimed to have the "deep teachings of God," but God said that they actually were holding to the "deep teachings of Satan!"

Nee's form of Gnosticism comes through the development of a rather complicated system, with its own specific terminology, which means that the uninitiated cannot really grasp the "deep teachings" of God. The focus on the intuition as the real means of grasping truth, rather than through the specifics (including the wording) of Scripture, is a definite type of Gnosticism, complete with its arrogance and exclusivity (regardless of intentions to the contrary). His claims that the conscience is based on one's intuition opens wide the door for being directed by a supposed inner voice from God, rather than taking God's written Word as the true basis of conscience training. The conscience is only as accurate as the training upon which it is based (see my recent article on this subject, entitled "Matters of Conscience: a Deeper Look").

The allegorical approach to interpretation is a part of the discovery of so-called "deeper truths." For one example, Nee, on page 29, compares the three-fold nature of man to the three parts of the temple (outer court, Holy Place, Most Holy Place)—as if God had made the comparison. Such allegorization is common to Nee and Witness Lee. Mentioning Witness Lee, who picked up the torch of Nee's theology, Lee is even more blatant in his Gnostic statements. Consider the following quotes from *The All-Inclusive Christ*:

> First of all, I would ask you to realize that according to the Scriptures all physical things, all the material things that we see, touch, and enjoy, are not the real things (Chapter 1, page 7).

> ...material objects: we are eating food, drinking water, putting on clothes; we are living in our houses and driving in our cars. I would ask you to realize and remember well that all these things are not real (Chapter 1, page 7).

> What about the earth? There was chaos upon the earth. Waste and void and deep waters were upon it. It was buried under the deep. So God came in to work; God began to recover the earth...Then He divided the water from the earth, and the earth came out from the waters on the third day. It was the third day when the Lord Jesus Christ came out of the depths of death. So, you see, this is a type. On the third day God brought the earth out of the waters of death. From this type you can realize what the earth is. The earth, or the land, is a type of Christ (Chapter 1, page 10).

Whenever you want to do something, whenever you enjoy
something, whenever you use something, you must immediately apply Christ. For instance, you are sitting on a seat. Do you
realize that this is not the real seat? This is but a shadow, a figure
point to Christ. Christ is the real seat. If you do not have Christ,
it means that in your entire life you have never had a seat. There
is no rest for you. You have nothing to rely upon. You have
something false, for Christ is the real thing (Chapter 2, page 19).

These quotes from Witness Lee show us two important pieces of
this dangerous, Gnostic-type teaching. One, the alleged lack of realness
of material things is very Gnostic in nature. Two, the typology (allegorization, in this case) is merely speculative, but a part of so-called deeper
truths. The only way we can be sure that an allegory is intended in Scripture is when the writer makes an allegorical application. For example,
in Galatians 4:24-26, God inspires Paul to use the following allegory:

These things may be taken figuratively, for the women represent
two covenants. One covenant is from Mount Sinai and bears
children who are to be slaves: This is Hagar. Now Hagar stands
for Mount Sinai in Arabia and corresponds to the present city
of Jerusalem, because she is in slavery with her children. But
the Jerusalem that is above is free, and she is our mother.

When God inspires a biblical writer to use an allegory and make an
application that we might not have otherwise thought of, that is his pre-
rogative. When non-inspired men do the same thing, they are assuming
what God has not said and are in danger of adding to the Scripture and
of being false prophets. Additionally, and this is not necessary Gnostic-
related, Lee is clearly premillennial in his interpretation of prophecy
(which I believe to be false, in spite of its popularity in the Evangelical
world).

Concluding Observations

Upon a close examination of the theology of Watchman Nee and
those who ascribe to his theology, I believe it to be biblically erroneous in
many ways, and thus clearly dangerous. This is not to say that the faulty
exegesis and danger was in any way intentional by him, nor is it to say
that his followers are intentionally deceived and deceptive, or unspiritual
in their overall desires or actions. However, regardless of intention, false
doctrine is false doctrine and therefore dangerous.

Recently, I heard a disciple commenting on Nee's books, saying
that they were "deep" and contained things that he never would have

thought of. I told him that there was a good reason for that—the Holy Spirit never thought of them either! But this brother provides a good example of how reading subtle but erroneous teachings can influence those without a real foundation of biblical knowledge. My hope and prayer is that this study can be profitable to those who have unknowingly ascribed to a false system of theology, and that it will help them to decide to adopt a much simpler and more accurate approach to Bible study by being willing to call Bible things by Bible names and accept the simple teachings of God's plan of salvation.

MATTERS OF CONSCIENCE: A DEEPER LOOK

BY GORDON FERGUSON

Common Misconceptions

The study of conscience biblically is a very interesting study, due partly to how misunderstood the subject actually is by many. For example, it is common to hear the old (mistaken) adage, "The conscience is a safe guide." It wasn't a very safe guide for Paul, who said before the Sanhedrin that he had "fulfilled my duty to God in all good conscience to this day" (Acts 23:1). That resulted in a slap in the mouth at the command of the High Priest, but it had resulted in something far worse prior to this—he had helped kill Christians while believing that it was a service to God. He later stated in 1 Corinthians 4:4: "My conscience is clear, but that does not make me innocent. It is the Lord who judges me." The conscience is a safe guide, only to the extent that it is properly trained by the Word of God.

Through the years, I have encountered several misunderstandings of just how the conscience was designed to function by God. Recently, I studied the Bible with a person who was deeply immersed in the teachings of Watchman Nee, teachings that I would call "neo-Gnosticism." (See Appendix V, "Watchman Nee's Teaching on Soul and Spirit: a Form of Neo-Gnosticism.") Essentially, his teaching is based on making a very sharp distinction between soul and spirit, and building an entire system on this distinction, which is very confusing to anyone not familiar with his system and its terminology. But as it relates to the subject of conscience, he says that the conscience is based on the intuition component of the spirit, which ushers in a type of Gnosticism by claiming to have something of a direct pipeline to God's truths through hearing his voice in our inner self. Many religious people believe that God somehow speaks directly to their spirits, in a way that is better felt than told, and their consciences are often quite misled as a result.

Another misunderstanding, or in this case, blatant misuse, occurred with a ministry acquaintance of mine who often played the "conscience card" if his opinions weren't carrying the day. If his ideas were accepted, he was happy; if they weren't, he had a "conscience" problem with the directions chosen by the rest of the leadership group, of which he was a part. This frequent appeal to conscience was nothing short of manipulation, and it probably won't surprise you to hear that he didn't keep his job long.

A Historical (almost hysterical) Example

Another misunderstanding and misuse of conscience takes me back to my old days in the Mainline Church of Christ. In that setting, a number of older leaders often mistook an immature or untrained conscience for a *sensitive* conscience, which supposedly demonstrated a high level of spirituality. As an anecdotal teacher, I can't help sharing an amusing incident in my life that illustrates this point all too well. Back in the late 1970s, I was preaching for a church, deep in the heart of the Bible Belt. Once, I took a week's vacation to go with my father and my young son on a hunting trip, during which time I didn't shave. Although beards were none too popular for ministers to have in those days, I decided to let mine grow for a while. And the negative reaction by some church members to my sporting a beard was nothing short of amazing! I suppose the "Hippie" years were in the too-recent past for them to see beards and rebellion as anything other than inseparably connected.

I remember one older member asking to meet with me, and he started the meeting with the question of whether anyone had ever told me that I was hard to get to know. I was trying to validate his evident feelings in any way I could, but unsure of just where he was coming from with such a question. About half an hour later, I figured it out. In essence, he said that he thought he knew me and that I was a great guy—but then I grew the beard, which showed that he didn't know me at all! Wow, that was an enlightening conversation! But it did show me how deeply some prejudices ran in that church at that period of history.

After a fairly short time, I shaved off the beard, but I was determined to address the issue of how I had supposedly "violated the consciences" of many members with my beard. It was obvious to me that the understanding of Paul's writing in 1 Corinthians 8-10, along with Romans 14, was woefully lacking. About six months later, I preached a sermon entitled, "The Sin of Beards and Bowties." At the time, large butterfly bowties were still on sale in stores, but quite out of style anyway (except to one announcer on a local TV news station). The night I preached the sermon, I wore one of the floppy things, and I knew that a young ministry student with a beard would be sitting in his normal place in the second row in front of the pulpit. Thus, I had the props all set up for my sermon!

I began the sermon by talking about the importance of example and influence, and the sin of causing brothers to stumble (an oft-repeated claim in situations like mine). The "Amens" started pretty early that night. I went on to show the biblical basis for not offending our brothers, by simply reading a number of verses in the chapters mentioned above. If you would like to read them, they are, in the order read: 1 Corinthians 8:1-2, 9, 12-13; 1 Corinthians 10:23-24, 32; Romans 14:13, 15, 19-21; 1 Corinthians 9:3-7, 11-15, 19-22; 1 Corinthians 10:31-33; and finishing with 1 Corinthians 11:1: "Follow my example, as I follow the example of Christ." I ended the readings with this statement: "If my bowtie bothers you, I ought to take it off; if Ralph's beard bothers you, he ought to cut it off! The chorus of "Amens" rose to a new level—quite a number of people were evidently rejoicing to see that I had finally seen the light! My next statement was that since it had been a very short lesson up to that point (about 7-8 minutes, as I recall), surely there must be other things on the subject to notice and study out in the context of the passages read.

From there, since the last passage I read was 1 Corinthians 11:1, I talked about the example of Christ in his earthly ministry. Certainly Jesus, like Paul, gave up many rights to influence people for good. Matthew 20:28 is a good passage on this point, as it states that "the Son of Man did not come to be served, but to serve, and to give his life as a ransom for many." Another good one is Matthew 12:20: "A bruised reed he will not break, and a smoldering wick he will not snuff out." However, some of the things Jesus did do seem to point in another, somewhat contradictory, direction. For example, Jesus often healed on the Sabbath Day. Exodus 20 and Deuteronomy 5 were very explicit—work six days and do no work on the Sabbath day. In fact, the Jews cut their teeth on the teaching that they shouldn't do anything on the Sabbath that they didn't absolutely have to do. It is not a mystery why some might have seen Jesus' work on the Sabbath as at least questionable. Yet, Jesus seemed to make a point of healing on the Sabbath. Sometimes, Jesus disrupted those gathered in the temple or the synagogues for the purpose of worshiping God to the extent that bedlam ensued.

Don't you think the people had at least some reasons for their feelings? There were six other days in which Jesus could have healed, but he insisted on Sabbath day healings! Even a more amazing situation was when the apostles picked grain on the Sabbath. Go back and read Exodus 16, which contain some very strong warnings about doing much

of anything on the Sabbath. Also read Numbers 15:32-36, where it describes a man being stoned to death at the command of God, simply
for gathering wood on the Sabbath day! What would you have thought
about the disciples gathering grain on the Sabbath day if you had grown
up with these passages? They could have prepared food the day before—
Israelites had been doing it for hundreds of years. Furthermore, Jesus
was criticized for the kinds of people he associated with, including prostitutes. (Likely, a minister in my 70s setting would have caused some
serious buzz through such associations!) He was also accused of being
a glutton and drunkard—but he didn't quit eating or drinking. The fact
that his behavior and practices drove some up the wall didn't stop him
from doing it. Why did he continue? We will answer that question a bit
later in the article.

The Importance of Context

Studying passages in their context is a must, especially when sensitive subjects are involved or when addressing misunderstood texts. Look
back at 1 Corinthians 8:4, 7-13, where the context gives a deeper insight
to this subject of influence. First, notice in verse 9 that the wrong use of
influence could cause someone to *stumble*. Verse 11 states that it could
cause them to be destroyed. (Romans 14:15 uses similar terminology.)
We must understand that there is a difference in causing someone to
grumble, and in causing them to *stumble*. Second, 1 Corinthians 8:9-10
shows exactly how someone was caused to sin in this setting. Bottom
line, they see your example and end up doing the same thing, but their
conscience won't allow them to do it without seriously damaging them.
So, to make the application to beards and bowties, it would mean, contextually, that my example or Ralph's example caused someone to wear
a bowtie or grow a beard when their conscience wouldn't allow it without producing guilt!

Third, note that the weak person is the one that is caused to stumble, not the strong person. My experiences growing up often showed the
supposed spiritually mature brothers raising issues about nearly everything, and thus backed others off on a given choice so that they wouldn't
be caused to "stumble." Frankly, those men were only grumblers, and
actually should have been the focus of church discipline, because in the
words of Titus 3:10, they were divisive. Fourth, Romans 14 makes the
other three points, but gives one additional point. It's about the attitudes
the strong should have toward the weak, and also about the attitudes the
weak should have toward the strong. Read verses 1-10 to grasp Paul's
line of reasoning. Note that in verse 1, we are dealing with matters of
opinion. The strong brother should not discount the conscience of the
weak brother. The weak brother, on the other hand, should not judge

the strong brother who has the stronger conscience and the freedom that goes with it. Either way, Romans 14 gives a clear call for tolerance towards each other. It should be quite obvious that my hearers in the long ago had looked at these passages in a surface way, and had often given some incomplete or even wrong applications of them. To summarize: (1) Paul was talking about causing someone to fall away; (2) the way that they were made to sin was by following someone's example when their conscience wouldn't allow it; (3) the weak person was the one caused to stumble, not the strong one; and finally, (4) in matters of opinion, we must develop and exercise tolerance toward one another with different viewpoints.

But how do we harmonize what Paul taught here with the examples of Jesus already noted? Paul is dealing with young Christians, whereas Jesus was dealing with those who were supposedly mature. Paul was arguing for giving the immature time to grow, while Jesus was not willing to placate the ones who claimed to be mature—the keepers and defenders of the law of God! I have found that the young are typically not the ones upset about such things as beards and bowties—they haven't had time yet to become traditionalized. It is most often the supposedly mature who appeal to conscience being violated.

In my lesson of long ago, I went on to discuss possible objections, which although strongly felt, were emotionally based instead of biblically based. I decided, as a result of that study, that I would try to imitate both Paul and Jesus. In a nutshell, I wanted to be very careful with those who were newer Christians and thus immature in their faith, but not be manipulated by older Christians who were not willing to change their minds and alter their consciences. Real maturity is a willingness to entertain the possibility of being wrong—of having a conscience that needs further training. Digging in one's heals in the kinds of issues that Paul would call matters of opinion is not a very mature practice. Hardening of the arteries is probably an inevitable part of aging; hardening of the attitudes should never be.

Consciences Can and Should Be Retrained

All in all, I would never advocate someone violating their conscience, even in an opinion area. I believe that is what Paul was warning against in the passages referenced. However, I will always try to help someone retrain their conscience in opinion areas. The reason I make this distinction and feel strongly about it is intensely personal. I was raised in a church of about 30 people, all of whom believed sincerely that taking communion from multiple cups, having more than one tray of bread passed and dividing the assembly into Sunday-school classes were all sinful practices. We were technically called a "One cup, no Sunday-school" type of Church of Christ. Once, we debated for six months whether we could change from using grape juice in communion to using wine, in order to have one couple join us on Sundays who were driving to another city to worship with a "wine, one cup, no Sunday-school church." Although I was a preteen at the time, or maybe a young teen, I still vividly remember some of the heated conversations between my parents and other members of that little church. The memories are not good ones, but after a number of decades, sometimes they can seem at least a little humorous. During those conversations, the questions of violating consciences came up often.

When I married at the ripe old age of 22, my (then) Baptist wife wanted us to attend church together. We at first agreed to switch off attending each other's church, which we did for a few months. When it was time to attend the Church of Christ, I chose one of the more typical ones, with multiple cups and Sunday-school, thinking that the little church of my childhood would be so different from what she was used to that it would seem too weird to her. After a few months, I just couldn't go to the Baptist church anymore, knowing how far off they were on the subject of salvation. In one service with a guest preacher, he had everyone close their eyes, and then asked those who wanted to accept Jesus to simply raise their hands. He kept telling us that people were being saved as they raised their hands. Although I honestly wasn't interested much in going to church anyway, I just couldn't stomach what I was observing in the Baptist church, and I told Theresa that I wasn't going to go with her anymore.

That could have been the end of it, and I could have used my Sundays for fishing—which was more to my liking anyway! But she said that she would just go with me to the Church of Christ (which was not particularly good news to me). But we started visiting various Mainline Churches of Christ at her insistence. It is a fact that the Baptist church teaching on salvation violated my conscience, based on passages about baptism and forgiveness of sins. And I believe that my conscience was correctly educated on that matter. It was not a matter of opinion.

However, like the folks being addressed in 1 Corinthians 8 and 10, I had conscience issues about other matters that were not as clear biblically—notably, the use of multiple cups and Sunday-school (which Paul could have called "disputable matters.") Fortunately for me, I became friends and fishing buddies with a preacher whom God used to change my life and my eternal destiny. I have written about him in the introductions of my books on *Surrender* and *Romans*. He introduced me to other Scriptures about conscience and patiently helped me think through it all. He basically said that conscience shouldn't be violated, but it could be re-educated, noting that those addressed in passages like 1 Corinthians

8 and 10 and Romans 14 were younger Christians with weak consciences in areas related to their backgrounds. Those like Paul had stronger consciences, which meant, in essence, that they had better trained consciences. I'm sure one of the passages my friend used was 1 Corinthians 4:4, which we have already quoted.

While abiding within the boundaries of our conscience is important, the conscience is not always correct in its conclusions, however strongly the conclusions may be felt. With my friend's help, I was able to retrain my conscience and accept a number of teachings that once violated my conscience. Those same principles he taught me served me well when I first encountered the discipling movement, and then later became a part of it. I did not violate my conscience (although at times it got "stretched" a bit!), but I did seek to ask the hard questions and try to deal with them biblically, and then prayed that God would help my conscience change in ways that it really needed to—moving from what would be classified as "weak" to "strong" (or at least "stronger" as the process continued).

Current Trends

In recent settings, I am hearing more about conscience than I have heard in a long, long time. Perhaps that is because some (most?) of us violated our consciences in our movement's past. But we have had far too many pendulum swings in the last several years, and this may well be among them. I would hope that matters of conscience would become more and more confined to biblically clear matters, not simply to what Paul calls disputable matters. People need retraining of their consciences far more than the strengthening of them in opinion areas. In the Mainline Church, we used to have an old saying: "In matters of faith, unity; in matters of opinion, liberty; and in all things, love." The problem I found with some folks was that their definition of faith issues was really broad. They didn't like to admit that very much of what they believed belonged in the opinion arena. The practical result was most often that they were able to hold others at bay—those who had different opinions. Otherwise, they reasoned, we would be asking them to violate their consciences.

I am not the judge of anyone's conscience. As Paul said, God is the one who judges. I am just pleading for consideration of possible weaknesses in how we are viewing conscience and conscience issues. My plea grows largely out of some of my own experiences in trying to work with others, and from my experiences in needing to retrain my own conscience—a painful but highly rewarding experience, for which I am most grateful. Had I not been open to that, I believe my life would have gone in quite different directions than it has, and I'm so thankful that my preacher friend (now deceased) was patient and loving enough to help me get past some things that were at first very difficult to deal with due to my background. And I do believe in looking back that my conscience was simply improperly trained in some areas, and hence, according to Paul's definition, it was weak. As we mature, I think our opinion areas should become less important to us. Learning to properly identify the differences between opinion and faith areas is pretty essential for unity and harmonious relationships. And as we do that, the strength of our emotions in opinion areas should lessen considerably. One thing that has helped me since I have been in our movement is to realize that when good brothers who know the Bible well have sincere differences, this fact alone makes it highly likely that these differences fall into opinion areas. And in opinion areas, I want to remain tolerant and open to being persuaded to go in other directions than I might opt for personally, in order to work together most effectively. That is a worthy goal, and clearly a biblical one.

A Caution to Leaders

Back when Wyndham Shaw and I co-authored the book *Golden Rule Leadership*, I wrote the introduction. Near the end of the introduction, I included the following caution:

WARNING!

The greatest danger in reading this book is to assume that you really already understand the principles being discussed and are currently putting them into practice. This is especially true for our most experienced leaders. We do not see ourselves as we are; we do not see ourselves as others see us. Our strong tendency is to think more highly of ourselves as leaders than we ought to think (Romans 12:3).

Guess who got offended by my cautionary remarks? Not young Christians—they were saying "Amen." But a number of older leaders were definitely offended. What does that say to us? It says to me that, as we age in leadership and years of service, we can be guilty of exactly what I penned in the quote above. In our former days as a movement, I was often cautioned about how I stated things, lest I offend the leaders. Now, I am again being given exactly the same cautions. Something is wrong with that, and I think terribly wrong. You mean I can "lay it out" strongly to the average members, but I have to be careful not to offend the older leaders? Wow! Must history repeat itself again? Leaders ought to be able to hear challenges more humbly than anyone.

Certainly, Paul argued in 1 Corinthians 8-10 that we must be willing to give up our "rights," and he used himself as a great example of such. But for whom was he anxious to give up his rights? It was the weak and immature ones in the fellowship who were struggling with their consciences over past pagan practices, and also for those not yet saved. Hence, he was willing to become all things to influence the ones in those categories and to give up all things in order to do so. But he was not willing to compromise or change his approach in teaching to placate the ones who should have been more mature. His question in Galatians 4:16 was, "Have I now become your enemy by telling you the truth?" Rest assured that he was not directing that question to young Christians. Frankly, my biggest concern for us as a movement is our tendency in the direction of some of the unsavory elements of the churches of which I used to be a part. I suggest that you look up every New Testament passage using the term *conscience*. The only places that I could find where it was warning against violating the consciences of others were in 1 Corinthians 8-10. Romans 14 contains the same concept, without using the word itself. In light of the context of who Paul's concern was about (immature Christians with weak consciences), and what the issues of controversy were (background pagan practices primarily), we need to be slow to play the "conscience card."

My best judgment about how to view and use money is not shared by all disciples, and that can bother me. My best judgment about the kinds of movies or TV shows to watch or allow our children to watch is not shared by all, which also bothers me. My best judgment about alcohol consumption (especially where and with whom it is done) is not shared by all of my brothers. So, once again, I am bothered. But I don't intend to let those differences of opinion cause me to violate my own conscience by joining in to their practices, nor do I intend to become bothered enough to let it affect my love and fellowship with those who have opinions and practices that vary from mine. What others do in opinion areas is ultimately their choice, and it is not about my conscience. In other areas more related to leadership decisions and directions, I am pretty flexible. If a real biblical issue is involved, we are going to have to hash that one out before proceeding, but if it is a judgment matter, I will, for the sake of unity, throw in my lot with majority opinion. Those are practical and workable paths to follow in our personal families and in God's family. Let's just keep conscience appeals out of places where they don't belong biblically. Generally, I like the old Restoration adage about faith and opinion, with this one change: "In matters of clear biblical doctrine, unity; in matters of judgment, freedom—but freedom exercised with a strong bent toward practical unity; and in all matters, love."

BIBLIOGRAPHY

Anton, Edward J. *Repentance*. Waltham, Massachusetts: Disciple-ship Publications International, 2005.

Beasley-Murray. *Baptism in the New Testament*. Grand Rapids: William B. Eerdmans Publishing Company, 1962.

Bristow, J.T. *Personal Illustrations*. Vancouver, Washington: Gospel Outreach Publishers, n.d.

Burney, Bob. *A Shocking "Confession" from Willow Creek Community Church*. Crosswalk.com, October 30, 2007.

Catechism of the Catholic Church. English Translation, United States Catholic Conference, Inc.—Libreria Editrice Vaticana. Liguori, Missouri: Liguori Publications, 1994.

Collins, Jim. *Good To Great*. New York: HarperCollins Publishers, 2001.

Department of Anthropology, The Smithsonian Institution. *Statement Regarding the Book of Mormon*. Washington: National Museum of Natural History, Spring, 1986.

Gibbons, James Cardinal. *The Faith of Our Fathers*. New York: P.J. Kennedy & Sons, 1917.

Goleman, Daniel, Richard Boyatzis, and Annie McKee. *Primal Leadership*. Boston, Massachusetts: Harvard Business School Press, 2002.

Hanko, Herman; Hoeksema, Homer C.; Van Baren, Gise J. *The Five Points of Calvinism*. Grand Rapids: Reformed Free Publishing Association, 1976.

Hybels, Bill. *Leadership Summit 07*. Oral presentation on the web site http://revealnow.com

Jones, Thomas A. *In Search of a City*. Spring Hill, Tennessee: DPI Books, 2007.

Jones, Tony. *The New Christians: Dispatches from the Emergent Frontier*. San Francisco: Jossey-Bass, 2008.

Jones, Tony. *The Sacred Way: Spiritual Practices for Everyday Life*. Grand Rapids, Michigan: Zondervan, 2005.

Journal of Discourses. Twenty-six Volumes. Liverpool: F.D. Richards, Latter Day Saints Book Depot, 1854-1886.

Lamb, Roger and Tom Jones, *"You Might Be Fighting God,"* Discipleship Magazine, Summer 1991, p. 23. This article is now in print as a part of First Principles, Kip McKean and Leigh Ann Vett, eds. Woburn, Massachusetts: Discipleship Publications International, 1992.

Langfield, Weldon. *The Truth About Mormonism.* Bakersfield, California: Weldon Langfield Publications, 1991.

Lanier, Roy H., Sr. *The Timeless Trinity.* Denver, Colorado: Roy H. Lanier, Sr. Publisher, 1974.

Mattox, F.W. *The Eternal Kingdom.* Delight, Arkansas: Gospel Light Publishing Company, 1961.

McConkie, Bruce R. *Mormon Doctrine.* Salt Lake City: Bookcraft, 1979.

Parkinson, Cally and Greg Hawkins. *Reveal: Where Are You?* Willow Creek Association, August 2007.

Rainer, S. Thom. *Breakout Churches.* Grand Rapids, Michigan: Zondervan, 2005.

Rainer, S. Thom and Eric Geiger. *Simple Church.* Nashville, Tennessee: B & H Publishing Group, 2006.

Rodkinson, Michael L. *Babylonian Talmud.* Boston: Talmud Soc., 1918.

Small, Dwight Hervey. *Christian: Celebrate Your Sexuality.* Old Tappan, N.J.: Fleming H. Revel Company, 1974.

Smith, Joseph, Jr. *The Book of Mormon.* Salt Lake City: The Church of Jesus Christ of Latter Day Saints, 1981.

_____. *Doctrine and Covenants.* Salt Lake City: The Church of Jesus Christ of Latter Day Saints, 1974.

_____. *Pearl of Great Price.* Salt Lake City: The Church of Jesus Christ of Latter Day Saints, 1974.

_____. *The History of the Church of Jesus Christ of Latter-day Saints.* Six Volumes. Salt Lake City: Deseret News, 1902-1912.

Stanback, C. Foster. *Into All Nations: A History of the International Churches of Christ.* Spring, Texas: Illumination Publishers International, 2005.

Wallace, Foy E. *God's Prophetic Word.* Oklahoma City: Foy E. Wallace, Jr., Publications, 1960.

Wikipedia.org web site.

RESOURCES FROM GORDON FERGUSON

The Power of Gratitude

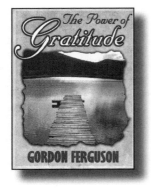

Gratitude is not just something nice to have. Gratitude is a pure and powerful expression of humility that transforms the mind and enriches the lives of those who see and feel it. Life has its negative elements, and many choose to focus on these with a complaining spirit. In a world where cynical and caustic comments seem to fill the air, some old-fashioned gratitude is badly needed.

In this insightful volume, Gordon Ferguson, a much-loved teacher and elder, shares lessons and examples from his own life. Some are heart warming, some are challenging. All of them help us to see ways in which we need to be grateful and show us the divine power that gratitude brings to our lives. This book brings into focus the life-changing power of gratitude that can change us to the core of our beings.

Price: $10.00 • 164 page softcover book • ISBN: 1577821246

Mine Eyes Have Seen the Glory
The Victory of the Lamb
in the Book of Revelation

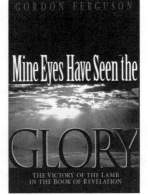

Mysterious. Confusing. Intriguing. Symbolic. Deep. Difficult. Literal. Futuristic. All these words and many others describe the final book of the Bible.

Misunderstood. Misinterpreted. Misapplied. These words speak of the "missed" message of Revelation in light of today's prevailing humanism, hedonism and hypocrisy.

Inspiring. Crucial. Radical. Victorious. Compelling. Challenging. Thrilling. Strengthening. These are a few of the right words—God's initial intent—about what is to happen in our hearts and in our souls after spending time with the apostle John on the island of Patmos as he reveals God through this revelation. In *Mine Eyes Have Seen the Glory*, Gordon Ferguson unlocks and unleashes God's powerful and timeless message—a message that will forever revolutionize our lives!

Price: $14.00 • 196 page softcover book • ISBN: 188453923

Available at www.ipibooks.com

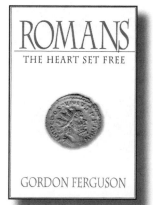

Illumination Publishers International

Toney Mulhollan has been in Christian publishing for over 30 years. He has served as the Production Manager for Crossroads Publications, Discipleship Magazine/ UpsideDown Magazine, Discipleship Publications International (DPI) and on the production teams of Campus Journal, Biblical Discipleship Quarterly, Bible Illustrator and others. He has served as production manager for several printing companies. Toney serves as the Editor of Illumination Publishers International. Toney is happily married to the love of his life, Denise Leonard Mulhollan, M.D. They make their home in Houston, Texas along with their daughter, Audra Joan.

For the best in Christian writing and audio instruction, go to the Illumination Publishers International website. We're commited to producing in-depth teaching that will inform, inspire and encourage Christians to a deeper and more committed walk with God. You can reach Toney Mulhollan by email at toneyipibooks@mac.com or at his office number, (832) 559-3658.

www.ipibooks.com